Shareholders' Agreements

Shareholders' Agreements

Ethical and Legal Perspectives on Freedom of Contract in Company Law

Edited by

Ana Perestrelo de Oliveira, Marta Boura and Catarina Coelho

Mohr Siebeck

Ana Perestrelo de Oliveira is Professor at the Faculty of Law of the University of Lisbon; Researcher at Research Centre for Private Law (CIDP).

Marta Boura is Guest Lecturer at the Faculty of Law of the University of Lisbon; Researcher at the Research Centre for Private Law (CIDP).

Catarina Coelho is Guest Lecturer at the Faculty of Law of the University of Lisbon; Researcher at the Research Centre for Private Law (CIDP); Ph.D.'s Scholarships holder of the CIDP

fct
Fundação
para a Ciência
e a Tecnologia

CENTRO DE INVESTIGAÇÃO DE DIREITO PRIVADO

This work is funded by national funds through FCT – Foundation for Science and Technology, I.P., within the scope of the project UID/06191/2025.

ISBN 978-3-16-200052-1 / eISBN 978-3-16-200053-8
DOI 10.1628/978-3-16-200053-8

The Deutsche Nationalbibliothek lists this publication in the Deutsche Nationalbibliographie; detailed bibliographic data are available at *https://dnb.dnb.de.*

Published by Mohr Siebeck Tübingen 2026.

Printed on non-aging paper. Typesetting: Laupp & Göbel, Gomaringen.

Mohr Siebeck GmbH & Co. KG, Wilhelmstraße 18, 72074 Tübingen, Germany
www.mohrsiebeck.com, info@mohrsiebeck.com

Foreword

The Boundaries of Shareholders' Freedom in Shareholders' Agreements

Ana Perestrelo de Oliveira, Marta Boura and Catarina Coelho

I. The Research Project and Preliminary Takeouts

I. Contractual autonomy (and, more broadly, the legal freedom of contract under private law) is currently under close scrutiny. Although it is recognized as a historical and axiological foundation of private law, its content and limits are not easily defined. This book aims to bridge the gap between academic theory and corporate practice, offering new perspectives on the efficiency, ethics, and adaptability of shareholders' agreements in a changing legal landscape.

This discussion attracts particular attention in the field of corporate law, mainly for two reasons. First, because the sector is marked by the rapid transformation of organisations, so debates about contractual freedom are constantly evolving and are repeatedly tested by the creation or adoption of new legal institutions, often driven by economic needs and demands. Second, some legal systems evidence that corporate law may diminish contractual functionality and efficiency in companies. As permissive tendencies increase, the question of how to balance flexibility and legal certainty (particularly under the numerus clausus system) remains unresolved.

By gathering contributions from leading scholars and practitioners across different jurisdictions, this volume stands out for its international and multidisciplinary approach, identifying both convergences and divergences in the treatment of shareholders' autonomy.

Widespread uncertainty about the limits of contractual freedom has fuelled scholarly disputes over which matters should be regulated in the articles of association versus shareholders' agreements. This debate has shaped progress in the field, helping to resolve doubts about the admissibility of shareholders' agreements and clarifying who may be a party to such agreements. It is also necessary to consider the compatibility of various clauses imported from international contractual practice to different jurisdictions (which creates significant obstacles for both national and international investors), as well as the ethical challenges posed by the parallel governance resulting from shareholders' agreements.

The works collected here are grouped around key themes: the relationship between shareholders' agreements and articles of association; the preservation of control and governance in family and venture capital contexts; the enforceability and legal constraints of such agreements; and the ethical and legal challenges posed by innovative contractual clauses.

These reflections shape the main goal of this project: to influence the practice of shareholders' agreements by promoting a reconsideration of efficiency and business ethics, while making use of the potential of the legal system.

II. At the International Conference held at the Faculty of Law, University of Lisbon, on 14 and 15 January 2025, we had the opportunity to explore the most pressing topics in corporate governance, independence, transparency, sustainability, and democracy – all central to the discussion we aim to address in this collective work. Both minorities, contractual freedom, conflict resolution, asset and value were keywords that emerged throughout, all meaning the one overall concept that we are trying to capture within the corporate world: control.

We received contributions from various jurisdictions, which further highlighted the importance of the debate and the common principles that unite us in discussing new trends and developments in economic and legal frameworks.

All in all, the question remains: how can we reconcile the contractual and corporate worlds in a way that does not breach corporate and civil law provisions, yet still addresses the practical demands of company law?

We hope this book will serve as a vehicle for further debate and innovation, inspiring both scholars and practitioners to rethink the boundaries of shareholders' freedom in light of contemporary legal, economic, and ethical challenges.

II. New Opportunities and Challenges within the Scope of Contractual Autonomy

I. A significant gap remains between academic perspectives and practical corporate realities, highlighting the need to reassess certain established dogmas. The law must keep pace with corporate practice and critically reflect on the challenges shareholders currently face.

This book seeks to explore the tensions arising from private autonomy and to clearly distinguish between truly unlawful shareholder conduct and actions that, while seemingly unbalanced, remain within the bounds of legality.

II. Another pressing issue is sustainable governance, which is increasingly relevant as companies act as market agents with responsibilities that extend beyond their shareholders to a broader range of stakeholders. Can shareholders' agreements serve as instruments to promote due diligence, environmental sustainability, and human rights?

All these matters raise the question of whether private autonomy is an adequate – or perhaps even preferable – means for addressing such issues, as opposed to relying on mandatory provisions, especially in an increasingly regulated field within the EU law framework.

III. Presentation of the Works

I. Turning to the works that shape this research, the first four papers were presented in the conference's first panel. We now have the opportunity to examine some of the most pressing issues related to control, asset locking, and the bidding effect in various contexts: generally, in family firms, in venture capital, and with regard to sustainability concerns.

Sebastian Mock's paper provides a comprehensive legal and comparative analysis of shareholders' agreements, focusing on their relationship to the articles of association, examining their differences and potential conflicts, as well as the legal effects, content, and enforceability of such agreements.

Paula del Val Talens' paper explores the role of shareholders' agreements in family-owned businesses, focusing on how these agreements help preserve family control, ensure intergenerational involvement, and structure governance and company organization.

Luca Enriques and Casimiro A. Nigro's essay examines why Italian corporate law is highly resistant to private ordering, particularly in the context of venture capital (VC) contracting. Building on their prior research, it demonstrates how this legal framework hinders the adoption of U.S.-style VC contracts, which are widely regarded as efficient and globally influential.

Maria Elisabeth Ramos' paper examines the role of shareholders' agreements in promoting sustainable corporate governance, particularly in the context of the EU Corporate Sustainability Due Diligence Directive and Portuguese law.

Given the importance of shareholders' agreements in these areas, the question was posed: can we opt out of corporate law?

As part of the roundtable discussion, Paulo Olavo Cunha and Carolina Cunha offer a perspective on the link between shareholders' agreements and board independence, combining both practical and theoretical approaches.

These agreements, especially when they are omnilateral, often seek to influence or direct the actions of the board or management bodies outside the formal mechanisms provided by company statutes or law.

The core problem lies in the potential conflict between private autonomy – allowing shareholders to organize their internal relations – and the legal principle of managerial independence. Most legal systems restrict or invalidate agreements that bind directors in the exercise of their management powers, aiming to safeguard the directors' fiduciary duties and the proper functioning of corporate governance. Even when all shareholders are parties to such agreements, the law typically maintains a clear separation between the shareholders' will and the autonomy of the management body, to prevent the creation of parallel governance structures and to protect the interests of the company and third parties.

The admissibility and enforceability of such agreements must always be balanced against the fundamental principles of corporate law, particularly the independence and responsibility of directors.

II. The next three papers, by Alexandre Soveral Martins, Francisco Mendes Correia, and José Ferreira Gomes, respectively, address legal constraints associated with shareholders' agreements, particularly in the contexts of private equity, venture capital, enforceability, and omnilateral agreements.

Alexandre Soveral Martins' paper analyses the practical challenges and legal constraints faced by private equity and venture capital investors when negotiating shareholders' agreements under Portuguese company law. It aims to guide foreign investors through the nuances of the Portuguese legal framework.

Francisco Mendes Correia's work discusses the normative content and foundations of the principle of separation between shareholders' agreements and articles of association, as well as the enforceability of shareholders' agreements under Portuguese company law. It aims to clarify the available remedies in cases of breach.

José Ferreira Gomes' paper explores the effectiveness of unanimous (omnilateral) shareholders' agreements across different jurisdictions, focusing on their relationship with company law and the principle of separation between shareholders' agreements and the company's articles of association.

During the conference, several thought-provoking questions were raised, sparking a lively debate on the role and limits of omnilateral shareholders' agreements.

A central question was whether the unanimous will of all shareholders should be sufficient to shape management, either directly or by influencing the directors' duties of loyalty and care. Even when all shareholders are in agreement, can their collective will override the core legal duties imposed on directors – duties that exist to protect not only the shareholders as a group, but also the integrity of the company as a separate legal entity and the interests of other stakeholders? Ultimately, the discussion returned to the concept of corporate purpose, which may be a key element in defining the limits of shareholder influence. While shareholders' agreements can play a significant role in shaping the company's direction, they cannot legitimately modify the fundamental duties of management or transform the company into a mere extension of the shareholders' will. The law draws a line to ensure that the company's purpose, the protection of minority and third party interests, and the integrity of the governance structure are preserved – even in the face of unanimous shareholder agreement.

This ongoing tension underscores the need for a nuanced and principled approach to the role of shareholders' agreements in corporate governance.

III. Finally, still within the context of the conference, this reflection concluded with a discussion of the termination of shareholders' agreements, further developments on corporate purpose, and the legal and ethical issues raised by deadlock provisions in shareholders' agreements.

Catarina Monteiro Pires' work examines the termination of shareholders' agreements under Portuguese law, focusing particularly on termination due to breach. It raises critical questions about the adequacy of general contract law remedies when applied to the unique nature of shareholders' agreements.

Paulo Câmara's paper addresses legislative responses to shareholder intervention in sustainability matters. He argues that while the broader EU framework on shareholder engagement in sustainability is adequate, EU takeover law responses are open to criticism, and ultimately advocates for a TOD reform.

Nicola de Lucas' paper examines the legal and ethical dimensions of Russian roulette clauses in shareholders' agreements, particularly in the context of business deadlocks and forced exits. It draws on comparative legal analysis and the landmark Italian Fintech case to explore whether such clauses must comply with fair pricing and how they align with business ethics.

Beyond the scope of the conference, and within the broader context of these discussions, Catarina Coelho's paper explores the legal admissibility, ethical implications, and practical consequences of including Russian roulette clauses in shareholders' agreements of closed limited liability companies under Portuguese law.

Taken together, the works presented in this book seek to reflect upon and critically analyse shareholders' agreements in light of the contemporary legal and practical challenges they raise. They aim to question the traditional dogmatic assumptions underlying these agreements and to open new avenues for debate within corporate law theory and practice.

In a time when ethics, sustainability, and contractual flexibility are increasingly central, we trust that this collective work will contribute to the progression of the debate and to the progress of balanced solutions for the future of company law.

Content

Shareholders' Agreements between Corporate and Contract Law

Sebastian Mock

Abstract: Shareholders' Agreements have a growing influence on the general understanding of corporate law since they bind not only the shareholders but also affect the constitution of the corporation and can have a severe impact on capital markets. Therefore, Shareholders' Agreements are increasingly subject to regulation in corporate, capital market and insolvency law on the national, the European and the international level. The following article provides an overview of the fundamental issues of shareholders' agreements and highlights the differences between shareholders' agreements and articles of association and their relationship to each other.

I. Shareholders' agreements and their status in the relation to corporate documents

Articles of association[1] represent the *constitution* of a corporation, regulating its existence, operation, structure, organization and relations among its shareholders, their relations toward the company and the powers of the corporation's bodies. Beside corporate documents, shareholders use to enter into special contractual agreements regulating their mutual relations. In practice, they are usually denominated as *bylaws* or *shareholders' agreements*.[2] A shareholders' agreement is an agreement of at least two shareholders establishing a contractual link in regard to their position as shareholder. The mere fact of *acting in concert* or the existence of joint interest between shareholders does not suffice as a shareholders' agreement but can nevertheless have the same consequences as a shareholders' agreement in e. g. capital markets law.[3] First of all it is necessary to define shareholders' agreements in a way that allows the distinction from articles of association. The distinction between the articles of association and a shareholders' agreement is sometimes hard to draw. According to a formal distinction, the articles of association and shareholders' agreement are distin-

---

[1] For the purposes of this analysis and unless stated otherwise the terms articles of association shall cover all types of deeds of establishment, memorandum of association and all internal corporate documents, i. e. *Satzung*, charter, bylaws.

[2] In German *Nebenabreden, schuldrechtliche Gesellschaftervereinbarungen* or *Syndikatsvertrage* (Austria) in Italian *sindicati azionari*.

[3] This is e.g. the case in German law (see *Mock*, in Mock/Csach/Havel (eds.), International Handbook on Shareholders' Agreements, 2018, 289, 309).

guished based on the formalization of a particular provision in a formal document regulated by corporate law adopted by a defined body. In such sense, the articles of association cover all arrangements incorporated into the formal document they are. Thereby, a shareholders' agreement is any other arrangement between shareholders that is – formally – not included in the articles of association. On the other hand, shareholders' agreements and articles of association might be distinguished regarding their actual content. Articles of association cover any arrangement that governs the corporation and/or has an effect on all shareholders. Any other contractual arrangements must be considered as shareholders' agreements. However, such simplistic criteria have their limitations as articles of association and shareholders' agreements may deal with similar aspect and therefore overlap.

Articles of association do not have to regulate only aspects of corporate law that are dealt with by the law as a possible content. The articles of association may thus include: a) the mandatory rules of corporate law, b) alterations from the non-mandatory corporate regulation, c) the non-mandatory rules, and last, but not least, also d) regulation of other issues that are not foreseen by corporate law regulation, but are formally included into the articles of association (for example various contractual arrangements, arbitration clause for disputes related to the share in a company). It shall not be ruled out that articles of association may also deal with issues that are very loosely connected with the participation of the shareholders in the corporation (for example, an obligation of shareholders to provide each other loans, authority and conditions for the use of company's services, etc.). Hence, the scope of the articles of association may be extended by the shareholders, even beyond the limits laid down by the law. Articles of association will thus establish an obligation containing not only the rules of a corporate constitutive nature, i. e. those that are inevitable or foreseen for the existence of a company, but also other rules that are not inevitable and that express the intended will of its shareholders. However, this applies *vice versa*, i.e. the shareholders may decide that they will not incorporate into the articles of association all the issues that are foreseen for this instrument. The corporation might have articles of association complying with the law but still its shareholders might have wished to execute an ancillary shareholders' agreement containing arrangements that should be contained in the articles of association (limitations on the transferability of shares, rules for appointing members of the company's bodies, profit sharing etc.). This approach is usually employed due to the fact that the articles of association are publicly accessible, while the shareholders' agreements are not available to the public.[4] Although the form does not predetermine the content, the selection of a particular form, or placement of a particular arrangement in the articles of association or in a shareholders' agreement may have consequences. Unless provided otherwise the placement of a particular arrangement into a certain formalized document is in general irrelevant for the validity of a particular arrangement. The particu-

[4] See III. for further details.

lar arrangement of non-corporate issues which is contained in the articles of association is not void only because it is contained in the articles of association and not in a separate agreement.[5]

II. Regulation of shareholders' agreements

Although the execution of shareholders' agreements has become a commonplace corporate practice, usually, they are not subject to a specific legislation.[6] Although the concept of shareholders' agreements itself is basically left undefined in many jurisdictions, the frameworks or various specific consequences of such agreements are defined.[7] National legislators usually regulate only the limits and possible consequences of shareholders' agreements, for example, in the area of fiduciary obligations of the company's authorised representatives, or in the area of the law of corporate groups, while the rest is subject to the general rules of the law of contract.

However, some legislators enacted specific regulations on shareholders' agreements and their approaches vary between generalization and *casuistry (Kasuistik)*. In the United States, for example, Section 7.32 MBCA applies a general negative model:

Section 7.32 MBCA states:
An agreement among the shareholders of a corporation that complies with this section is effective among the shareholders and the corporation even though it is inconsistent with one or more other provisions of this Act in that it:

(1) eliminates the board of directors or restricts the discretion or powers of the board of directors;
(2) governs the authorization or making of distributions whether or not in proportion to ownership of shares, subject to the limitations in section 6.40;
(3) establishes who shall be directors or officers of the corporation, or their terms of office or manner of selection or removal;
(4) governs, in general or in regard to specific matters, the exercise or division of voting power by or between the shareholders and directors or by or among any of them, including use of weighted voting rights or director proxies;

[5] Constitutive elements of a company will obviously not qualify for being a subject of shareholders agreements. It will be, for example, useless if a business name, registered office or amount of registered capital or the line of business are contained in the shareholders' agreement. This will not void the document but it will rather make such provision of the shareholders' agreement obsolete, since in order to accomplish their intended effect, such questions must be contained (also formally) in the articles of association.

[6] This is e.g. the case in German law (*Mock*, [supra note 3], 289, 292), shareholders agreements are delimited "in legislation", for example, in Article 36 of the draft model law UNCITRAL on a simplified business entity of 2015. (*UNCITRAL Draft model law on a simplified business entity.* A/CN. 9/WG. I/WP. 89.)

[7] See e.g. the Irish Companies Act of 2014.

(5) establishes the terms and conditions of any agreement for the transfer or use of property or the provision of services between the corporation and any shareholder, director, officer or employee of the corporation or among any of them;
(6) transfers to one or more shareholders or other persons all or part of the authority to exercise the corporate powers or to manage the business and affairs of the corporation, including the resolution of any issue about which there exists a deadlock among directors or shareholders;
(7) requires dissolution of the corporation at the request of one or more of the shareholders or upon the occurrence of a specified event or contingency; or
(8) otherwise governs the exercise of the corporate powers or the management of the business and affairs of the corporation or the relationship among the shareholders, the directors and the corporation, or among any of them, and is not contrary to public policy.

an example of a positive approach existing since 2017 is the Slovak law.[8]

Section 66c Slovak Commercial Code (Shareholders' agreements) states:
Parties may, by a written shareholders' agreement, agree mutual rights and duties resulting from their share in the company, in particular mode and conditions of the exercise of the rights related to the share in the company, mode of the exercise of the rights related to the company governance,
conditions and extent of the involvement in the changes of the share/registered capital, and ancillary arrangements related to the transfer of the share in the company. The conflict between a decision of the company's body and the shareholders' agreement shall not make such a decision void.

Besides this example, which might be interpreted as determined by the local culture and legislative technique and thus superfluous[9], other national legal systems show a lack of positive regulation expressly allowing shareholders' agreements.[10]

III. Advantages and disadvantages of shareholders' agreements

Shareholders' agreements have become quite common in the current corporate practice. The reasons for concluding shareholders' agreements vary. The confidentiality or *absence of publicity,* of shareholders' agreements is considered as one of their major advantages. Contrary to the articles of association they need not be filed with the

---

[8] See in detail *Mrázová*, in Mock/Csach/Havel (eds.), International Handbook on Shareholders' Agreements, 2018, 551, 553 ff.

[9] See also for Slovak law *Mrázová*, (supra note 8), 551, 553 ff. and for Danish law *Neville*, in Mock/Csach/Havel (eds.), International Handbook on Shareholders' Agreements, 2018, 233, 236.

[10] This is e.g. the case in Austria (*Arlt*, in Mock/Csach/Havel (eds.), International Handbook on Shareholders' Agreements, 2018, 153, 157), Belgium (*Matthijs*, in Mock/Csach/Havel (eds.), International Handbook on Shareholders' Agreements, 2018, 179, 180 f.) or Germany (*Mock*, [supra note 3], 289, 292).

public register and thus are not available to the public or third parties. Shareholders' agreements show a certain degree of flexibility since their amendment is not subject to any special formal procedure as it is required for the amendment of other corporate documents. Another advantage is also a wide availability of contractual instruments of securing and enforcing rights and duties resulting from the shareholders' agreements. Last, but not least, the reason for entering into shareholders' agreements may also be the need to determine the relationship between some of the shareholders differently from the relations towards other shareholders. Shareholders' agreements also frequently involve other persons that are not bound by the articles of association.

The major disadvantages are the contractual nature of shareholders' agreements and consequently their limited effect upon third parties (especially upon assignees and share purchasers). Moreover, shareholders' agreements require a quite complicated amendment mechanism compared to the majority principle for the amendments of articles of association. Also, it is usual to apply corporate consequences from a breach of obligations imposed by the shareholders' agreement (e.g. the exclusion of shareholders). As the national reports show, the absence of domestic case law might also be considered disadvantageous, to a certain extent, although the fact itself does not seem to limit the use of shareholders' agreements.

When searching for the reasons why shareholders' agreements are concluded, one has to consider wider structural links between the purpose of a company itself and the interests of those who have made up, manage or control it. It is well-known that especially registered companies basically serve as a tool to produce a benefit defined by their shareholders, i.e. profit, but it is also known that there is a kind of a wall standing between the company, its assets and its shareholders, known as "asset locking". In other words: the shareholders, on the one hand, define the purpose of the whole organization, but afterwards the organization lives its own autonomous life and the shareholders may only influence its activities indirectly. This concept of division of the company's assets from its shareholders is a more general justification of the necessity to make shareholders' agreements whereby the shareholders are trying to compensate their future limited influence on the company's management to a certain extent *ex ante*, at least, on a contract basis. Law & economics analyses indicate that such contracts may *ex ante* decrease not only the risk of future disputes, but they may also provide the space for a later re-negotiation and application of the principles of contract law within the less flexible corporate law.[11]

[11] See e.g. *Chemla/Ljungqvist*, An Analysis of Shareholder Agreements, 5 Journal of the Economic Association 93 (2007).

IV. Shareholders' agreements and their impact on the company

A problem of representation that has been described many times (i.e. *agency problem*)[12] points out that despite the unifying purpose of the whole organization there will always be a structural difference, at least, between the interests of the shareholders, the company, the members of its bodies, the creditors, and the like. Regardless of the extent to which it is possible to interpret the concept of the company's interest functionally and to let it cover also wider social interests, and even without considering what the interests of all shareholders and the company itself are and how they can get into conflict with the interests mentioned above, the statutory concept of dichotomy of interests of the shareholders and those of the company must be respected. Considering the fact that they are clearly differentiated, the analysis admits that these interests are kept distinct. On the other hand, the interest of the company is supposed to prevail over the interests of all shareholders in order that the company could accomplish its purpose to protect third persons (creditors, employees, etc.). Further, it is obvious that members of the company's bodies are bound by the purpose and goal of the company itself, hence, they must take into account the will of the shareholders expressed by the company's purpose. Where the influence of a shareholder is to be strengthened, typically in various kinds of corporate groups, the loyalty of members of the company's bodies shifts toward the corporate interest. It should also be pointed out that a certain degree of loyalty binds also the shareholders themselves, not only because of the fact that they are parties to the articles of association, but also due to the fact that it is prescribed by the standard of fair conduct toward the company. Moreover, diverse interests may also arise, inter alia, among the shareholders toward one another.

Already in the 1930s, economic academia started to pose a rhetoric question as *to whom the company management does actually serve*. The problem became a topic during a period of so called *managerial capitalism*, i.e. at the time when the company basically served as a tool of profit maximization controlled by the management massively exploiting (scarce) resources. This concept then served not only to understand the functionalities of the company as such, but mainly to gradually re-define the standards of fiduciary duties of members of the company's bodies. To simplify, experts try to find out whose interests should be pursued/protected by the company's bodies. If one realizes that the process was accompanied with a gradual change of the concept of responsibility of members of the company's bodies, i.e. from subjective to

---

[12] See e.g. *Armour/Hansmann/Kraakman*, in Kraakman/Armour/Davies/Enriques/Hansmann/Hertig/Kanda/Pargendler/Ringe/Rock, The Anatomy of Corporate law, 3rd edition, OUP 2017, Chapter 2; also see *Sjåfjell*, Towards a Sustainable European Company Law, Kluwer 2009, 37 ff.; see also (from a German context) *Bachmann/Eidenmüller/Engert/Fleischer/Schön*, Regulating the Closed Corporations, Berlin, 2014, 28 ff. (conflicts of shareholders in closed corporations); or Roth/Kindler, The Spirit of Corporate Law, Munich 2013, 71 ff.; in Czech see, *inter alia, Havel*, Obchodní korporace ve světle proměn, Praha 2010, and the literature quoted therein.

absolute liability, hence, the objectivized and identifiable standard was becoming all the more important, it is no surprise that the attention of experts focused on whether the management is to pursue:

- only and only the interest of the company,
- the interest of shareholders or their majority (so called *shareholders model*),
- the interest of stakeholders in a more general sense, or such stakeholders as creditors, employees, etc. (so called *stakeholder model*), or
- various forms of enlightened models (*enlightened shareholders model*)[13], or later even wider models established on the basis of corporate social responsibility (*CSR model*) [14] and the like (e.g. *productive coalition model*)[15].

It is needless to say that the further development gradually oscillated between various approaches and/or their combinations and the model which prevailed finally was the one combining all of the above models also in relation to their socially sustainable development (similarly a coalition/cooperation model). Such a solution is pragmatic and foresees various nuances depending on the purpose selected for a particular company, for example, whether a public interest exists in respect of its activities, etc. Especially so if one realizes that even today the management of companies is vested with non-corporate organizations, such as trusts that also enter in the shareholders' agreements.

Substantially, the company is therefore an arranged structure which becomes the (meeting) place for various unarranged interests. If one connects such a concept of the company with the contractual aspects arising out of shareholders' agreements, the question of a conflict of interests or complicacy of identification of such conflicts may grow significant. It is then disputable if the existence of contractual covenants outside corporate documents represents only the establishment of a parallel world of contractual obligation outside the company or even of a distinct category of a third kind. Obviously, the discussions about models of corporate governance are closely connected with shareholders' agreements since the external strengthening of the shareholders' positions may shift the company more toward the shareholders model, i.e. it may result in the strengthening of a utilitarian perception of the benefit of *the owners* of the company. At the same time, however, it cannot be expected that the resulting corporate structure would pursue or show only a single interest, because there would still be a rule that although the statutory grounds of the company established by the articles of association are wrapped up by the contractual net of shareholders' agreements, the company's bodies must nevertheless perform their statutory duties and must pursue wider interests than just those that would be pursued by the

[13] See e.g. *Sjåfjell*, (supra note 12), 88 ff.

[14] See the comparative study in *Güler/Crowther*, in Guler/Crowther, Global Perspectives on Corporate Governance and CSR, 2009, 1 ff.; *Sacconi/Blair/Freeman/Verceli* (eds.), Corporate Social Responsibility and Corporate, 2011.

[15] *Johnston*, EC Regulation of Corporate Governance, CUP, 2009, 59 ff.

shareholders. In other words, the complicated and intertwined relations among partial components of the company's governance would not result in creating a single uniform interest and in eliminating the agency problem.

The dichotomy of interests of all the shareholders and the company is not – conceptually – interfered with by the shareholders' agreement. The shareholders' agreement does not result in the change of the interest, nor does it create any common collective corporate interest that would prevail over the interests of the shareholders and that would automatically by itself define or interfere with the interests of the company for the purposes of determining the liability of members of the company's bodies. Even the agreement among all shareholders does not have any relevance for the articles of association.[16] The existence of the shareholders' agreement, however, will facilitate the identification of the shareholder's interest, or the interest of several or of all shareholders. Where the company's body proceeds in accordance with the shareholders' agreement it could be expected not to prefer any of the shareholders who are parties to the agreement. That still does not mean that it proceeds in compliance with the interest of the company.

V. Differences between the articles of association and shareholders' agreements

Both shareholders' agreements and articles of association have a contractual basis. They are established by a consent of shareholders, and they are dependent on that will. Their operation is, however, completely different. To put it simply, these are two parallel worlds, each having their own rules that are not directly related, although they might cross each other. As mentioned before, besides a formal distinction between the articles of association and shareholders' agreements (the articles of association being a formalized contract meeting some requirements as to its form and content, whose amendment and operation are subject to a separate regulation) a substantive distinction might be proposed between corporate and non-corporate issues. Corporate issues cover the structure and functioning of the company and involve provisions which are considered as a possible or inevitable content of the articles of association as set by corporate law. In contrast, non-corporate (contractual) provisions regulate other issues of an obligatory nature regardless of where such provisions are contained in the articles of association or in the shareholders' agreements. From such a perspective, a corporate issue may be regulated in a shareholders' agreement,

[16] From a point of view of German or Czech law, however, it should be pointed out that case law has repeatedly admitted a direct influence of shareholders' agreements on the articles of association (see e.g. arrangements of all shareholders contained in the shareholders' agreement regime may result in an *ad hoc* piercing the rule contained in the memorandum of association in Czech law (*Bohumil*, in Mock/Csach/Havel (eds.), International Handbook on Shareholders' Agreements, 2018, 219, 229) and German law (*Mock*, supra note 3], 289, 307).

but also *vice versa*, a contractual (non-corporate) issue may be contained in the articles of association. Distinguishing according to a material criterion will play a role in considering particulars necessary for the validity of a given legal act, its effect, possibility of changes and legal consequences of defects or remedies available. It will also be important for the evaluation of the relation between the resolution of a general meeting and the articles of association. The fundamental distinctions between the articles of association and the shareholders' agreement may be outlined as follows.

1. Different content and formal requirements for corporate and non-corporate provisions

The formation of a shareholders' agreement is subject to regulations governing legal conduct and its restrictions. Besides general prohibitions and limitations which are imposed by the law in relation to the content of contracts, other restrictions that respond to a stricter nature of some sections of the corporate law are to be taken into account. The law often regulates the content of the articles of association by its mandatory rules (the concept of *Satzungstrenge*[17] and its more or less persuasive derivatives). The mandatory or cogent nature of a particular provision (rule) of corporate law, however, does not automatically make the provision of the shareholders' agreement contravening such a regulation void.[18] It is always necessary to examine the reasons why a particular arrangement in articles of association is prohibited, or why it is prohibited to deviate from a particular rule by an arrangement in the articles of association. Where a statutory prohibition is aimed to prevent a particular result (constitutive elements or *status* of the company), but also aims at basic construction elements of individual forms of companies (for example, a prohibition to split a share, rules of maintaining the capital or the basic division of functions of the company's bodies), then an arrangement leading to such an undesired result is void even if it is part of a shareholders' agreement.

It may be concluded that it is not possible to agree, within a shareholders' agreement, on any arrangements that would interfere with the mandatory rules of the company, i.e. the rules that are considered so significant by the law that they are forming the very substance of a company. At the same time, however, even if such rules are agreed, they will not be void automatically, but they might be considered as having no effect externally and leading to specific consequences *inter partes*. The same might be said about those rules contained in the articles of association that could possibly contravene the non-mandatory rules. Even these rules may remain valid, but only in the contractual regime without having any influence upon third

[17] This is e.g. the case in Austria (*Arlt*, [supra note 10], 153, 153) and Germany (*Mock*, [supra note 3], 289, 290 ff.).

[18] See e.g. in German law (*Mock*, [supra note 3], 289, 290 f.).

persons. These considerations may be important when discussing sanction schemes pertaining to such rules, or resulting from their violation.

Arrangements where shareholders' agreement threaten the company's interest not available to the shareholders themselves should be viewed critically. For example, a shareholders' agreement, whereby shareholders obligate themselves not to initiate an *actio pro socio* or derivative suit should be void (especially if the breach of such a duty would be sanctioned by a contractual fine). Regardless of whether such an arrangement would amount to an *ex ante* waiver of rights (which might be – in some jurisdictions – prohibited) or a limited *pactum de non petendo*, the arrangement in question should be void since it interferes with the interests of the company and the creditors. Its execution interferes with the company's interest which is not available to the shareholders and not even to the company itself. Nevertheless, in many jurisdictions the discussion is pending on a possibility to waive the rights related to a share in the registered company, i. e. on a possibility to agree, for example, on a share without a profit-sharing right, without a voting right, etc. Even such discussions usually result in a conclusion that it is not possible to waive those rights which basically consist in the protection of minority shareholders, or in the retaining of control in the company.

Also, the application of general corporate substantive-law mechanisms among shareholders might be an option. For example, the content of corporate documents will be subject to a prohibition to abuse rights, and especially in some jurisdictions it might be a ban on abusive disadvantaging of some of the shareholders. The shareholders' agreement is of a contractual nature allowing the contractual modification of the legal status and it represents voluntary, rather than mandatory, assumption of obligations (except for the arrangements that would vest the right to determine the content of this covenant with the majority). It is therefore protected by contractual mechanisms (good morals, fair business practices, ban on the abuse of a right, and the like).

In other cases, however, there is no reason why the mere fact that an arrangement in shareholders' agreements contravening the rules of the corporate law or the law regulating legal entities should inevitably result in its nullity. Nevertheless, it remains disputable if an inclusion of a particular provision in the shareholders' agreement which, if contained in the articles of association, would have to be in a prescribed written form (for example, in form of a notarial deed). In general, it may be stated that private law does not require that an act related to another act which is subject to a stricter statutory requirement of a written form would also have to comply with the same statutory requirement of a stricter written form. The fact that the articles of association require a stricter written form would still not imply that a similar contractual regulation must comply with the same formal requirements.[19]

---

[19] See e. g. in German law (*Mock*, [supra note 3], 289, 293 ff.).

2. (Limited) Binding effect of shareholders' agreements and articles of association

A difference between the articles of association and shareholders' agreements is also the different extent to which the company, the shareholders and other persons are bound by them. Articles of association bind all shareholders as well as the company itself. They are also binding upon the shareholders who did not vote for the amendment to the articles of association if the quorum necessary for the change of the articles of association has been achieved, and all these entities are also entitled to derive their rights from the articles of association. The binding effect of the articles of association is inseparably connected with the share in the company *(causa societatis)*, and it therefore binds every person acquiring a share in the company. The articles of association also bind members of the company's bodies since they are bound to proceed in compliance with the given corporate documents. On the contrary, shareholders agreements bind only the persons that expressed their consent with them, and they do not bind those who did not express their consent thereto. It is not inevitable that all shareholders were also parties to the shareholders' agreement. On the other hand, it is not excluded that the shareholders' agreement can also bind third persons.

a) Effect on the corporation and its bodies

The boundaries of the binding effect of shareholders' agreements might be illustrated on three entities, the corporation itself and the members of its bodies, the purchasers of shares and third parties. First of all, shareholders' agreements do not automatically bind the corporation, unless the company (and other parties) agreed thereto.[20] The conclusion of a shareholders' agreement is not subject to the consent of a general meeting. However, the company may still derive its rights from such an agreement in accordance with the regulation on contracts for the benefit of third parties on condition that the shareholders intended to grant the company such a benefit. Similar rules will also apply in cases where a member of the company's body is a party to such a shareholders' agreement. The contractual position is personally determined and does not extend to all members of the body. It will always be a specifically designated person who agreed to the shareholders' agreement, rather than any person who is holding an office of a member of the company's body. As was already mentioned, the involvement of the corporation and its bodies in the shareholders' agreements is possible, but they must not exceed so called *statutory powers*, i.e. the core mandatory rules of general regulation of the powers of the company's bodies, including a ban on interference of third parties in the company's management. In other words, the structure of obligations built within the shareholders' agreement may not result in contravening the core mandatory rules on corporate governance which guarantee

[20] On the contrary, a UNCITRAL Model Law on a simplified business entity of 2015 provides in its Article 36 that the shareholder's agreement will bind the company if the company was notified of their existence. UNCITRAL Draft model law on a simplified business entity. A/CN. 9/WG. I/WP. 89.

that governance and ownership of shares will be distinguished and which also guarantee the obligation of due performance of the company's bodies members' duties.

b) Effect on purchasers of shares

Second, even the share purchaser will not automatically become a party to the shareholders' agreement. The share purchaser could acquire the position of a party to the shareholders' agreement only under the rules of the law of contract which basically requires consent of other shareholders to the change of the entities who are parties to the agreement. On the contrary, the rights and duties agreed in the articles of association are "rooted" in the share, because the articles are published and everyone ought to know what properties are bought when acquiring the shares. Where the share is being sold only in the regime of articles of association, it is being sold under the conditions defined in the articles of association and in the law. The rights and duties defined in the shareholders' agreement bind only the parties to that agreement, which obviously also determines the public perception of the status of the share and the company. The legal provisions on how a shareholder may become a party to the agreement vary in different jurisdictions. For example, in Italian[21] and Czech law[22] a cession of the shareholders' agreement is possible. Based on a share transfer agreement between the transferor and the transferee, it will be possible to assign also the claims resulting from the shareholders' agreement if the rights and duties resulting from the agreement are assignable. For the transfer of other rights and duties it will be necessary to execute an agreement whose parties will also include other stakeholders (debtor). On the contrary, the articles of association will usually also bind the assignees. The question of the assignee being bound by articles of association should be distinguished from the meritorious or contractual nature of a covenant contained in the articles of association. Special rules applying to the binding status of the assignee may be identified with the registered ancillary covenants in the shareholders' agreement within the joint stock company in relation to the shares which may be effective also toward third persons.

c) Effect on third parties

Finally, third parties can be parties of shareholders' agreements (e.g. creditors). The covenants agreed with third parties are always of non-corporate nature. However, the participation of a third party standing outside the shareholders' structure and its influence on the company may lead to the specific legal consequences or restrictions, for example, in respect of the question of a possible factual influence on the company governance. Hence, these cases of shareholders' agreements are usually *joint ventures*

---

[21] See for Italian law *Malberti*, in Mock/Csach/Havel (eds.), International Handbook on Shareholders' Agreements, 2018, 425, 434.

[22] See for Czech law *Bohumil*, (supra note 16), 219, 230.

or other forms of consortium structures, basically in a regime of a civil partnership. Similar structures may also be created within arrangement proceedings (restructuring) of a company in crisis, while such models may serve to prevent the threat of bankruptcy etc. (within a more general concept of *standstill of lock-up* agreements).[23]

3. Different mechanisms for the change of corporate and non-corporate arrangements

Company law generally lays down the minimum quorum necessary to execute an amendment to the articles of association. The change of corporate documents is not necessarily subject to unanimous vote, in common, majority vote or qualified majority vote will suffice. Articles of association may be changed by a formal voting process by the general meeting of shareholders, or by passing a resolution outside the general meeting. The shareholders' agreement may be changed by a consent of all of the persons concerned. However, a possibility to agree to majority decision-making on the common matters is not excluded. The shareholders' agreement, by itself, does not effect a majority decision-making concerning its change. This difference, however, exceeds the framework of formalities distinguishing between the articles of association and the shareholders' agreement, and it is also manifested in different conditions of the amendments to corporate and non-corporate arrangements included in the articles of association. Even if contractual (non-corporate) arrangements are included in the articles of association, this will not change its nature, and majority voting thereon will not automatically suffice or is expected. However, a more complex position is to be taken when a corporate matter (for example, an establishment of the right of pre-emption or another restriction of transferability of shares) may be located either in the articles of association or in the shareholders' agreement and thus the matter might appear both contractual and corporate. From the shareholders' decision to include a particular corporate arrangement within the articles of association, one should derive the intent of shareholders to attain not only a contractual nature of that arrangement but especially the corporate nature thereof. The worlds of the shareholders' agreement and of a corporate document are not fully separated. As will be explained later[24], a change or an attempt to change the articles of association may eventually effect a shareholders' agreement, and *vice versa.*

4. Different mechanisms for the enforcement and the consequences of the breach of a shareholders' agreement

The consequences of a breach of the shareholders' duties resulting from the articles of association are defined by the law for each of the types of corporations (for exam-

[23] For details see *Havel*, in Mock/Csach/Havel (eds.), International Handbook on Shareholders' Agreements, 2018, 111 ff.

[24] See F.II.

ple, a duty to pay late-payment interest, to refrain from competitive activities, a possibility of excluding a shareholder). However, the law usually does not provide for the specific consequences of a breach of shareholders' agreements. Common contractual tools will therefore be used. The injured party should basically have at its disposal the whole range of contractual remedies (damages, withdrawal from the contract, objections of default, liability for delay, etc.). In practice, shareholders' agreements are often enforced by a representative of a shareholder authorised by a power of attorney who will exercise the shareholder's rights instead of the shareholder (or several shareholders) and who is bound by the instructions resulting from the shareholders' agreement. Nevertheless, in the above differentiation it is also necessary to take into account the content of the arrangement, or the nature of the obligation breached, and not only its location either in the articles of association or in the shareholders' agreement.

As stated before, [25] an inclusion of a non-corporate arrangement in the articles of association will not affect the contractual nature of such an arrangement. It will remain a contractual covenant that is enforced as a contractual arrangement and binds the parties to such a covenant. If the shareholders opted for a contractual remedy for the breach of a certain obligation resulting from the articles of association and directed at the remaining shareholders, it would amount to a contractual covenant regardless of where it would be placed. And similarly, a provision of articles of association which would bind the shareholders to provide each other loans or which would impose subsidiary obligations upon the shareholders toward each other, unrelated to their corporate shares, would not become a corporate arrangement but remains contractual. A corporate arrangement operates in the world of corporate law and it allows a corporate enforcement instrument only if it is included in the articles of association. The corporate effect (i.e. an exclusion of a shareholder) is not only bound with formal requirements (provision in the memorandam of association or articles of association), but also to material prerequisites (a corporate issue). For example, a duty to pay an extra fee provided for only in the shareholders' agreement will not allow of initiating the process of exclusion against the shareholder in breach of such a duty.

The possibility of enforcing duties or claims resulting from the shareholders' agreement or from the articles of association is associated also with a question of possible protective measures to be employed by the entities affected. Shareholders are protected against changes of the articles of association by an action to declare a resolution of the general meeting passing it as void, and they are protected against the shareholders' agreement or its changes by an action to determine a legal act void. Both of these actions have different condition (for example, varying term of time for bringing an action) and they are addressed against different entities.

---

[25] See IV.

5. Termination

A significant difference between the articles of association and shareholders' agreement also rests in the possibility and the mechanisms of their termination. Shareholders' agreements may be terminated regardless of the duration of the company or a share in the company, by an agreement of shareholders or even unilaterally. It is, however, necessary to take into account a connectedness of the shareholders' agreement with the status of a shareholder of a company. It is, inter alia, disputable if a particular party may withdraw from the shareholders' agreement in full, for example, in the case of a substantial breach of its duties by another shareholder. In our opinion, it is necessary to examine if the parties, when entering into the shareholders' agreement, might have intended, even in an implied manner, to bind the shareholders' agreement with the status of a company's shareholder, and not to allow him/her to terminate the agreement unilaterally, without terminating his/her share in the company. On the contrary, the status of a shareholder is firmly bound to the articles of association. Shareholders are allowed to withdraw from the articles of association only exceptionally, and exclusively along with the transfer of their share in the company or their exit in other way. It is possible neither to agree, nor to unilaterally effect the termination of the articles of association during the life of the company.

6. Interpretation

Another difference between the articles of association and shareholders agreements might be a varying approach to their interpretation. Although it may be generally stated that the world of the articles of association and the world of shareholders' agreements are quite varying worlds, or varying animals, [26] their common contractual basis and their mutual interconnection cannot be omitted. Articles of association basically contain not only provisions pre-defined by the law, but they also contain covenants that exceed the statutory requirements and they include also rules which have been agreed by the shareholders in a regime of autonomous will, but which they intend to maintain only in a regime of external agreement. Such rules are the rules that, although resulting from contractual arrangement of shareholders, acquire as if "meritorious" effect by their being included in the articles of association, which has an impact upon their interpretation. Ancillary shareholders' agreements standing outside statutory rules are sometimes called *sideletters*.[27] A statutory default regulation of the content of the articles of association[28] is supposed to offer such a

---

[26] *Cadman*, Shareholders' Agreements, 2004, 2.

[27] Here the concept of *sideletters* is understood as the concept of the law of contract which is the concept that is superordinate to possible shareholders' agreements as well as ancillary provisions of the articles of association.

[28] I assume that the silence of the articles of association themselves implicitly attracts into their content a range of statutory rules, the "content of articles of association" should therefore be viewed more generally.

normative solution on which the parties would agree if they had time and funds for detailed negotiations, and which, at the same time, guarantees a certain degree of protection of the minority and the creditors (in a more general sense, also other categories of good morals and public order). On the contrary, shareholders' agreements are foreseen to result from negotiation and from searching for a precise solution not relying on the protective network of dispositive rules of the law. While the articles of association are a manifestation and an embodiment of statutory rules with an increased occurrence of cogent rules, shareholders' agreements are a manifestation of autonomous will.[29] It is obvious that the rules which the shareholders have agreed in excess to the statutory delimitation of the articles of association, but which, in spite of that, have been included in the articles of association, are the rules that are more like corporate (statutory) rules, although it is not always so, and so an overlap of corporate (statutory) rules and shareholders' agreement may occur in the articles of association. The above note on the substance of the articles of association, or shareholders' agreement is important for their *ex post* interpretation. It is logical that although the shareholders are trying, through these agreements, to settle the problems *ex ante*, their concrete application will take place thereafter, hence at the time when there will already be no harmony between the parties to the agreement. It is generally assumed that the interpretation of the two instruments must be distinct. This is because the articles of association inevitably require an interpretation where objectiveness is of a higher degree due to the very nature of the instrument, which distinguishes it from a more subjective interpretation of the shareholders' agreement. Similarly, it is necessary to distinguish registered companies from personal companies, etc. For example, the interpretation of articles of association of public companies/joint stock companies is less dependent on the will of the founders compared to the closed companies where no change of shareholders' structure has occurred, or to the shareholders' agreements,[30] which are basically bound with their founders. Nevertheless, it is necessary to say at the same time that although making a difference between the two ruling systems, they still result from the will and intentions of the same persons, and they therefore cannot be separated. Both structures thus make up a single, more general set of rules, the individual layers of which are related to one another and should be perceived in a more holistic way. Under certain circumstances it may be quite artificial to view the articles of association as separate from the shareholders' agreement and from its background, which should enable the courts, when interpreting the articles, to take shareholders' agreements into consideration.[31] The German case

[29] It is also possible to find a different, or more complicated constructions, for example, when a statutory framework of such agreements exists, see above, for example Section § 7. 32 MBCA.

[30] See for example German law (*Mock*, [supra note 3], 289, 307) and Austrian law (*Arlt*, [supra note 10], 153, 173).

[31] See for example English law (*Zakrzewski*, in Mock/Csach/Havel (eds.), International Handbook on Shareholders' Agreements, 2018, 259, 283 ff.).

law permits – in certain occasions[32] – that the circumstances which are outside the scope of the articles of association, including the shareholders' agreements, should be taken into consideration when it is generally possible to expect that the members of the company's bodies were aware of them. However, when interpreting the articles of association, it is necessary to focus more on the fact that they regulate statutory (corporate) issues and by being published their effect is *erga omnes*. Nevertheless, it is not possible to omit their contractual background manifested not only in the possible ancillary provisions contained in the articles of association, but also, for example, in the shareholders' agreement (especially so if the company itself is a party to such an agreement).

7. Shareholders' agreements in the case of structural changes

The consequences of structural changes of a company (change of legal form, merger, consolidation, splitting up, etc.) have a disputable impact on the validity and duration of shareholders' agreements. It is possible to start from the fact that if a particular provision is included in the articles of association, then if, as a result of the change, the original articles of association are replaced by new ones, the previous one terminates. The validity and duration of shareholders' agreements will be examined on a case by case basis according to contractual mechanisms (i.e. impossibility of performance), however, an automatic termination of this agreement is not inevitable.

8. Shareholders' agreements in the bankruptcy of the company

It is possible to assume that the shareholders' agreements may change their function in the situation where the company or any of the parties enters bankruptcy proceedings. The foremost rule is that the bankruptcy of a company not being a party to such an agreement has no direct effect because such an agreement only binds the parties. Nevertheless, it will change the reasons and mechanisms of the agreement among the parties. It is quite common practice, especially in the life of bigger or economically interesting companies, that before the filing for the company management, with the support of its owners and major creditors, to try to find an informal solution of the whole situation. If, for example, the company which is funded by banks falls in a state of economic insufficiency or is threatened by bankruptcy, the bank will identify such a condition based on the agreed contractual instruments and will subsequently initiate an internal process within which it will seek for a possible solution that will generally presuppose not only the engagement of the company but also its shareholder or parent companies. Since the reason of the problem often rests in the current lack of income it is not necessary that the company should end up in bankruptcy. It is

[32] See for German law *Mock*, (supra note 3), 289, 307; for Greek law *Psaroudakis*, in Mock/Csach/Havel (eds.), International Handbook on Shareholders' Agreements, 2018, 317, 337 f.

therefore the company itself which initiates various internal restructuring measures (sale of unnecessary assets, closure of unprofitable establishments, decrease of personnel costs, sale of a part of a business, etc.). Shareholders agreements are therefore often modified for such purposes and amended by new schemes, or other new covenants are added, now already with the engagement of creditors. So-called *standstill* agreements are a common instrument, i.e. agreements between the company, shareholders and major creditors, to the effect that the current increase of the amount of debt by interests is frozen, in other words the current amount of debts is fixed for a defined period of time (e.g. for six to twelve months). Similarly, in order to ensure the continuity of such agreements, various *lock-up* agreements are arranged, i.e. agreements restricting a possible transfer of the *position of a bank*, especially the assignment of its claims to third persons. The subsequent fate of these agreements will depend mainly on their economic success.

In some jurisdictions, within bankruptcy proceedings the claims of shareholders become subordinate and they may be satisfied only after the satisfaction of claims that are not subordinate. Only those claims of the shareholder toward the company may be subordinate which are related to the position of the shareholder, but also any others to the which the shareholder is entitled. If such a situation occurred it may result in that also other claims against the company resulting from shareholders' agreements will qualify as subordinate. Subordination shall mean a subordinate order of sequence of satisfying such claims in respect of other claims. If the company that is bankrupt were a party to the shareholders' agreement, the nature of the agreement may change in the course of insolvency proceedings. First of all, its nature will basically amount to an agreement that has not been mutually performed, yet, and its fate will be in the hands of the official receiver, or a person authorised to dispose of the debtor's assets. This option is used in many European jurisdictions, entitling the official receiver to terminate agreements which would unreasonably burden the debtor and would prevent a sound economic solution – the agreement may, of course, provide for such a solution, and it will either terminate automatically or it provides for its own survival, even without the company as its party. The official receiver may, of course, resist the shareholders' agreement, or its part in a regime of relative ineffectiveness, *actio pauliana*, should the company put some entity in advantage in relation to the bankruptcy, or, on the contrary, if the company disadvantaged anyone in relation thereto.

VI. Collisions between shareholders' agreements and articles of association

The articles of association and shareholders' agreements represent two worlds that are to a great extent, however, not fully, linked to each other. Their collision or intersection is not excluded, and they may supplement and replace each other, but they may also change each other or influence each other in another way.

1. Contradiction between the articles of association and shareholders' agreements

On an abstract level, there might occur a contradiction between the wording of the articles of association and shareholders' agreements. This conflict may already reside in the fact that the corporate document regulates a particular question in a particular way and the shareholders' agreement does so differently. The contradiction itself between the articles of association and the shareholders' agreement will not automatically make any of these documents void. Regarding the parallel nature of their impact, these documents may be contradictory or colliding otherwise. Although legal regulations do not deal with a collision, it is possible to derive certain conclusions. For example, shareholders can agree in a shareholders' agreement to a different extent of the competition clause compared to that which results from the articles of association. Such an agreement could be concluded by only some of the shareholders among each other or just toward one of the shareholders. A competition ban agreed on a contractual basis should only have *inter partes* effect and its breach should basically not result in the rights of the company itself, unless such an agreement complied with the requirement of a contract in favour of a third party. It is even possible that the parties to a shareholders' agreement would intend to provide exactly for an issue that cannot be agreed in the articles of association. For example, in many jurisdictions articles of association cannot exclude the transferability of certain types of shares. Nevertheless, this will not prevent the shareholders from agreeing to a limitation or exclusion of transferability with contractual effect *inter partes*. The contradiction between the articles of association and shareholders' agreements will not result in the invalidity of the articles of association. As has been already stated the fact that a certain arrangement may not be included in the articles of association (or it contravenes another mandatory rule) does not cause the invalidity of the colliding part of the shareholders' agreement.[33] It is always necessary to examine why the regulation of a particular question in the articles of association is inadmissible.

2. Impact of shareholders' agreement on the change of the articles of association

Although, in general a conflict between shareholders' agreements and the articles of association will not make any of these documents void, such a collision may affect their content. The articles of association will be amended by a formal procedure intended for that purpose, by adopting a decision of the general meeting on their change in the future. The shareholders may also adopt such a valid decision that contravenes the provision of the articles of association. The conflict itself between the resolution and the articles of association does not always result in an invalidity of the resolution as the resolution might be an ad hoc deviation of the articles of association or a general pro future amendment thereof.

---

[33] See IV.

A resolution of the general meeting may qualify as an amendment to the articles of association, either in general and for the future, or just for a particular case. The content as well as formal requirements applicable to the amendment to the articles of association must be met, however, and the shareholders must intend either to deviate from the articles of association *ad hoc* and to establish a rule exactly for a particular case without changing the content of the memorandum of association or articles of association (so called piercing of the memorandum of association or articles of association, *Satzungsdurchbrechung*[34]), or to manifest an intention to change the articles of association for the future and in general. In this respect discussion is pending whether an *ad hoc* decision of all shareholders whereby the shareholders would not intend to change the articles of association for the future, but only to establish a particular condition deviating from the articles of association, must meet all formal, procedure and content requirements, as if it was an amendment to the articles of association. The German[35] case law, in particular, but also the Czech case law admits the piercing of the articles of association as a special shareholders' agreement deviating in a particular case from the articles of association without meeting the requirements necessary for the amendment to the articles of association, those are supposed to be required only when the shareholders intend to establish a new legal status, i.e. to change the articles of association for the future (so-called *Satzungsdurchbrechung*).[36] The Slovak case law, for example, has not been fully established, yet. After

[34] See for Germany *Mock*, (supra note 3), 289, 292 f.

[35] See for Germany *Mock*, (supra note 3), 289, 292 f.

[36] According to the Judgment of the Supreme Court of the Czech Republic of 22 April 2009, case ref. 29 Cdo 2254/2007: "The Supreme Court does not find the reason why the shareholders should be able to word out a part of the content of the right to a settlement share (maturity, in particular) in the agreement to terminate a share, pursuant to Section 61 of the Commercial Code in the wording effective in the relevant period, whereas their intent concerning the remain elements of such a content (especially, defining the mode of determination of the amount of the share and the mode of its payment) would have to be determined by the shareholders in the memorandum of association or articles of association. Especially so, if their will – as in the case pending – was not aimed at the determination of a general regime of such a deviation (for an unspecified range of future cases), but rather at the enforcement of a single-case solution related to a single, concrete shareholder. An amendment to the memorandum of association or articles of association would not be suitable for such a purpose, if it was subsequently – after approving an agreement pursuant to Section 149a of the Commercial Code – necessary to review it again. Instead of the interpretation of the provision of Section 61 subsection 2 of the Commercial Code in the relevant wording proposed by the appellant, the Supreme Court therefore concludes that the said provision should be interpreted so as the memorandum of association or articles of association may, in advance, determine the mode of determination of the settlement share differently from the statutory provisions and thereby secure the shareholders in respect of how their settlement share is to be determined in the case of termination of their share in the company. That provision, however, does not prevent all the shareholders from agreeing in a particular case on the mode of determination of a settlement share of a shareholder whose share in the company is to terminate, of course, on condition that such an agreement will not contravene the law, nor will it evade it (i.e. it will not damage the company's creditors, for example), and it will not be contrary to good morals or fair trading practices. It must be noted, however, that the said decision may also be interpreted so that the shareholders' agreement creates a covenant, besides the memorandum of association (articles of association), which determines a reference rule

certain flexible hints,[37] however, it seems to be of a more rigid position.[38] It is, however, beyond any doubt that in order to change the articles of association – including their *ad hoc* piercing or general factual change – it is not enough if the shareholders' intent to adopt a regulation parallel to the existing contractual sphere, but it is rather required that the will of the shareholders was aimed at the adoption of such regulation that would amend the memorandum of association. It remains unclear if a conclusion of or an amendment to the shareholders' agreement which establishes a rule deviating from the one foreseen by the articles of association or articles of association may be considered as a decision that would pierce or factually amended the articles of association. In our opinion, the shareholders' agreement does not have a character of a decision of the shareholders that is necessary in order to pierce or change the arti-

to consider the compliance of the settlement share with good morals or fair trading practises." See also *Bohumil*, (supra note 16), 219, 229 f. for further details.

[37] According to a decision of the Supreme Court of the Slovak Republic in the case referenced as Obdo V 79/2003, an assignment of a business share to a third person is valid, although the memorandum of association has not provided for such a possibility, but the assignment occurred with a consent of all shareholders. Quoted as: "The memorandum of association is a manifestation of the common will of shareholders and all the shareholders jointly have the right to amend it also in way that they will proceed in a particular case differently from its wording." In this case it is a fusion of law-making amendment to the memorandum of association and *ad hoc* piercing of the articles of association. The Supreme Court of the Slovak Republic retained the general level of admissibility, and did not examine if that would also cause an amendment of the memorandum of association for the future, or only an adoption of an *ad hoc* solution contravening the memorandum of association. See *Mrázová*, (supra note 8), 551, 558 ff. for further details.

[38] It might be sometimes demanding to consider and decide if a particular decision of the general meeting represents an amendment to the memorandum of association (articles of association), a decision within the existing memorandum of association (articles of association), or whether it is such a decision that will alter the wording of the memorandum of association (articles of association) only for the purposes of this single case. Professional public has been attracted by the case where a resolution of the general meeting on the removal of one from several members of an authorised body without appointing a new member in its stead, the Supreme Court of the Slovak Republic considered it as a decision on the amendment to the memorandum of association – a decrease of the number of members of an authorised representative body which requires a higher quorum to be valid (judgment of the Supreme Court of the Slovak Republic, case reference 1 Obo 95/2002, ZSP 9/2004, also see the note annexed in the particular journal). Such a procedure is incorrect (a contrary approach was taken, for example, the Supreme Court of the Czech Republic in its judgment of 30 October 2002, case ref. 29 Odo 269/2002). It is not possible to derive the intention to amend the memorandum of association from the very fact that the shareholders have decided to remove a director. The said decision was specific as to the facts in that the subject of the resolution of the general meeting designated as "the amendment to the memorandum of association" in the part where the memorandum of association specified the names of the company's directors. Even that, however, does not allow of concluding that the shareholders intended to amend the memorandum of association since the specification of the names of directors could be only a formal expression or could result from an incorrect interpretation of an obligation to state the names of first directors in the memorandum of association (and the shareholders could think that the memorandum of association should reflect the change of the person of the company's director, from the first to the last). It should therefore be examined if by specifying the names of directors in the memorandum the shareholders really intended to increase the quorum necessary to remove a member of a statutory body. See *Mrázová*, (supra note 8), 551, 558 ff. for further details.

cles of association. It may be assumed that in the case where a particular question deviating from the articles of association is provided for in the shareholders' agreement, its parties might not have intended to amend the articles of association, not even in form of a single piercing, but only to establish a contractual regulation standing besides the corporate document. With regard to the parallel existence and scope of the articles of association and the shareholders' agreement a subsequent shareholders' agreement basically does not amend earlier articles of association and neither does it *vice versa*.

It is also unclear if one could consider shareholders' agreements as agreements on the future amendment of the articles of association (*pactum de contrahendo*). The agreement imposing upon the shareholders an obligation to amend the articles of association should be basically considered an agreement on the exercise of the voting right at the general meeting. But in the situation where it is possible to amend the articles of association also otherwise, for example in a contractual form by an agreement of all shareholders on the amendment to the articles of association, it should be also possible to conclude an agreement on the future amendment to the articles of association. Such arrangements shall render the doubts about the enforceability of voting rights agreements obsolete. Of course, one condition is that the formal and content requirements of a *pactum de contrahendo* have been met.

3. Conflicts between resolutions of the general meeting and shareholders' agreements

On the level of particular cases, a conflict between the corporate and contractual acts may arise in the case where the shareholders have voted at the general meeting differently from what has been agreed in a shareholders' agreement. According to (often criticised) German[39] or even Austrian[40] case law the conflict of a decision of the general meeting with the agreement of all of the company's shareholders is a reason to render such a decision void as if the articles of association have been violated. On the contrary, for example, the Slovak law provides explicitly for such cases that a conflict of a decision of the company's body with the shareholders' agreement will not make such a decision void.[41] This means that even an agreement made by all shareholders does not have the effect of a corporate act. The Slovak law, however, is intentionally silent about the consequences that may result from such a conflict. The consequences of a breach of the shareholders' agreement will remain contractual (for example, damages, contractually agreed legal consequences, and the like).

The shareholders' agreement may exceptionally have some consequences also outside its contractual framework. Shareholders' agreements could be considered as a (voluntary) restriction of shareholders' right. However, this will obviously be an ex-

39 See for Germany *Mock*, (supra note 3), 289, 312.

40 See for Austrian law *Arlt*, (supra note 10), 153, 174.

41 See for Slovak law *Mrázová*, (supra note 8), 551, 569 and for Danish law *Neville*, (supra note 9), 233, 257.

traordinarily rare case occurring, for example, when deciding on the payment of a dividend in the situation where the shareholder concerned would grant his consent in the shareholders' agreement to restrict his right. It would qualify as a manifestation of a contractual type of agreement, but its consequence would appear on the level of corporate law and through the mechanisms of corporate law. The reason why such a resolution should not restrict the rights of a shareholder should therefore not be such that the given result derives from the shareholders' agreement, but rather that the shareholders have granted their prior consent with such a restriction. The interference would obviously have to be such which allows of a consent having been granted in advance, regardless of the technicalities of the voting process, within the meaning of which the question itself could be decided upon only after some time has passed after the granting of such a consent.

4. Invalid decision of the general meeting (shareholders) as a valid shareholders' agreement?

A consenting manifestation of the intent of the shareholders which does not meet the prerequisites of a valid resolution may be considered as a shareholders' agreement.[42] In general, however, it is not possible to state that any invalid resolution of the general meeting should be automatically considered as the shareholders' agreement. One must start from the fact that the members of the general meeting, through their voting, have expressed their will to vote at the general meeting and to pass a resolution rather than to enter into an agreement defining their mutual rights and duties. For example, a resolution on such a change of the articles of association whereby the shareholders would introduce the pre-emption right to their business shares would be declared void because the voting would impair the rights of the shareholders injured. It would obviously not be possible to assume that the voters intended to establish the pre-emption right also among the other shareholders, unless such an intention could be derived from the circumstances of a particular case. The unlawful and therefore void resolution of the general meeting should be never considered as a shareholders' agreement because the reasons of nullity should not admit a possibility of transformation of a corporate act into a contractual act.

a) Content of shareholders' agreements

The content of shareholders' agreements may focus on various detailed issued among shareholders (a narrow definition) or they may deal with issues among shareholders

---

[42] See, e.g., the judgment of the German Federal Court of Justice as of 15.3.2010 – II ZR 4/09, NZG 2010, 988 stating that shareholders can agree on the amount of an appraisal right for the membership in a closed corporation (GmbH) in a shareholders' agreement or in the articles of association. Also see *Ulmer*, Schuldrechtliche Gesellschafterabrede zugunsten der GmbH – Geeignetes Ersatzgeschäft für formnichtige Satzungsdurchbrechung?, in Liber Amicorum Winter, 2011, 687 ff.

as well as toward third persons or the company itself (a wider definition), which means that various *joint venture/consortium, etc.* are also ranked with such agreements.

What is generally agreed by shareholders in terms of a narrow definition of the shareholders' agreement?

1. A more detailed and extensive definition of rights and duties of shareholders:
   a) a more detailed specification of the types of shares even without defining the kind of the share that must be contained in the articles of association,
   b) introduction of specific rights and duties of shareholders not ranked with specific kinds of rights, or
   c) rules for voting at the general meeting (for example, *pooling* – agreements on the exercise of a voting right, or *voting trust* – an arrangement on the separation of the right to vote from the ownership right to a share whereas the title to a share is transferred under fiduciary rules upon a trustee under the trust who will then exercise the voting right with the effect that the right to a profit is retained by the original beneficiary – owner)[43];
2. Rules of company governance:
   a) for example, the rules of structuring and appointment of members of corporate bodies, the right of deployment (*Entsendungsrecht*), the right of appointment (*Nominierungsrecht*), the rules of concern cooperation, the rules concerning determination of a reward (e.g. option schemes, etc.), of course, on condition that they have been approved by the articles of association,
   b) rules for dealing with so called *deadlock,* i.e. the situation where, due to an internal conflict among shareholders or bodies, the functioning of bodies or the company itself is being blocked (e.g. Russian roulette, *Texas shoot-out*, freezing of certain rules, etc.), even in the situation where such a condition has been foreseen by introducing so called the right to veto;
3. Rules for the termination of a shareholders' share in the company – *call options, put options, tag along, drag along,* price fixation, various forms of the right of pre-emption, etc.;
4. Protection of minorities, typically by increasing the rights of a minority shareholder in terms of the right to be informed or the right to deploy its own member of a statutory body, and
5. Rules for dispute settlement (out-of-court-settlement, conciliation proceedings, mediation, arbitration, etc.).

[43] I am aware that this solution employed, for example, in the U.S. law clashes with the Continental law mainly in terms of non-existence of the legal concept of trust or discussion of whether it is possible to separate the voting right and ownership right in this manner. I believe, however, that the concept of trust, including a fiduciary transfer, are solutions that do not interfere with the principle of unity of share because through them the owner is deprived of ownership for a certain period of time, but s/he does so on a fiduciary basis, and not otherwise. This conclusion is also supported by the existence of the concept of fiduciary transfer of a right, etc.

Any shareholder' agreement must be further considered according to particular legal regulations, and the limitations and restrictions of the given legal concepts will be drawn mainly from the rules of that particular jurisdiction. Therefore, if the parties agree on the right of pre-emption to the business shares it may be necessary to examine the compliance of such an arrangement with the rights related to the pre-emption arrangement. In the case of an obligation to provide additional funds to the company there should be examined the prerequisites required by the law for such financing (extra fee, gift, loan), in the case of an obligation to pay a contractual fine it is necessary to examine the requirements for a particular arrangement to be valid, etc. From a point of view of its purpose, the content of the shareholders' agreement will therefore often depend on the parties. The law does not require that all the company's shareholders should be parties to the shareholders' agreement. It is possible that only some of the shareholders will enter into shareholders' agreements. It is even not excluded that a party to a shareholders' agreement could be the company itself, members of its bodies or prospective shareholders, or any third persons (in general, funding creditors). Regardless of the wording of the law, the parties may use their shareholders' agreements for varying purposes that will appear in the content and wording of the provisions of the agreement. The general content of shareholders' agreements could be systematized according to a function which they fulfil, or according to partial goals which they pursue. In this perspective, the above survey of usual particulars of shareholders' agreements may be classified as follows.

5. Shareholders' agreements as a tool of company governance

By entering into a shareholders' agreement its parties arrange for their mutual rights and duties, but the shareholders may not only agree on the mutual rights in the shareholders' agreement, but also the mode of exercise of their rights toward the company. The law outlines general rules for the manner and conditions of the exercise of rights related to their share in the company whether of a proprietary or non-proprietary nature. Hence, the shareholders' agreement may become another manner of company governance.

a) Arrangements on a specific exercise of voting rights

Shareholders' agreements often include agreements on the exercise of voting rights in various forms. Shareholders' agreements may agree, in advance, on a general voting procedure for voting or on a particular voting. It is possible to establish a voting consortium in which some of the shareholders will agree that before the voting at the general meeting itself they will meet separately and will decide by a majority vote on how they will vote at the general meeting (or some of the members of a consortium will be granted the right of veto). Even the shareholders who did not make up the majority are then under a duty to vote at the general meeting as it was decided by the majority of the consortium. Voting arrangements whereby shareholders undertakes to vote in accordance with the instruction of another shareholder, or in compliance with the majority vote of the consortium of shareholders are usually admissible.

The validity of agreements on the exercise of voting rights whereby the shareholder undertakes to observe a voting instruction of a third person is not admitted without reservations. The validity of agreements on the exercise of voting rights concluded with third persons should not be excluded *a priori*. Even the uniformity principle, or a prohibition to split the share or a general impossibility to transfer to a third person the voting rights should not prevent a contractual agreement under which a shareholder is bound to abide by a third person's voting instruction.[44] Sometimes, such an agreement has reasonable grounds (for example, an undertaking not to remove a person, without a due reason, who is a member of a supervisory body delegated by the funding creditor). However, agreements whereby the exercise of the voting rights would be decided upon by a person that is precluded from their exercise (the company itself, members of its bodies), or that would be excluded from the exercise of the voting rights if such a person were a shareholder will obviously not be admissible. An agreement to fulfil the third person's instructions could collide in certain cases with a duty of corporate loyalty of the shareholder that should prevail over his contractual obligation *inter partes*. In such cases it is necessary to realize that the Czech law,[45] taking the German law for its model, contains a ban on binding instructions interfering with the governance of registered companies. Hence, if another shareholder or a third person would attempt at giving binding instructions to the company's bodies, through various contractual structures, concerning the company's governance, it should be treated only as a recommendation that may be rejected by a member of the statutory body within the framework of a due care concept. At the same time, however, the person issuing such instructions exposes itself to the company law, including a possible conclusion that it may be harmful effect that may result in a duty to compensate damage or to assume liability. However, if such instructions are issued within the existing concern, they are basically binding and the statutory body of the controlled entity may reject them only if the harm caused by them was not supposed to be remedied in terms of the company law.

Agreements on the exercise of the voting rights are also connected with the problem of votes buying. It remains unclear if an agreement on the exercise of the voting rights should be valid if the shareholder was supposed to obtain a special reward

44 Other way round, for example, the decision of the Appellate Court in Warsaw as of 5.1.2006 – I ACa 630/05, under which the binding of a shareholder's a voting by instructions of another person is contrary to the prohibition to split the business share, and is therefore void. This conclusion of the Court is, however, criticised in the Polish doctrine (see *Gasinski*, in Mock/Csach/Havel (eds.), International Handbook on Shareholders' Agreements, 2018, 479, 500f.). Even the Austrian practice arrived as a similar conclusion in relation to a partial assignment of the voting rights from one business share to another person, see the judgment OGH of 13 October 2011, case ref. 6 Ob 202/10i. See *Arlt*, [supra note 10], 153, 158ff. for further details.

45 See *Bohumil*, (supra note 16), 219, 224ff. for further details.

(consideration) for a particular way of voting. Some assume that such an agreement should be invalid on the ground of a prohibition to split the business share, or a ban on the "assignment" of voting rights. In the German doctrine, the invalidity of agreements on the exercise of voting rights in a private limited liability company is derived from the contravention with good morals in the case where the shareholder undertakes to vote for a specific reward.[46] This is motivated not only by the effort to remove a corruptive aspect but especially by the protection of a duty of the shareholder's loyalty toward the company. If the shareholder votes on the ground of special advantaged rendered, he is doing so by preferring his own benefit to the benefit of the company and his exercise of the voting right is considered as being unfair. The general rule should be that the shareholder must always prefer the benefit of the company to its own benefit. It would be unfair, however, for the shareholder to prefer its own benefit at the expense of the other shareholders and the company itself. Similar, the agreement on the exercise of the voting rights for a reward may not result in avoiding the voting rights assignment ban, especially in the case of long-term agreements. However, the invalidity of the shareholders' agreement itself need not inevitably make a decision of the company's body void for this particular reason, but an unfair voting should not be taken into account.

The legal consequences of the breach of agreements on the exercise will always be limited to the contractual level. In our opinion, an agreement on the exercise of the voting rights is not an agreement on the future voting at the general meeting and it should not be governed by the rules on the agreement to enter into a future contract. In particular, it should not be possible to achieve, by a bringing an action before the court, to replace or manifest the will of a shareholder during the voting at the general meeting. The reason for that is, that a breach of an agreement to exercise the voting rights is accomplished by voting contrary thereto, or by not voting where voting should be effected. A decision of the court replacing the manifestation of the will as a result of the breach of an agreement to enter into a future contract will be operative in the future where by its becoming effective it will replace a legal act which was not executed (in the case of an agreement to enter into a future contract, such an act is the conclusion of the agreement itself). As a result of such a decision, however, there may not occur a backward change of one manifestation of will (voting contrary to the agreement) to another manifestation of will (voting in accordance with the agreement). On the contrary, the claimant will be able to seek the performance of the obligation to vote in a certain way. However, if the procedural law admits the approach according to which a judgment imposing a duty to perform a particular act will always replace such an act/manifestation of will even regardless of a possible substantive-law absence of an option to replace such an act/manifestation of will so that such

[46] In the area of the law of public limited liability companies/joint stock companies the situation is simpler since the sale of the votes of shareholders is a public law transgression/administrative offence pursuant to Section 405 AktG, and hence is void due to its contravention of the law. See *Mock*, (supra note 3), 289, 296 ff. for further details.

a final judgment should be taken into account at the later voting at the general meeting as an act of voting of the obligated shareholder.

b) Agreements on the appointment of members of corporate bodies (appointment agreements)

Shareholders take part in the company governance especially by the exercise of their rights at the general meeting, but also outside the general meeting. This will include, in particular, agreements on the ways of submission of proposals, procedures for deciding on certain questions, for example, in form of preliminary negotiations in a particular body, but also in deciding on the staffing company's bodies. Shareholders may, for example, agree that the company's bodies will be composed of a particular number of persons appointed by particular parties. In contrast to a common agreement on the exercise of the voting rights in this case it will not be an agreement on the election of a particular person to an office, but also an undertaking to agree with such a person as will be proposed by a particular party to a shareholders' agreement. A potential candidate need not be (and neither will it actually be) specified. That candidate does not have a position of third party – beneficiary and cannot by himself invoke the performance of such an agreement, or claims resulting from their breach. One may derive from the fact that the parties perceive the candidacy of a particular person as subject of their legal relationship, rather than taking a candidate as the subject of that legal relationship. The rules applicable to the agreement in favour of a third person will not apply.

c) Agreements on profit-sharing or other benefits in favour of shareholders

Shareholders may also agree on rules whereby they will govern the company's performance in their own favour. This includes, basically, dividends, settlement shares or other admissible performance in favour of shareholders. Such agreements will become effective only after all the shareholders agree. This will not be a disposition accompanied with the right to a share in profit (by assigning the right to pay the dividend), which is sometimes restricted by the law but it is a non-corporate agreement on the changes of the shares of profit or other performance. Such an agreement could also be a part of the articles of association. However, even the shareholders' agreement cannot exclude or amend the rules restricting the performance of the company in favour of the shareholders (a prohibition to return a contribution, prohibition or restriction to pay a dividend or other equity capital of the company), that are laid down in order to protect the company or its shareholders. If decision-making on the performance in favour of shareholders is in competence of a general meeting (profit sharing/dividend), this part of the shareholders' agreement will basically qualify as an agreement on the exercise of voting rights.[47] In other cases, where the perfor-

[47] See G.I.1.

mance is considerably independent of decisions of a general meeting (for example, conclusion of agreements with shareholders, agreements to decrease the right to a settlement share or functionally equivalent performance related to termination of a share in a company), such agreements will be different from classic agreements on the exercise of the voting rights. Because they may also be considered as a certain waiver of rights, even toward the company itself.

d) Shareholders' agreements on the funding of the company

In shareholders' agreements parties may also agree on how they will participate in the (further) funding of the company (e. g., conditions of additional contributions in excess of the contributions to the registered/share capital, granting donations or loans to the company as well as the mode and extent by which they will take part in the changes of the registered/share capital). As has been suggested, such arrangements are often connected with the agreements concluded within the process of handling a threatening bankruptcy of a company, [48] although they sometimes also appear in form of an "unenforceable" *comfort letter.*

For example, it may be an agreement on the nominal increase of the registered/share capital from the sources of the company and on the mode of division of proportions of their share after a possible increase of the share/registered capital. The shareholders could agree that they will agree provide the company with other funds, for example, by efficiently increasing the share/registered capital in the case where the company is in the crisis or its crisis would threaten. The parties are not excluded from agreeing on a division of the extent of liabilities among themselves to pay the contribution. The obligation to pay the funds may also be an obligation to provide the funds either in form of internal as well as external resources. A legal approach to these arrangements may be complicated and it will obviously depend on a kind of pooling up of the share capital to which the shareholders commit themselves and a degree of legally binding force or legal consequences of such an arrangement. One may take into consideration an agreement to enter into a future contract (an undertaking to conclude a loan contract, but also an undertaking to amend the articles of association), but also a contract containing a condition precedent (a loan whose effect is conditioned by a certain critical financial position of the company). In the above cases the company should itself be a party to the shareholders' agreement. In the case where the shareholders undertake to fund the company one could also consider an agreement in favour of a third party where the company would be such a third party beneficiary. In that case the company itself would not be a party to the shareholders' agreement. It is also possible that the company, already as a party to the shareholders' agreement would be directly entitled as beneficiary under such an agreement. A complicated nature of the forced implementation of a funding obligation will depend on the character of the undertaking assumed. The company as beneficiary could be en-

[48] See VII.I.d).

titled toward the shareholders bound to render the company funds from a loan or to conclude with the company a loan contract. In such a case, it will be a classic contractual relationship. A more complicated situation will occur if the shareholders undertake in the shareholders' agreement to pay up new contributions. A consent to the shareholders' agreement itself will not amount to the assumption of the obligation to pay up a new contribution, not even a conditional one because the new contribution will mean a change of the amount of the registered/share capital which must be first decided by a general meeting. Thus, the shareholders' agreement itself does not establish the company's entitlement to be paid a contribution that it would be able to enforce the performance by an action in court. The agreement on the conditions and the extent of the participation in the changes of the registered capital binds the shareholders involved to vote in a particular way on the issue in question at the general meeting. Such an undertaking, however, has only a contractual nature. It is a contractual undertaking aimed to effect certain corporate conduct. A third person may also become a party to the agreement that may afterward request from the shareholders to issue a decision to increase the registered capital under the conditions of the agreement and to enable such a third person to become a shareholder of the company.

6. Shareholders' agreements related to the transfer of shares

Shareholders' agreements will very often involve arrangements related to various restrictions of the sale or another kind of a transfer of the share in the company (business share, shares of stock), especially in form of various pre-emptive rights, options, restrictions or determinations of potential transfers.

a) Arrangements related to the transfers of shares provided in the articles of association

When determining the issues related to the transfer of the share in the company discussions are focused on whether such an arrangement has substantive or contractual consequences. The conceptual distinguishing between substantive and contractual consequences, however, is not quite precise and it is obscuring the problem in the corporate context rather than clearing it up. Contractual consequences of a breach of the arrangement on the restriction of transfer will traditionally mean the *inter partes* consequences without binding or otherwise relating the third person, assignee of an object or a right thereto while being in breach of a given restriction. The substantive law consequences of the arrangement will mean two different things. First, the binding force or effect of such an arrangement also toward a third person not involved in the arrangement, for example, toward the assignee of a thing. Second, the invalidity of the act whereby a breach would be accomplished. It is generally assumed that is a particular arrangement has only contractual consequences, it is related only to the contractual parties and its breach does not result in nullity. Nullity is not associated with the substantive (factual) nature of an arrangement, most probably, because it is a sanction or legal consequence which is also related to the person not involved in the arrangement. In company law, however, one should not get lured by the simplification of the law of contract, and not only because the articles of association or the articles of association bind *per se* each assignee of a share, i.e. it is not possible to talk about a third person not involved in the articles of association at all. Moreover, the different consequences of the agreement to restrict the right of assignment of a share in the company need not result from a different understanding of the qualities of that agreement or the consequences of its breach (substantive or contractual), but they may be associated with different qualities of the given object of the assignment (assignability as a property of the object). For example, the agreement to prohibit further transfer of ownership (of a thing) has completely different consequences of its breach than the agreement on the prohibition of further assignment of a claim. The reason is not the substantive or contractual nature of these agreements but modification of the content of the given legal position (right of ownership, claim). Although ownership may not be changed by agreement of subjects, the content (properties) of a claim may be changed in such a way. It is possible to create such a claim which will extinguish upon the assignment. A contractual prohibition of the assignment could represent just that type of agreement. Even that, however, should not become grounds for the nullity of the assignment of a claim, if any, only for the liability for defects (non-existence of the object of the assignment). This should be taken into account also in the relation to the share in the company. The substantive or contractual consequences are thus more of a description of the functioning and effect rather than the reason of such consequences. A change of perspective is therefore necessary. The point is not whether a breach of such an agreement has substantive or contractual consequence, but rather if it is possible to change, in the articles of association, the properties of the share in the company (shares of stock, business shares). The admissibility of such an arrangement should be measured by the fact if the law allows to "close" the company and its shareholders' structure *(closed company)*, or to determine the conditions of the assignability of its shares. The limit would be a ban on the closing of the company (public limited liability companies). If it is possible to exclude or restrict the assignability of a share in the company it is also possible to determine in the articles of association a special mechanism related to the assignment of that share. Such a mechanism would qualify as the exclusion or restriction of the assignability of a business share or a share of stock.

This is from the consequences of the breach of such an arrangement derive. More correct is therefore the approach of the Czech Supreme Court,[49] also adopted by a part of the Slovak case law,[50] under which the right of pre-emption to a business share

[49] Judgment of the Supreme Court of the Czech Republic of 4 April 2000, case ref. 29 Cdo 2811/99; see *Bohumil*, (supra note 16), 219, 227 for further details.

[50] Judgment of the Regional Court in Bratislava of 1 October 2013, case ref. 2 Cob /238/2012; see *Mrázová*, (supra note 8), 551, 561 f. for further details.

determined in the articles of association is treated as a restriction of the assignability of a business share. An offer made to the other shareholders to purchase that share is therefore considered as the objective prerequisite of the assignability. This approach seems to be more persuasive compared to the approach of the Slovak Supreme Court according to which a breach of the right of pre-emption to shares of stock has only contractual consequences.[51] Distinguishing, made by the Slovak Supreme Court, between the substantive and contractual consequence of a particular arrangement obviously resulted from the application of the concept whose consequences – in the non-corporate world – are usually distinguished on such grounds (pre-emptive right). Such distinguishing, however, will not help us if the shareholders included in the articles of association a concept that is typical in the private law, for, example, an obligation to inform other about the intended assignment, time specification of a possibility to transfer the shares of stock (open or closed period of a year), various options, etc. However, this will not mean that the parties would not be allowed to determine, even in the articles of association, such rules to dispose of their shares in the company whose breach would only have contractual consequences.

With each particular provision of the articles of association related to the transfer of the share in the company one has to decide if it amounts to corporate restriction of the assignment of a share or an arrangement of parallel contractual (or even substantive or substantivized) regime. One should expect that by placing a particular arrangement related to the transfer of the share into a corporate document the parties intended to achieve its corporate effect, hence (in the extent admissible for a particular company) to condition or restrict the transfer of the share in the company, and not only to attain such consequences with which this institute is – in non-corporate world – commonly associated. Hence, they changed the properties of the share in the company. And therefore, if nothing else results from a particular arrangement in the articles of association it will be a condition of assignability a breach of which should make the assignment void. Moreover, not every arrangement related to the assignment of the share should be considered as corporate restriction of the assignment – i. e. as corporate agreement on the change of the properties of the share. Shareholders are free to incorporate in the articles of association such a rule that will not be considered as restriction of the assignability of the share in the company, but only as a specific duty of a shareholder having contractual consequences. Nevertheless, that should not be presupposed, but should be specifically proved. In other words, from the fact that the shareholders included in the articles of association a particularly named concept related to the assignment of the share in the company (for example, pre-emptive right), one should not automatically assume that one should apply the legal regulation of the consequences of its breach. That also means that if shareholders included an atypical concept in the articles of association admissible on the ground of their contractual freedom (for example, duties to inform connected with

[51] see *Mrázová*, (supra note 8), 551, 567 for further details.

the intended assignment), will not be applied only to the consequences resulting from the law of contract, but it should be determined if it qualifies as corporate restriction of the assignment or only as additional contractual regime.

b) Shareholders' agreements on the transfers of shares

The regulation of the rights and duties related to the assignment of the share in the company contained in the articles of association should be distinguished from the regulation of such rights and duties contained in the shareholders' agreement. Corporate practice knows a lot of such covenants, such as pre-emptive rights, rights of re-purchase (specified mechanisms for assignments of others), mandatory assignments and various agreements to enter into future contracts, options, *drag-along* or *tag-along* arrangements, regularly connected with various supportive mechanisms of price determination (*shoot-out* etc.). Subsidiary arrangement related to the assignment would have corporate effect and could be considered as restrictions or conditions of the assignment of the share only if they met a condition of formal corporate document, i.e. if they were contained in the memorandum of association or in the articles of association. However, the cases where the memorandum of association or articles of association have been "pierced" in an admissible extent will also be considered as articles of association. As has resulted from the above, the arrangement standing outside a corporate instrument may not change the properties of the share in the company. One therefore has to consider their consequences according to general rules of the law of contract distinguishing between the traditional categories of substantive and contractual consequences. Such arrangements have always only contractual consequences in the shareholders' agreement and they will not bind third parties unless those became parties to the shareholders' agreement. Consequences of a breach of the contractual obligation related to the assignment of the share in the company will manifest itself only in the contractual sphere (as a rule, by a duty to pay damages or a contractual fine) and only exceptionally also in form of absolute nullity in the case of a breach of the right to re-purchase.

c) Collisions between shareholders' agreements and articles of association related to the assignment of shares

It may happen that a particular contractual provision for the assignment of a share in the company contained in the shareholders' agreement will collide with the statutory provisions related to the assignment of such a share or with the articles of association. A situation may occur where the shareholders will agree in the shareholder's agreement a certain limitation of the right to dispose of the share in the company, although they may not take into consideration any such limitation in the articles of association or the articles of association, or they will explicitly determine in these documents that no limitation of the assignment exists. Collision of these provision will result in the nullity of the shareholders' agreement and the rules agreed therein regulation the right of disposition of the share in the company. Consequences of violation of one or another will become manifest in their separated worlds. It will therefore be possible that the assignment of the share will become effective, however, there will occur a breach of the shareholders' agreement establishing the right to damages. Shareholders' agreements may also serve to agree the rules that would be inadmissible in the memorandum of association or articles of association. Such practice is manifested in the arrangements relate to the assignment of the share in the company. In relation to this one refers to the interpretation of the relationship between the shareholders' agreement and articles of association. A short excursion in this respect should be made to the German case law where a decision of the Federal Court of Justice was passed,[52] which laid down that an agreement between the shareholder and the joint stock company will be void if the shareholder is imposed a duty to transfer its shares to the joint stock company free of charge although the shareholder itself acquired them for a financial consideration.[53] It seems, however, that the reason of such a prohibition is just a coincidence of circumstances and the transaction context (a duty to transfer the shares in the company free of charge if those were acquired of a financial consideration), rather than a conceptual prohibition of an "ancillary" agreement on a mandatory duty to transfer the share in the company in favour of the company that is subject to strict conditions within the meaning of the German law on the joint stock companies (public limited liability companies).

7. Shareholders' agreements regulating the enforcement of rights and duties; dispute resolution

Shareholders' agreements also contain provisions related to dispute resolution and enforcement (execution) of rights and duties of shareholders. In such cases shareholders basically try to minimalize the risks of a violation of duties resulting from the share in the company in the shareholders' agreements, either by exerting factual and economic pressure to perform them or by ensuring various legal simplifications during their implementation. The aim is to achieve that the exercise of the rights and execution of duties should not be decided in ordinary proceedings before a court, but rather that an *ex ante* solution should be offered that will exclude a possibility to bring an action in a particular case or will diminish the motivation of the persons concerned to initiate such a dispute, because a lengthy court proceedings may cause long-term damage to the operation of the company. The parties to the shareholders' agreement have a wide range of tools available to reach that goal. These include arrangements on self-executory mechanisms of enforcement of shareholders' agreements (power of attorney to perform the rights of the shareholders, including an au-

---

[52] Federal Court of Justice as of 22.1.2013 – II ZR 80/10, NZG 2013, 220.

[53] German law on the joint stock companies allows that a joint stock company should be forced to receive/take over the shares *(Zwangseinziehung)* – § 237 German Stock Corporation Act (AktG).

thorisation to transfer the share in the company while some them being already contained in the statutory law.

Arbitration clauses are common practice in shareholders' agreement. Disputes between shareholders, companies and its directors are generally arbitrable.[54] The inclusion of an arbitration clause into the shareholders' agreement underlines its contractual nature. However, some specific types of corporate disputes are either non-arbitrable or only arbitrable subject to specific limitations and conditions (declaration of nullity of a shareholder meeting resolution, disqualification of directors or disputes about liquidation or winding up of the company).[55] Parties to a shareholders' agreement might seek arbitration in order to enforce voting rights agreements. A possibility to declare the resolution of a shareholders meeting in breach of a voting right agreement null by an arbitral award might be an important step towards the enforceability of such covenants. However, the arbitrability of such claims is controversial. First of all, the declaration on the nullity of a shareholders meeting resolution has *erga omnes* effects while arbitration produces *inter partes* effects only. Unlike a statutory court, an arbitral tribunal can have no powers vis-à-vis persons that are not bound by the arbitration agreement. Nonetheless, such limitation does not render the arbitrability of such matter impossible. Since shareholders can revoke or amend the resolutions of their meeting, there is no compelling reason for such disputes to be non-arbitrable *per se*. The conditions under which such disputes are arbitrable have been well developed by German[56] and Austrian[57] case law and legal literature.[58]

Austrian courts and literature adopted a more streamlined positive attitude towards the arbitrability of such disputes already in 1950.[59] In Germany, two landmark cases are to be brought into attention. In 1996, the Federal Supreme Court affirmed the general arbitrability of disputes for declaratory relief on the nullity of shareholder meeting resolutions.[60] The particular conditions necessary for the arbitrability of

[54] *Born*, International Commercial Arbitration, 2nd edition 2014, 1029 and the case law and literature cited therein.

[55] *Born*, (supra note 55), 1029.

[56] German Federal Supreme Court as of 6.4.2017 – I ZB 23/16 (*Schiedsfähigkeit III*), NJW 2017, 657; German Federal Supreme Court as of 6.4.2009 – II ZR 255/08 (*Schiedsfähigkeit II*), BGHZ 180, 221 = NJW 2009, 1962; German Federal Supreme Court as of 29.3.1996 – II ZR 124/95 (*Schiedsfähigkeit I*), BGHZ 132, 278 = NJW 1996, 1753.

[57] Austrian Supreme Court as of 16.12.2013 – 6 Ob 43/13m, Zak 2014/148 S 78 – Zak 2014, 78; Austrian Supreme Court as of 13.6.1990 – 7 Ob 548/93; Austrian Supreme Court as of 29.6.2006 – 6 Ob 145/06a.

[58] See e.g. *Duve*, Arbitration of Corporate Law Disputes in Germany, in Böckstiegel/Kröll/Nacimiento (eds.), Arbitration in Germany – The Model Law in Practice 2007, 1006; *Pitkowitz*, The Arbitrability of Corporate Disputes under Austrian Law – Still Open Questions? In Austrian Yearbook on International Arbitration 2014, Vienna 2014, 33.

[59] Ruling of the Austrian Supreme Court, file No 2Ob276/50. repeatedly confirmed afterwards. See rulings of the Austrian Supreme Court, file No 7Ob221/98w; file No 6Ob145/06a and decisions cited above.

[60] German Federal Supreme Court, (supra note 57) ("Schiedsfähigkeit I").

such disputes have been elaborated in a Federal Supreme Court ruling from 2009[61] and were confirmed in 2017.[62] These conditions ought to provide enough arguments for an *erga omnes*-like effect of an arbitral award. The most relevant ones might be helpful reflected by other jurisdictions as well. According to the conditions set by the German Federal Supreme court:

- All shareholders must be parties to the arbitral proceeding. All shareholders must be informed of the proceeding and must have the right and the possibility to participate in the proceeding.
- The appointment of the tribunal must be left to an independent appointing authority or the shareholders must have the right to participate in the appointment of the tribunal.
- The setup of the arbitral proceeding must prevent parallel proceedings and irreconcilable rulings on the same subject. It is thus required that all potential disputes concerning one particular resolution are concentrated in the same proceedings.
- It is advisable that all shareholders and the company itself including its bodies are parties to the arbitration agreement and thus bound by it.

In Germany, these conditions were incorporated into the model arbitration clause and the rules prepared by the German Institute for Arbitration and its Arbitral Rules.[63] Similarly, arbitration clauses are strengthening the enforcement possibilities of contractual arrangements concerning the rights and obligations of parties related to the sale of their shares (rights of first refusal, pre-emption rights, piggy-back clauses, put or call options and other arrangements).

---

61 German Federal Supreme Court, (supra note 57) ("Schiedsfähigkeit II").

62 German Federal Supreme Court, (supra note 57) ("Schiedsfähigkeit III").

63 *Deutsche Institution für Schiedsgerichtsbarkeit* (*DIS-Ergänzende Regeln fur gesellschaftsrechtliche Streitigkeiten 2009*), available under www.disarb.org.

Shareholders' Agreements in Family Firms

Paula del Val Talens

Abstract: Family firms rely on shareholders' agreements as a tool to both reinforce and to preserve the influence of the family over the company. This contribution examines the role this kind of agreements play in ensuring family control and transgenerational involvement by looking at the features that companies ruled by families share. It also places shareholders' agreements within the matrix of sources governing family companies, namely, as regards the articles of association and family protocols. The chapter then explores the topical contents of shareholders' agreements undersigned by family members, this is, family voting pools, provisions regarding the transfer of shares, and provisions relating to the composition of the board of directors.

I. Introduction

Family firms qualify a *real type*, as opposed to legal forms or legal types.[1] As it is the case for real types, family firms are seldom tackled directly by legal provisions and, therefore, are hardly defined by the law. This is not to say that they are never addressed by legal provisions since a number of relevant illustrations arise in the comparative framework. Family firms are sometimes addressed under succession law to ensure the unity and continuity of the family business upon death.[2] In such scenarios, the law usually enables testators to allocate the firm entirely in the hands of a sole heir or a number thereof so that the firms is passed on to the next generations (art. 1056.II of the Spanish Civil Code). Another notable example of this trend is the Spanish Royal Decree 171/2007, of February 9, regulating the disclosure of family protocols.[3]

In contrast to the regulatory framework, the defining features of family firms have long been established by legal scholarship.[4] Recent interdisciplinary endeavours have

[1] See, for this approach, *Fleischer*, NZG 2017, 1201, 1204; *Bong*, Gesellschaftsrechtliche Wirkungen einer Familienverfassung, 2022, 11–12.

[2] See *Kalss* in Kalss (ed.), Company Law and the Law of Succession, 2015, 3, 4; *Kalss*, in Fleischer/Prigge (eds.), Family Firms and Family Constitution, 2023, 198, 199ff.

[3] Real Decreto 171/2007, de 9 de febrero, por el que se regula la publicidad de los protocolos familiares, "BOE" núm. 65, de 16/03/2007.

[4] *Kalss/Probst*, Familienunternehmen, 2013, 14–20; *Kalss* (fn. 2), 4; *del Val Talens/Gimeno Ribes*,

produced conclusive findings.[5] Against this background, a family firm is one whose members and those actively controlling the business are attached to each other by kinship or marriage. Since it is common for the firm to take the form of a limited liability company, such linkage refers to shareholders and directors. In addition, to qualify as having family nature a firm must seek intergenerational involvement as to ensure that the firm is passed on to the next generation of the family, which shall remain in control thereof.

It is against this conceptual framework that our contribution discusses the specific role that shareholders' agreements play in family firms. To this end, we asses shareholders' agreements in light of the defining features of family firms (II). This section analyses their legal placement within the organisational framework of a family firm, namely, a family company (a public or a private limited liability company). We then discuss the subjective and substantive scope of shareholders' agreements in family firms (III). The analysis is grounded on commonly accepted practice and legal scholarship within the comparative framework by providing illustrations from several European jurisdictions (Germany, Italy, Spain, and Portugal).

II. Role and Placement of Shareholders' Agreements in Family Firms

This section conceptualises the influence of shareholders' agreements on the governance of a family company against the theoretical backdrop on the presiding features of family firms (1). It then observes shareholders' agreements within the matrix of legal sources that shape any given family company (2).

1. The Role of Shareholders' Agreements in Light of the Features of Family Firms

Whether shareholders' agreements play a significant role in family firms must be assessed against the features of this kind of businesses. First, within the European business environment, family firms are predominantly closed companies, often adopting the form of private limited liability companies.[6] These are typically reliant on adaptable contractual arrangements.[7] Although such tailored arrangements may sometimes be embedded in the articles of association, an agreement running parallel to the latter may offer a higher degree of adaptability and, thus, better accommodate the preferences of a family firm.[8]

---

in Fleischer/Recalde/Spindler (eds.), Family Firms and Closed Companies in Germany and Spain, 2021, 23, 57.

[5] *Fleischer,* in Fleischer/Prigge (eds.), Family Firms and Family Constitution, 2023, 3 ff.; *Bong* (fn. 1), 19–25.

[6] *Bachmann/Eidenmüller* et al., Regulating the Closed Corporation, Berlin, 2014, 5–6.

[7] *McCahery/Vermeulen,* Corporate Governance of Non-Listed Companies, 2008, 144.

[8] Similarly, *Hueck,* Die Familienverfassung – Rechtliche Konturen eines Instruments der Governance in Familienunternehmen, 2017, 97.

This assertion shall be nuanced in light of certain comparative law considerations. In some jurisdictions, the articles of association of private limited liability companies may enjoy a higher degree of flexibility that those of a public limited liability company – compare the difference between German public and private limited liability companies (§ 23 Abs. 5 Aktiengesetz, for Germany) with the lack of distinction for Spanish public and private limited liability companies (art. 28 Ley de Sociedades de Capital, for Spain)[9] – . Therefore, the adaptability argument may be valid for family firms that adopt the form of stock companies (public limited liability companies), but would be less persuasive for family-owned private limited liability companies.[10] This nuance should not be generalized, as the difference in the degree of flexibility between company types is not the rule in all jurisdictions.

Second, since family firms aspire to maintain family control over the company, it is well established both by the management and legal scholarship that they are naturally averse to third-party access to the company. This shows in their common reluctance towards both equity finance and accessing capital markets.[11] In this vein, given that shareholders' agreements are kept confidential among shareholders, family firms will be prone to them as a tool to maintain secrecy over certain tools that hinder the entry of third parties and, more generally, protect family control from being compromised.[12] From the business perspective, shareholders' agreements can help preserve trade secrets or prospective policy guidelines.[13] From a governance perspective, shareholders' agreements can lay down family coordination mechanisms ensuring family control over outside shareholders or vis-à-vis the fragmentation of the family into branches.[14]

Third, shareholders of family firms are impacted by affective commitment. Affective commitment, as an emotional attachment to the family firm, provides family members who are also members of the company with a sense of belonging and loyalty towards it. This explains why family firms may sometimes rely on so-called moral enforcement mechanisms. As opposed to legal enforcement mechanisms, these may stem from the influence a matriarch or patriarch may have upon their descendants or the fear of causing family conflict, disappointing their elders, or disengaging from the family legacy or the family values. Moral enforcement mechanisms can and are sometimes documented as part of a family protocol, the legal core of which are indeed shareholders' agreements. As a result, shareholders' agreements may formally

---

[9] Real Decreto Legislativo 1/2010, de 2 de julio, por el que se aprueba el texto refundido de la Ley de Sociedades de Capital, hereinafter LSC.

[10] *Wicke/Berkefeld*, in Bochmann/Scheller/Prütting (eds.), Münchener Handbuch des Gesellschaftsrecht. Recht der Familienunternehmen, 6th ed., vol. 9, 2021, 676, 678, para. 3.

[11] *del Val Talens/Gimeno Ribes* (fn. 4), 59–61,

[12] *Embid Irujo/Martínez Sanz*, RdS 7 (1996), 11–12; *Wicke/Berkefeld* (fn. 10), 678, para. 3; *Hueck* (fn. 8), 97; *Mock*, in Fleischer/Recalde/Spindler (eds.), Family Firms and Closed Companies in Germany and Spain, 2021, 205, 207. See also, pointing in this direction *J. Feliu Rey*, RdS 54 (2018), 246 ff.

[13] *Wicke/Berkefeld* (fn. 10), 678, para. 3.

[14] *Wicke*, ZGR 2012, 450, 483; *Mock* (fn. 12), 210–211.

appear documented alongside with moral duties arising from affective commitment. Hence, the latter may exert certain influence upon the interpretation of the former, and even upon legal enforcement mechanisms as a whole.

2. Legal Placement of Shareholders' Agreements in Family Firms

To further explore the issue, we now turn to the way shareholders' agreements interact with the broader framework of regulations affecting the latter. Here, the scholarly literature has observed that family firms are subjected to a multi-layered framework or matrix of legal sources. This framework or matrix combines normative commitments based on both company and contract law, on one side, and moral commitments, on the other side.[15] The normative layers of the matrix are typically comprised of i) mandatory legal provisions regulating a family company; ii) the partnership agreement or company contract; iii) the articles of association with iv) the family protocol, the core legal part of which is a shareholders' agreement; v) and sometimes even internal board regulations or provisions establishing how the general meeting may be conducted. This matrix of sources can be regarded as a legal embodiment of the well-known three circle model proposed by *Tagiuri* and *Davis*.[16]

The placement and interaction of shareholders' agreements within such a framework is probably not confined to family firms but rather concerns any company to which a shareholders' agreement runs parallel.[17] The distinctiveness of family firms lies in the richness of its matrix of sources, especially due to the presence of moral obligations. When assessing each level of regulation vis-à-vis shareholders' agreements within family firms, the following results are yield. As regards level one, mandatory company law may be more stringent or more widespread in the case of public or stock companies than in private limited liability companies. This idea simply underlines the choice of the latter as a preferred type of company for family firms. We further discuss the relationship between family shareholders' agreements and the articles of association, on one side, and that between the former and the family protocol.

a) Family shareholders' agreements vis-à-vis the articles of association

At the second level, that concerning the articles of association, a tension emerges between them and shareholders' agreements. This tension balances flexibility and the

[15] This layer approach in *Kalss/Probst* (fn. 4), 54; *Fleischer*, ZIP 2016, 1509, 1509–1510. A similar approach, on pilars *McCahery/Vermeulen* (fn. 7), 4 (setting the ground for FF). For a similar approach from the Spanish perspective, *Vicent Chulià*, RDPat. 5 (2000), 21, 36; *Fernández del Pozo*, RdS 29 (2007), 156. See also *Alonso Espinosa*, RDM 283 (2012), 33, 47–48.

[16] *Tagiuri/Davis*, FBR 1996, 1999 ff.

[17] See *Fleischer* (fn. 15), 1510; *Fleischer* (fn. 5), 19 highlighting that the nomenclature in Spanish and Italian underlines the idea that shareholders' agreements run alongside the articles of association.

coherence of the system of sources. The discussion on the former revolves around which of them (whether the articles of association or shareholders' agreements) affords more flexibility; this is, is more easily adaptable and therefore should be preferred by family firms. In theory, company law typically provides sufficient leeway for shareholders to tailor the organisation of the company in accordance with their preferences and their needs (in Spanish private and public limited liability companies, art. 28 LSC; in the German private limited liability company, § 45 GmbHG).[18] However, the articles of association as well as their amendments are submitted to substantive judicial or registral scrutiny. In their examination, the competent authority will evaluate their consistency with mandatory company law. Despite the theoretical flexibility the articles provide, since shareholders' agreements need not be registered or even disclosed, they are naturally exempt from this kind of legality scrutiny and therefore offer – at least in this regard – more leeway to adaptability.

A second aspect of the quest for flexibility refers to the consensus necessary to amend each of them (the articles of association and the shareholders' agreement). Under domestic company law, the articles of association can generally be amended by a qualified majority of shareholders. In turn, the modification of shareholders' agreements is typically subjected to contract law, which generally requires that all signatories to an agreement consent. Notwithstanding the above, in a number of jurisdictions – such as Germany and Spain –, shareholders' agreements may qualify as partnership agreements.[19] Whenever this is the case, some countries deem acceptable that the partnership agreement itself alters the unanimity requirement and provides for amendments thereof by the majority instead.[20] As a result, the domestic framework is largely responsible for shaping the degree of flexibility afforded to shareholders' agreements as opposed to articles of association.

As for the coherence between the articles of association and shareholders' agreements, three key issues must be considered. First, it is widely accepted in the literature that the articles of association should be adapted to conform a shareholders' agreement.[21] To the extent admissible by applicable company law provisions, transposing merely contractual provisions into the articles would render them fully enforceable under company law.[22] The idea is emphasized in the context of family firms, where a significant portion of the family will be involved in the agreement or the agreement may be omnilateral. The extent to which such adaptation is possible is variable and relies entirely on the content of the shareholders' agreement being aligned with mandatory company law. It may also depend on the position of the do-

---

[18] *Fleischer* (fn. 5), 18.

[19] *Wicke* (fn. 14), 484; *Hueck* (fn. 8), 96; *Mock*, in Mock/Csach/Havel (eds.), International Handbook on Shareholders' Agreements: Regulation, Practice and Comparative Analysis, 2018, 277, 281–283.

[20] For Germany see *Mock* (fn. 12), 219.

[21] *Fernández del Pozo* (fn. 15), 164; *J. Valenzuela Garach*, in Pérez-Serrabona González (ed.), Derecho societario, derecho privado y empresa familiar, 2023, 117, 123.

[22] *Vicent Chulià* (fn. 15), 42.

mestic authority in charge of the Commercial Register. In Spain, very detailed provisions aimed at establishing *ad personam* safeguards for family members, typically included in shareholders' agreements, may be denied registration.

Second, but in close connection, in some countries it is commonly advised to enact family protocols into the articles of association. The protocol may take the form of a preamble to the articles of association.[23] In other countries, to the contrary, this practice is not followed as the protocol's is deemed unsuitable content of the articles.[24] Simply mentioning the existence of a family protocol and referring to them may be similarly admissible in both types of jurisdictions.

Yet, most jurisdictions share the view that family protocols – and the shareholders' agreements that they contain – enjoy certain interpretive value vis-à-vis the articles of association as long as the interest of third parties is not at stake.[25] The scope of their interpretive value is generally reflected upon by comparing onminlateral and non-omnilateral agreements. Legal scholarship insists that the interpretation of the articles of association shall not rely entirely on a non-onmnilateral agreement;[26] other interpretive tools such as the partnership agreement should be similarly considered.[27] However, this in turn acknowledges certain interpretive value to non-omnilateral shareholders' agreements.

Interestingly, on a general basis, the articles of association of companies are to be interpreted objectively.[28] Claiming that the articles may be interpreted in light of a family protocol or a family shareholders' agreement entails a subjective understanding of an otherwise objectively interpretable document. This explains why the suggestion that family protocols or family shareholders' agreements shall be relied upon to interpret the articles of association has been met with resistance in Germany,[29] and to a lesser extent in Spain.[30]

The principle of objective interpretation shows some signs of openness in family contexts. Recent legal scholarship promotes a slightly more flexible perspective by comparing family protocols to circumstances known by all shareholders and direc-

[23] *Fleischer* (fn. 15), 1518. For similar practices in Italy, *Malberti*, in Mock/Csach/Havel (eds.), International Handbook on Shareholders' Agreements: Regulation, Practice and Comparative Analysis, 2018, 413, 434.

[24] For Spain, *Fernández del Pozo* (fn. 15), 168.

[25] RDGRN 4 May 2005 [RJ\2005\5539]; *Fernández del Pozo* (fn. 15), 168; *Fernández del Pozo*, RDM 284 (2012), 53, 95; *Noval Pato*, Los pactos onminlaterales: su oponibilidad a la Sociedad, 2012, 125; *Pérez Millán*, in Mock/Csach/Havel (eds.), International Handbook on Shareholders' Agreements: Regulation, Practice and Comparative Analysis, 2018, 567, 582.

[26] *Perez Millán* (fn. 25), 582.

[27] *Fleischer* (fn. 15), 1517; *Hueck* (fn. 8), 252 ff.

[28] *U. Noack*, Gesellschaftervereinbarungen bei Kapitalgesellschaften, 1994, 70–75; cfr. *Schockenhoff*, ZGR 2013, 76, 87 ff. As regards family protocols, *Bong* (fn. 1), 325 ff. and 354. For Spain, *Noval Pato* (fn. 25), 38 ff.; *del Val Talens*, RJN 95–96 (2015), 629 ff.

[29] See *supra* n. 28.

[30] *Paz-Ares*, Actualidad Jurídica Uría & Menéndez 5 (2003), 40–41.

tors or to omnilateral agreements in private limited liability companies.[31] Their interpretive value is today accepted whenever the protocol is referred to by the articles of association.[32] A more overt strategy for interpretive nuance is the express inclusion of family-oriented criteria within the articles of association. In Spain, the DGRN/DGSJP, the governing body of notaries and registrars, upheld a provision in the articles of association of a family company which required that the articles of association and other rules on the functioning of the company were interpreted in accordance with the purpose of preserving the family business and assets.[33] In contrast to simply enacting the family protocol or relying on the prevailing scholarly view on the interpretation of the articles in light of shareholders' agreements, the drafters chose to set – in a way, objectively – their own family-related interpretive standards. The meaning of the clause was far from clear but was a distinct indication of the family's intentions. Besides, the resolution confirms that the existence of a family protocol may be indeed mentioned by the articles of association.

Within the family company's matrix of sources, shareholders' agreements and articles of association are not hierarchically related,[34] but rather have a different objective and subjective scope. This statement shall of course be nuanced in light of an onmilateral shareholders' agreement. In practice, shareholders' agreements often assert their own precedence over the articles of association.[35] Again, the objective value of such provision on the articles of association and, more generally, its corporate enforceability is rather limited besides the specific case of omnilateral agreements.

b) Family shareholders' agreements and family protocols

The legal nature of family protocols, sometimes also called family constitutions, has been at the centre of the academic debate for some time now. As a complex document laying down the foundations and principles that preside the governance of a family firm, family protocols contain a bundle of contracts alongside with moral commitments by means of which a family firm is governed.[36] Due to the diversity of their content, there is broad consensus that family protocols cannot be ascribed a single

---

[31] *Fleischer* (fn. 15), 1518 in light of BGH, Urteil v. 26.11.2007 (II ZR 227/06) and Urteil vom 18.12.1986 – VII ZR 22/86. An equivalent approach in Spain can be found in *Noval Pato* (fn. 25), 125.

[32] *Fleischer* (fn. 15) 1518; *Bong* (fn. 1), 354.

[33] The provision read in Spanish, "Mientras se mantenga la actual caracterización, como empresa ligada de modo exclusivo a la familia de los fundadores, la interpretación y aplicación de sus estatutos y normas de funcionamiento habrá de respetar la finalidad de conservación de la empresa y patrimonio familiares".

[34] *Fernández del Pozo* (fn. 15), 170. Similarly, referring to independence, *J. Valenzuela Garach* (fn. 21), 123. On this discussion, vis-à-vis omnilateral agreements, *Noval Pato* (fn. 25), 88.

[35] *Wicke* (fn. 14), 483.

[36] *Kalss/Probst* (fn. 4), 53–55; *Serrano Cañas*, El cambio generacional en empresas familiares, 2013, 51.

legal nature.[37] From a legal standpoint, and for the purposes of our analysis, the core of family protocols are indeed shareholders' agreements.[38] This is not to imply that both shall be entirely assimilated as suggested by the Spanish provisions on the disclosure of family protocols, according to which this is the most common hypothesis.[39] The most authoritative scholarly analyses indicate that family protocols encompass contractual, moral, and mission-driven components, requiring an *ex casu* legal assessment of each provision.[40] In fact, for the purposes of the Spanish regime on the disclosure of family protocols, merely morally binding protocols are excluded from its scope of application.[41]

Even though one is usually part of the other, their personal scope may sometimes differ. Shareholders' agreements within a family firm may sometimes be undersigned by non-family shareholders (art. 29 LSC). In turn, family protocols may be subscribed by family members who do not hold shares to the family company. In this vein, under Spanish law, a family protocol is regarded as a bundle of agreements signed by shareholders or by them and third parties (art. 2.1 RD 171/2007).

As mentioned, in Spain, family protocols may be disclosed on a voluntary basis (art. 2.3 RD 171/2007). Each company shall only disclose one protocol (art. 2.3 RD) and the power to decide upon this kind of publicity is vested on the firm's administrative organ (art. 3.1 RD 171/2007). The decision to disclose or withhold publicity shall be grounded in the interest of the company (art. 3.1 RD 171/2007). Evidently the signatories of the family protocol as such – namely, those who are also shareholders – do not hold authority upon the corporate channels through which the formalities for the disclosure of a protocol are managed.[42] This somehow differs from the disclosure of shareholders' agreements in public listed companies, where any of the signatories is equally entitled to notify the agreement. All in all, any provisions on disclosure set in an omnilateral agreement within a family protocol should be taken into account as a clear-cut reflection of the interest of all shareholders. Besides, in both Spanish private and public limited liability companies the general meeting may instruct the board of directors on administrative matters (art. 161 LSC), hence, to disclose or refrain from publicising the family protocol. As long as their personal data are made available as part of the family protocols, the board will require the signatories' consent (art. 3.2 RD 171/2007).

The Spanish provisions on the scope of disclosure are difficult to interpret and have caused considerable confusion around the ways in which the existence of the protocol and the contents thereof shall be made public. First, the administrative body of a

---

37 *Fleischer* (fn. 15), 1519. For Spain, *J. Valenzuela Garach* (fn. 21), 129.

38 Cfr. *Fernández del Pozo* (fn. 15), 147.

39 Preamble of Real Decreto 171/2007, de 9 de febrero, por el que se regula la publicidad de los protocolos familiares: "como pacto parasocial, en hipótesis más frecuente sin más límites que los establecidos, con carácter general, en el ordenamiento civil y específico, en el societario".

40 *Fleischer* (fn. 15), 1519; *Fleischer* (fn. 3), 18; *Bong* (fn. 1), 284–285.

41 *Vicent Chulià*, RJC 1 (2008), 51, 67.

42 *Fernández del Pozo* (fn. 15), 170.

company can decide upon disclosure of the protocol through the website that the company has indicated to the Register (art. 4 RD 171/2007). It is unclear whether this shall be the same corporate website registered in accordance with company law provisions (art. 11 bis LSC) because article 4 RD 171/2007 refers to an abrogated general provision on corporate websites, which was surprisingly deleted due to its lack of use in practice very shortly after RD 171/2007 came into force.[43] This appears to be a systematically correct solution to the loophole.[44]

Second, the board of directors may also notify the register, as for the information to be included in the company's registry record, whether a family protocol exists and whether it is available through the corporate website (art. 5.1 RD 171/2007). The Register will simply disclose the existence of a family protocol and the indication whether it is available on the company's website. The content of the protocol is not made public through the Register, which cannot require the board to submit it (art. 5.2 RD 171/2007).

As a third alternative, the family protocol can be disclosed through the annual accounts (art. 6 RD 171/2007). The protocol can be attached to the documents submitted with the filing of the annual accounts (art. 6 RD 171/2007). Here again, doubts arise regarding the scope of powers of the Register upon examination of the family protocol.[45]

The Spanish provisions on disclosure of family protocols also highlight the interplay between family protocols, within which family shareholder agreements are contained, and resolutions of the company bodies (the general meeting and the board of directors). Whenever the company passes a resolution in accordance with a disclosed family protocol, this circumstance must be stated in the public deed and duly recorded in the Commercial Register (art. 7 RD 171/2007). This may be the case, for instance, if the articles of association need to be amended to preserve coherence with a family shareholders' agreement or if the voting pool appoints a family member to the board in accordance with the protocol's contractual provisions. The provision only applies as long as the protocol has been disclosed in accordance with RD 171/2007. Since the Royal Decree foresees different ways, doubts arise as to the kind of publicity that must have been complied with in order for article 7 RD 171/2007 to take effect. While some claim it only accounts for fully disclosed protocols, others consider that the content of the protocol need not be publicly available for the provision to apply.[46] Once again, the underlying rationale of article 7 RD 171/2007 is to foster the interpretation of corporate provisions in line with a *pro familia* interpretive principle. Here,

---

[43] Art. 9 *Ley 34/2002, de 11 de julio, de servicios de la sociedad de la información y de comercio electrónico* abrogated by *Ley 56/2007, de 28 de diciembre, de Medidas de Impulso de la Sociedad de la Información.*

[44] See *Martínez Rosado*, Los pactos parasociales, 2017, 209.

[45] *Serrano Cañas* (fn. 36), 68–69.

[46] *Fernández del Pozo* (fn. 15), 165; *Fernández del Pozo* (fn. 25), 91.

it does so by providing a formal ground to interpret resolutions in alignment with the family protocol.[47]

The failed Spanish regime on the disclosure of family protocols should be observed within a shift towards increased *juridification* of family protocols and constitutions,[48] which has prominently focused on establishing their legal nature and the implications thereof. Spain was quick to join this trend, although arguably only favouring a formal approach as a means of advancing the issue.

III. The Scope of Shareholders' Agreements in Family Firms

Shareholders' agreements in family firms they are distinctive from both a subjective and a substantive standpoint. We therefore examine the nuances of their personal scope (1) and then explore the content they most commonly encompass (2).

1. Subjective Scope

Shareholders' agreements in family firms are typically undesigned by those shareholders belonging to the controlling family, but sometimes non-family members may also be part of them.[49] As discussed, the subjective scope of family agreements may differ from that of the family protocol. This is primarily due to the fact that third parties who are connected to the company (such as shareholders or directors), but who do not belong to the family will be generally excluded from the latter. In the same vein, whereas a family protocol may be addressed at the foundational or controlling family as a whole, a shareholders' agreement may sometimes be only undersigned by a branch or another smaller group of family members.[50]

Taking from the matrix of sources as an adaptation of *Tagiuri* and *Davis*'s representation, simultaneously belonging to more than one circle – here, that of the family and that of the company – entails that the concerned person will arguably be bound by both company and family commitments. The composition of each group could undergo variations. The family may grow through marriage and birth, with may come alongside with transfers of shares to family members or third parties, which in turn may also happen upon death of a relative. This explains why adherence and withdrawal mechanisms are a key component of shareholders' agreements in family firms. On the company's side, proper coordination with a family shareholders' agreement or even a family protocol may be ensured through ancillary obligations.

---

[47] See Preamble of RD 171/2007: "permitir con ello una más adecuada interpretación de los acuerdos adoptados."

[48] *Fleischer* (fn. 5), 20.

[49] *Hueck* (fn. 8), 94. Similarly, *Fernández del Pozo* (fn. 15), 160; *J. Valenzuela Garach* (fn. 21), 124 and 126.

[50] *Wicke/Berkefeld* (fn. 10), 680, para. 6.

This type of auxiliary duties for shareholders can be attached to the shares through the articles of association. Here, they would impose shareholders to undersign a family protocol.[51] The issue has been intensively discussed under Spanish law, where the debate has revolved around the proper content of such ancillary obligations and the effective disposal of her shares.[52]

2. Substantive Scope

The international scholarly literature on family shareholders' agreements similarly highlights three main types of provisions that are usually found in them.

a) Voting arrangements

Voting arrangements are the backbone of this type of agreements.[53] Through them, family signatories undertake to vote together and determine the direction of their vote at the general meeting of the company to which they are shareholders. In this way, they ensure that family members pertaining to the pool vote in accordance with the shareholders' agreement.[54] By creating a voting pool the family members may retain the majority of the voting power in the company and therefore ensure family control over it. They may as well facilitate the exercise of power by one or several family branches.[55]

Voting pools are usually encompassed by provisions aimed at ensuring that signatories respect voting commitments and cast their vote as agreed. These may take the form of a family assembly prior to a general meeting in which family members discuss and agree on their voting position or simply confirm previous voting policy.[56] Domestic law constraints may also justify this kind of periodic meetings. For instance, in Spain, a proxy should be awarded for every single general meeting unless the general power to represent the shareholder is contained in a public deed (art. 183.2.II LSC).[57]

---

[51] *Fernández del Pozo* (fn. 15), 163; *Sánchez Ruiz*, in Sánchez Ruiz (ed.), Régimen jurídico de la empresa familiar, 2010, 43, 51–52. RDGSJFP 26 June 2018 [RJ\2018\36]. Monographically, *J. Feliu Rey*, 54 (2018), 666 ff.; *Pérez Millán*, RDM 311 (2019), 477, 486–788. For Germany, *Wicke* (fn. 14), 484; *Hueck* (fn. 8), 95.

[52] RDGSJFP 26 June 2018 [RJ\2018\36]. See *Fernández del Pozo* (fn. 15), 163; *Pérez Millán* (fn. 51), 486 et seq.

[53] *Mock* (fn. 12), 213; *Fleischer* (fn. 5), 19. From the Spanish perspective, *Sánchez Ruiz* (fn. 51), 51–52;

[54] *Klein-Wiele*, NZG 2018, 1401, 1403.

[55] *Wicke/Berkefeld* (fn. 10), 680, para. 6. *Noval Pato* (fn. 25), 49.

[56] *Vicent Chulià*, in Derecho mercantil de la Comunidad Económica Europea: Estudios en homenaje a José Girón Tena, 1991, 1205, 1233; *Fernández del Pozo* (fn. 15), 149, *Fernández del Pozo* (fn. 25), 88; *Trinks*, in Kindler/Laimer/Perathoner (eds.), Gesellschaftsrechtliche Nebenvereinbarungen in Europa, 2nd ed., 2024, 532, 554, para. 41.

[57] Similarly highlighting this point *Pérez Millán* (fn. 25), 574.

Both to facilitate the casting of the votes and to ensure compliance with the voting arrangement it is frequent for a proxy to be authorised, sometimes during the family assembly.[58] Proxy voting will play a more significant role in companies that are not entirely controlled by a single family, or where multiple family branches are organized into different shareholders' agreements or into distinct voting pools. In this way, a family representative or one for each family branch[59] may attend the meeting on behalf of the members of the voting pool and cast their votes in accordance with the family agreement. This explains why their role is particularly highlighted when the descendants belonging to the third generation join the company.[60] The pool should also expressly regulate their operating rules. Again, since the pool may qualify as a partnership under domestic provisions, decisions shall be adopted unanimously unless otherwise expressed by pool regulations providing for majority decisions.[61]

At the domestic level, non-revokable proxies are heavily discussed as a measure against free-riding. A non-revokable proxy entails that a shareholder who granted a proxy may not revoke the representative's authority, namely, by attending the general meeting themselves. Under company law, personal attendance of a shareholder will *ex lege* revoke the proxy (in Spain, art. 185 LSC).[62] The question arises whether this provision may be departed from by agreeing on a non-revokable proxy. In Spain, under article 186.5 Reglamento del Registro Mercantil (hereinafter RRM), the articles of association can enable non-revokable proxies in private limited liability companies. In such case, the company shall only acknowledge attendance of the representative – here, the designated family or pool representative – .[63] The proxy may then only be revoked in accordance with the provisions regulating how the voting pool operates and not simply by the shareholder attending the general meeting themselves.[64]

The issue is that article 186.5 RRM is a regulatory-level rule that should not repeal or deviate from the mandatory legal provision laid down in article 185 LSC.[65] The former provision does not apply to public limited liability companies although authors sometimes advocate in favour thereof.[66]

---

[58] *Fernández del Pozo* (fn. 15), 149; *Fernández del Pozo* (fn. 25), 88.

[59] *Fernández del Pozo* (fn. 15), 169 and fn. 74; *Sánchez Ruiz* (fn. 51), 52.

[60] *Wicke/Berkefeld* (fn. 10), 680, para. 6.

[61] See for Germany, *Klein-Wiele*, NZG 2018, 1401, 1402–1403; *Wicke/Berkefeld* (fn. 10), 680 and 687, para. 7 and 21. For Spain, *Alonso Ledesma*, in Alonso Ledesma (ed.), Diccionario de Derecho de sociedades, 2006, *Sindicato de voto*, 1029, 1033. For Italy, *Malberti* (fn. 23), 430 after Cass. Civ. sez, 20 September 1995, n. 9975, para 4.

[62] *Sánchez Ruiz* (fn. 51), 52. More broadly *Vicent Chulià* (fn. 56), 1240–1244. See, for Germany, *Klein-Wiele* (fn. 61), 1404.

[63] *Fernández del Pozo* (fn. 15), 177.

[64] *Pérez Millán* (fn. 25), 574.

[65] *Serrano Cañas* (fn. 36), 78–79.

[66] *Fernández del Pozo* (fn. 15), 177; *Serrano Cañas* (fn. 36), 78.

b) Provisions regarding the transfer of shares

Provisions regarding the transfer of shares are similarly relevant for family members who undersign a shareholders' agreement.[67] The interdependence between the latter and the articles of association becomes especially evident here. Indeed, the articles of association will lay down the corporate rules applicable to the transfer of shares. Provisions regarding the transfer of shares within a family shareholders' agreement typically balance family control with preserving equality among family members or branches while ensuring liquidity for family members.

As a matter of fact, this kind of clauses will primarily aim at ensuring that shares cannot be easily transferred outside the family pool, jeopardizing family control over the company. In turn, members of the family may have conflicting interests and personal affinities should also be factored in. This may often be the case when different family branches are involved in the company as the firm is passed on to the next generations: One may think of rivalries between siblings or of parental preferences. Here, provisions on the transfer of shares can be relied upon to preserve the power balance between family branches,[68] for instance, by ensuring that their shares remain in the hands of relatives belonging to the branch. At the same time, the scholarly literature highlights the role of liquidity in family firms.[69] Like provisions on profit distribution, provisions on the transfer of shares should facilitate that family members who have lost affective commitment are able to disinvest.[70]

These clauses often take the form of pre-emption rights for family members favouring all of them generally or only the concerned family branch.[71] To ensure coherence with the corporate framework, these provisions can rely on share classes laid down by the articles of association. In close connection to the latter, share transfer may also be subjected to authorisation clauses. By virtue of such provisions signatories to the agreement shall seek authorisation from their counterparties to the pool before transferring them. The authorisation may be granted by a majority or unanimous vote of the signatories to the agreement or may only concern the members of a given branch.

Although formally and substantively different, all provisions on the transfer of shares are mutually interdependent.[72] As a result, they may be separately considered in abstract terms, but can only be incorporated into the agreement after careful joint consideration of their interaction. We examine some of the most commonly highlighted examples in the international scholarly literature on family firms. Lock-up

[67] *Mock* (fn. 12), 213; *Pérez Millán* (fn. 25), 592; *Fleischer* (fn. 5), 19.

[68] *Sánchez Ruiz* (fn. 51), 60.

[69] From a Portuguese perspective, *Norton dos Reis/Alves*, in VII Congresso Direito das Sociedades em Revista, 2023, 273, 275–276.

[70] As a result, *Vicent Chulià* (fn. 56), p. 13; *Iribarren Blanco*, RdS 53 (2018), para. 2.

[71] *Fleischer* (fn. 5), 19. See also *McCahery/Vermeulen* (fn. 7), 153. Sometimes foreseen as rights of first refusal, *Pérez Millán* (fn. 25), 579.

[72] *Valmaña Cabanes*, El régimen jurídico del protocolo familiar, 2014, 155.

clauses prevent shareholders from transferring their shares *inter vivos*.[73] Although differences arise at the domestic level, most jurisdictions are concerned with the excessive length of such attachments being contrary to principle (cfr. art. 1705 CC).[74] This explains why they are generally accepted as long as the prohibition is confined to a period of time.[75] The temporary framework ranges between two (art. 108.3 LSC, for Spanish private limited liability companies) and five years (art. 123.4 RRM for Spanish public companies).[76] Domestic company law sometimes lays down additional safeguards such as granting a withdrawal right or unanimous approval by the general meeting (cfr. artt. 108.4 LSC and 2355 c.c. for Spain and Italy). In practice, shareholder agreements' may set longer temporary thresholds, but tend to abide to the time constraints laid down by the law to ensure enforceability.[77] Within this constellation, mutual hostage provisions may be relied upon whenever the family members work through their differences to solve any conflict.[78] In turn, forcing a signatory to sell their shares may be a corporate solution to a family conflict, for instance, whenever someone abandons the family as a result of divorce.[79]

The following may be considered among the clauses that limit access based on the profile of prospective shareholders. Lock-out clauses prevent third parties, but also persons not fulfilling the criteria selected by the family agreement from accessing the company.[80] The requirements may refer to the prospective acquirer's education or experience,[81] but also to family ties or even age. Among the latter, so-called young access provisions appear to gain momentum.[82] These are clauses aimed at ensuring that younger family members access the company at a specific point in time, which favours intergenerational involvement. Granting access to successors may also help preserve equality between family branches.[83] If they coexist with pre-emptive rights established by the agreement itself or by the articles of association in favour of current shareholders, it will be necessary to provide for the waiver or repeal of such rights in order for these clauses to be effective. Branch balance can be preserved through a right of first refusal benefiting the members of the family branch.[84]

These provisions are supplemented by contractual mechanisms concerning the valuation of shares. The comparative framework is somewhat asymmetric, but common practice remains relatively homogenous. Like the articles of association, the

[73] *McCahery/Vermeulen* (fn. 7), 152–153; *Sánchez Ruiz* (fn. 51), 60.

[74] *Valmaña Cabanes* (fn. 72), 163.

[75] *McCahery/Vermeulen* (fn. 7), 153.

[76] *Pérez Millán* (fn. 25), 579.

[77] *Pérez Millán* (fn. 25), 579; *Trinks* (fn. 56), 555, para. 44.

[78] *McCahery/Vermeulen* (fn. 7), 152.

[79] *Sánchez Ruiz* (fn. 51), 60; *Valmaña Cabanes* (fn. 72), 162.

[80] *Sánchez Ruiz* (fn. 51), 60; *Valmaña Cabanes* (fn. 72), 161.

[81] *Sánchez Ruiz* (fn. 51), 60.

[82] *Sánchez Ruiz* (fn. 51), 60. Similarly, *Lamandini*, Cont. imp. 2004, 282, 287–288.

[83] *Sánchez Ruiz* (fn. 51), 60; *Lamandini* (fn. 82), 287–288.

[84] RDGRN 1 October 1993 [BOE n. 268, 9 November 1993, pp. 31569–31571]. *Alonso Espinosa* (fn. 15), 69.

agreement may lay down the criteria and calculation systems to establish reasonable value (art. 114.2.b) RRM). Whenever departing from the latter is deemed lawful, below-market valuations in case of buy-back by family members is a prototypical solution.[85]

c) Provisions regarding board composition

Voting pools and provisions affecting the transfer of shares ensure that the majority of the voting power attached to the shares and expressed through the general meeting remains in the hands of the controlling family. To achieve a similar effect within the administrative organ or the board of directors, shareholders' agreements also foresee provisions on the composition of the board.[86] These secure the continuity of family dominance on the board and, if required, the power balance between family members. Essentially, these clauses seek that the board of directors accommodates both family preferences and family members.[87] For this purpose, they are designed to facilitate the nomination of family members or persons associated to them as directors. Whenever necessary, they will be aimed at preserving an equal or balanced presence of all family branches.

Of course, since the power to appoint directors lies with the general meeting, provisions on board composition heavily rely on voting pools to achieve the majority required under company law.[88] Only as long as family shareholders comply with them will a given family member be successfully appointed to the office in accordance with the provisions we analyse.[89]

As regards their contents, provisions may consider four core issues. First, as long as company law provides for different organisational options for the company's administrative body, a shareholder's agreement may compel signatories to ensure that a board composed with enough positions to host enough family members or branches remains in place.[90] Second, the agreement will instruct the voting pool to favour the appointment of family candidates. This may entail exclusively appointing family members or also favouring candidates proposed by them.[91] Candidates should fulfil any requirements laid down by mandatory company law and the articles of association. Third, the agreement could similarly establish the criteria under which appointments will be decided. Through them, power balance between branches can be preserved by allocating equal seats to the board for each family branch or simply by ensuring that all branches are represented.[92] Fourth, the agreement may also estab-

[85] *McCahery/Vermeulen* (fn. 7), 153. See also *Pérez Millán* (fn. 25), 592.

[86] *McCahery/Vermeulen* (fn. 7), 154; *Mock* (fn. 12), 213.

[87] *Fleischer* (fn. 5), 19. Simlarly, *Fernández del Pozo* (fn. 15), 148.

[88] *Vicent Chulià* (fn. 56), 1236; *Martínez Rosado* (fn. 44), 313.

[89] *Fernández del Pozo* (fn. 25), 97.

[90] *Serrano Cañas* (fn. 36), 63–64; *del Val Talens/Gimeno Ribes* (fn. 4), 59 and 62.

[91] In Portugal, *Norton dos Reis/Alves* (fn. 69), 278. In Spain, STS 17 November 2020 (n. 613) [RJ\2020\5282]; *Gimeno Ribes*, RdS 61 (2021), para. II.3.

[92] *Lamandini* (fn. 82), 287.

lish the appointment mechanism through which the family candidate shall access the board[93] or simply state that one of the parties or the branches shall be entitled to appoint directors.[94] This can take the form of a contractual minority appointment mechanism, but may also rely upon corporate channels such as ordinary resolutions of the general meeting or minority appointment mechanisms under the applicable company law (i. e., the Spanish *sistema de representación proporcional* [art. 243 LSC]).[95] In practice these clauses are often encompassed by correspondent provisions in the articles of association.

Shareholders' agreements may sometimes consider particular positions within the board such as executive directorates, the chairpersonship or the secretary.[96] Here, branch balance shall be compatible with clauses reserving key positions to family members with a demonstrated vocation and/or suitable professional experience.[97] Along these lines, it may be the case of larger undertakings that professionalisation concerns or legal requirements recommend setting aside family members and appointing directors who are not connected to the controlling family.[98] In turn, provisions on board composition may assign the chairpersonship to a family member,[99] sometimes an elderly person with authority such as the matriarch or patriarch.

The main concern raised by contractual clauses dealing with board composition has to do with the influence that signatories to a shareholders' agreement may exercise upon directors who were appointed on its grounds. The terms of discussion slightly differ from one jurisdiction to another, but the concern is shared across all the legal systems under consideration. Directors appointed as a result of a shareholders' agreement shall still act independently and in the interest of the company. From the Spanish perspective, shareholders' agreements cannot dictate the way in which directors (not even family appointed ones) shall vote within the administrative body nor how they should behave.[100] Instead, both the power division between the board and the general meeting, and director independence shall prevail.[101]

In the comparative framework, article 17.2 of the Portuguese Companies Act (*Código das Sociedades Commerciais*) is very revealing in this regard. The provision states that shareholders' agreements shall not address the behaviour of other persons in the exercise of administrative of supervisory functions. As a result, shareholders'

[93] *McCahery/Vermeulen* (fn. 7), p. 154.

[94] STS 17 November 2020 (n. 13) [RJ\2020\5282], FD I.

[95] STS 6 March 2009 (n. 138) [RJ\2009\2794]; STS 17 November 2020 (n. 13) [RJ\2020\5282], FD I.

[96] STS 5 March 2009 (n. 131) [RJ\2009\1633]; *Paz-Ares Rodríguez*, RDM 325 (2022), para. I.

[97] *Lamandini* (fn. 82), 287.

[98] *Lamandini* (fn. 82), 287–288.

[99] *Lamandini* (fn. 82), 288.

[100] *Vicent Chulià* (fn. 56), 1235–1236; *Alonso Ledesma* (fn, 61), 1033; *Martínez Rosado* (fn. 44), 338–351.

[101] *Vicent Chulià* (fn. 56), 1235–1236; *Martínez Rosado* (fn. 44), 338–351; *Trinks* (fn. 56), 555, para. 43. See also *Paz-Ares Rodríguez*, InDret 4 (2010), 1, 14–20.

agreements may not instruct directors how to behave, which in turn poses doubts as to the admissibility of the scope of any provision regarding directors in shareholders' agreements under Portuguese law.[102]

Provisions on family directors can also consider interactions between them an any family body, such as a family council, instituted either through a shareholders' agreement or through the articles of association.[103] In connection to the threat to director independence, reluctance towards family bodies is grounded on their risk of interference upon the powers vested on the company bodies by the law.[104]

IV. Overview

1. The analysis has underlined the ways in which shareholders' agreements accommodate the defining features of family firms, namely, of family companies. Adaptability and confidentiality are the two main reasons why a family-owned or controlled company may resort to shareholders' agreements. Although aligned with a current trend aimed at grounding family protocols, provisions encouraging their disclosure or that of the relevant contractual provisions they usually contain, such as the Spanish RD 171/2007, have not been successful.

2. Whenever in place, shareholders' agreement may be embedded at the core of a family protocol. They will then both exert some influence in the interpretation of the articles of association, but common practice still recommends either referring them in the articles (Germany) or including the interest of the family as an interpretive criterion (Spain).

3. Voting pools, provisions regulating and restricting the transfer of shares and clauses relating to the composition of the administrative body of the family company are the three main contents of agreements between family members holding shares to a company. Clauses that establish how signatories shall vote generally sustain provisions on share transfer and board composition. For this reason, they are usually reinforced by family meetings and proxy mechanisms. Provisions regulating share transfer demand stronger coherence with the equivalent clauses on the articles of association. Finally, shareholders' agreements shape the composition of the board in family firms, especially, to ensure balance among family branches. Still, mandatory company law provisions on directorial behavioural draw a blurry line on their admissibility.[105]

---

[102] *Cunha*, in Countinho de Abreu (ed.), Código das Sociedades Comerciais em Comentário, vol. I, 2nd ed., 2021, Art. 17, 325–326.

[103] *Fleischer* (fn. 5), 18.

[104] As a result, *Fernández del Pozo* (fn. 15), 150–151. Similarly, *Alonso Espinosa* (fn. 15), 65.

[105] This paper is part of Research Project PID2024-158762OB-I00.

No Private Ordering Please, We're Italian[1]

Luca Enriques and Casimiro A. Nigro

Abstract: Private ordering enables investors to design firm-specific governance arrangements. Aided by specialized lawyers, sophisticated contracting parties can engage in complex private ordering exercises yielding agency cost-minimizing governance structures. Venture capital ("VC") contracting is a notable example. Through decades-long iterations, US VC contracts have emerged as the best real-world solutions to the challenges of financing high-tech firms, informing transactional practice globally. Yet, the law, corporate law included, can hinder the "transplant" of US VC contracts. In a companion paper, we provide systematic evidence that German and Italian corporate laws literally crash contracting parties' ambitions to transplant US VC contracts. Importantly, we spotlight that blackletter corporate law provisions are less often to blame for this outcome than (widely accepted) scholarly interpretations. Corporate law in action is thus "über-mandatory". This essay complements our previous research by asking how Italian legal culture can explain this character. We note that Italy's internal legal culture grants legal professionals wide discretion in interpreting and applying the law to complement statutory provisions with a number of implicit mandatory rules and principles. External legal culture, in turn, explains legal professionals' (and chief among them legal scholars') inclination to build a "system" of mandatory corporate law rules. To begin with, the long-standing predominance of banks' role in corporate finance created demand for rigid corporate laws. Second, legal professionals' inclination to extend mandatory corporate law is consistent with their self-interest as it increases demand for legal services and, hence, their rents. Third, few Italian legal scholars appear to trust markets and decentralized rulemaking as efficient and fair tools to allocate resources, consistently with the dominant political ideology. Lastly, Italian legal scholars aspiring to establish their academic reputation and advance their careers face stronger incentives to identify novel mandatory requirements that constrain private ordering – thereby demonstrating their mastery of the legal system – than to advocate for legal deference to existing private ordering solutions, which may be perceived as trite and unoriginal.

De te fabula narratur.
Horace, *Satires*, I, 1, 69–70

---

[1] This chapter is a reprint of the article with the same title published in The Italian Law Journal in 2025. We acknowledge our debt to the many people whose comments have greatly improved the output of the project on corporate law as a determinant of VC contracting and investments in one of the companion papers. This specific essay has benefited from additional comments by Peter Agstner, Antonio Capizzi, Camilla Crea, Alberto Mingardi, Mario Notari, Tobias Tröger, and Andrea Zoppini. Benedetta Maini has provided valuable research assistance.

I. Introduction

In many jurisdictions including Italy, the law can be conceptualized as a nested structure reminiscent of a *matryoshka* doll. In this analogy, the legal regime applicable to a specific case represents the innermost doll, encased within a larger, more comprehensive structure: the "system". This system can be understood as a rationally ordered, all-encompassing virtual repository of legal rules, concepts, and principles.[2] It is collectively shaped by legal professionals – including scholars, practitioners advising private parties, and, most authoritatively,[3] judges – who continually refine and articulate its contents. The system is the result of how, consistent with a jurisdiction's "internal legal culture",[4] legal professionals apply their jurisdiction's metarules[5] to combine, organize, and rationalise the raw materials of the relevant legal sources in a coherent intellectual construction. Our third *matryoshka* doll comprises those legal sources, namely the constitution, EU Treaties and secondary legislation, domestic legislative acts, governmental regulations, customs, and whatever else a jurisdiction recognizes as a valid legal source. Legal sources, in turn, are shaped by "external legal culture", a combination of politics, market forces, ideology, and philosophical ideas[6] that can be viewed as the fourth and largest *matryoshka* doll: as such, it shapes not only legal sources but also the system and, ultimately, the legal regime that applies to the individual case.

This analogy should illuminate the relevance to this special issue of the Italian Law Journal on Italy's legal culture of an ongoing research project on corporate law and venture capital ("VC") contracting that we have been working on together with Tobias Tröger.[7] In companion papers we show that Italy's corporate law (similar to

---

[2] The idea of a "system" of rules has its origin in Savigny's scholarship, which Italian legal scholars made their own in the second half of the 1800s. See, eg, *Lipari*, Le categorie del diritto civile, 2013, 21 f.

[3] To be fair, it is at least open to debate whether courts' authority is above legal academics' when it comes to identify what the law in action is that applies to a specific case, but it is safe to say that, in the absence of precedents from the Italian Supreme Court ("Corte di Cassazione") and possibly even from its Joint Divisions ("Sezioni Unite"), lawyers will find the answer in the writings of top legal academics to be as relevant for their case as, if not more relevant than, case law from lower courts.

[4] *Sunde*, in Koch/Kjølstad (eds.), Handbook on Legal Cultures, 2023, 13, 24 (defining internal legal culture as "the ideas and expectations and the institutional practices of those regularly engaged with the legal culture").

[5] *Legrand*, International and Comparative Law Quarterly 45 (1996), 52, 57 (defining metarules as "the rules developed by a legal system (or, more accurately, by the actors within a legal system) in order to help it manage its body of rules").

[6] See *Sunde* (fn. 3), 24. "external legal culture […] is the part of legal culture that is influenced by primarily non-legal actors and activities, such as politics, economy, or communication technology".

[7] *Enriques/Nigro/Tröger*, Venture Capital Contracting as Bargaining in the Shadow of Corporate Law Constraints, ECGI Law Working Paper No. 833/2025, 2025, www.ssrn.com/abstract=5183235 (15.6.2025); *Enriques/Nigro/Tröger*, Can U.S. Venture Capital Contracts Be Transplanted to Europe? Systematic Evidence from Germany and Italy, ECGI Law Working Paper No. 848/2025, 2025, www.ssrn.com/abstract=5287685 (15.6.2025); *Enriques/Nigro/Tröger*, in Broughman/de Fontenay (eds.),

Germany's) rejects virtually all the elements of the sophisticated contractual framework that US legal practitioners have elaborated over decades to govern the relationships between VC funds ("VCFs") and entrepreneurs within VC-backed start-ups.[8] By identifying the corporate law rules, concepts and principles that determine such an outcome, we also gain insight into how the system originating them is built up.

This essay builds on our previous research's findings to shed light on what determines Italian corporate law in action, namely the internal and external legal culture of Italian (corporate) law scholars. It shows that they widely share an almost unfettered inclination to "find" new implicit legal rules, concepts, and principles that have little to no explicit basis in the relevant legislation and are almost invariably of a mandatory nature. As an outcome, corporate players find themselves trapped inside a corporate law regime that looks like a labyrinth of restrictions. In other words, Italian corporate law displays an "über-mandatory" structure.

This essay explains how internal and external legal culture explains such a structure. First, it sheds light on the toolkits that legal professionals use to build this system of mandatory rules. Second, it identifies four external forces that contribute to shaping such a system. First, the long-lasting predominance of banks' role in the market for corporate finance has resulted in a demand for rigid corporate law, whilst the lack of alternative, more modern, forms of market-based financing until very recently has simultaneously implied a lack of demand for more flexible corporate law. Second, legal professionals' inclination to extend the domain of mandatory corporate law is consistent with their self-interest: the more expansive the net of mandatory rules and principles, the higher the demand for legal services and, hence, the higher legal professionals' rents. Further, a political culture favourable to private ordering is largely alien to Italian legal elites. The prevailing view among legal scholars is in fact one that deeply distrusts markets as a tool to allocate (rights to) resources. Finally, Italian legal academics who aim to establish themselves as well-respected scholars among their peers have strong incentives to elaborate new mandatory rules and principles.

The remainder of this essay is organized as follows. Section II summarizes the results of our research on VC contracting under German and Italian corporate laws. Section III zooms in on the mandatory structure of Italian corporate law to show that, despite recent reforms, Italian legal scholars use local metarules to find new implicit mandatory requirements that constrain private ordering in significant respects. Section IV provides four non-mutually exclusive explanations for the resulting über-mandatory structure of Italian corporate law. Section V concludes.

Research Handbook on the Structure of Private Equity and Venture Capital Investments, forthcoming. For the sake of brevity, we do not discuss German law and legal culture throughout this essay.

[8] See *Enriques/Nigro/Tröger*, Can U.S. (fn. 7).

II. Our Findings

Our research project, now comprising three papers in addition to this essay,[9] delves into the question of how corporate law matters for the development of VC markets.

In one of our companion papers, we refine the theory that corporate law can support (hinder) efficient VC contracting and thus possibly enhance (curb) VC activity because of its relative flexibility (inflexibility). We offer a primer of the multiple mechanisms by which rigid corporate law affects the adoption of the presumptively efficient VC contracts governing the VCF-entrepreneur relationship in the US.[10]

Our analysis rests on the premise that sophisticated market participants are fully capable of safeguarding their interests, especially when advised by specialized legal counsel. This assumption applies not only to experienced actors such as VCFs but also to the fund-raising firms and their founders.[11]

Consistent with this premise, we then outline the key features of an ideal pro-VC corporate law.[12] We define corporate law as optimally flexible for VC contracting if it (a) adopts a hands-off approach regarding the legality and enforceability of private ordering solutions that shape VC deals, (b) refrains from employing *ex post* gap-filling mechanisms that might restrict the exercise of resultant rights in ways inconsistent with the economic rationales underlying VC contracts, and (c) provides remedies in the case of abuse in the exercise of such rights. If corporate law exhibits those features, contracting parties can delineate their rights and obligations via contract with a high degree of certainty.

Delaware corporate law conforms nearly perfectly with this pro-VC corporate law model. The Delaware General Corporation Law has an enabling nature because of the explicit choice of its lawmakers. Building on that premise, all players involved in the process of interpreting and applying corporate law – scholars, lawyers, and courts – obey metarules largely favourable to private ordering.[13] As a result, Delaware corporate law in action allows contracting parties to shape any aspect of their business relationship as they see fit, including the prescriptive contents of the fiduciary duty of loyalty. At the same time, Delaware corporate law ensures that parties stick to contractual promises by policing abuse strictly but also consistently with the economic logic of the relevant transaction.[14] Under this framework, contracting parties can plainly rely on private ordering to both predetermine their own expected behaviour and to more accurately anticipate how the other party will act.[15]

VCFs and entrepreneurs have built upon Delaware corporate law's enabling nature to create a sophisticated contractual framework with two primary objectives: first, to

---

[9] For references, see fn. 7.

[10] *Enriques/Nigro/Tröger*, Venture Capital (fn. 7), 11 f.

[11] *Enriques/Nigro/Tröger*, Venture Capital (fn. 7), 12 f.

[12] *Enriques/Nigro/Tröger*, Venture Capital (fn. 7), 11 f.

[13] *Enriques/Nigro/Tröger*, Venture Capital (fn. 7), 8 ff.

[14] *Enriques/Nigro/Tröger*, Venture Capital (fn. 7), 20 f.

[15] *Enriques/Nigro/Tröger*, Venture Capital (fn. 7), 21.

address the severe problems of uncertainty, information asymmetries, and moral hazard that characterize the funding of highly innovative projects;[16] and, second, to align VC-backed firms' lifecycles with the organizational and operational features of VC funds.[17]

Through decades of iterations, US VC contracts have reached high levels of standardization and ultimately emerged as the best real-world solution to the challenges bedevilling the financing of high-tech projects.[18] Economic theory thus predicted that US VC contracts would gain popularity across jurisdictions over time, serving as a model for value-enhancing private ordering.[19] Transactional practice globally has to date confirmed these predictions.[20]

Outside the US, however, the applicable legal regime, including corporate law, may limit VCFs' and entrepreneurs' ability to transplant US VC contracts. The more prescriptive a given corporate law is, the harder it is for contracting parties to transpose into their contracts such clauses and/or functionally equivalent arrangements – that is, arrangements that enable contracting parties to achieve (1) the same practical result as the model solution (2) without incurring higher costs.[21] When functionally equivalent arrangements are also unavailable, for instance due to anti-avoidance rules, contracting parties must content themselves with arrangements lacking either of those features, or both (hereinafter, "alternative arrangements").[22]

Rigid corporate law can prevent contracting parties from resorting to private ordering to allocate control and cash-flow rights as they see fit via constraints that stem from either "absolute" or "relative" prohibitions.[23] Absolute prohibitions rule out not only the relevant US clause itself but also, possibly via general anti-evasion principles or other doctrines, any alternative arrangements.[24] Relative prohibitions rule out the viability of a specific US-style contractual arrangement and functionally equivalent solutions but allow contracting parties to resort to alternative arrangements.[25] Relative prohibitions may admit alternative arrangements, for instance, subject to specific provisos to the original US clause or to their finding place in shareholder agreements rather than in the VC-backed firm's corporate charter.[26]

Relative prohibitions imply that market participants can only enter VC deals under a suboptimal contractual framework. Although, admittedly, we cannot say by how much this efficiency gap is bound to increase VC-backed firms' cost of capital, at

---

16 *Enriques/Nigro/Tröger*, Venture Capital (fn. 7), 7 f.
17 *Enriques/Nigro/Tröger*, Venture Capital (fn. 7), 8 f.
18 *Enriques/Nigro/Tröger*, Venture Capital (fn. 7), 25 f.
19 *Enriques/Nigro/Tröger*, Venture Capital (fn. 7), 27.
20 *Enriques/Nigro/Tröger*, Venture Capital (fn. 7), 27.
21 *Enriques/Nigro/Tröger*, Venture Capital (fn. 7), 13.
22 *Enriques/Nigro/Tröger*, Venture Capital (fn. 7), 14.
23 *Enriques/Nigro/Tröger*, Venture Capital (fn. 7), 14 f.
24 *Enriques/Nigro/Tröger*, Venture Capital (fn. 7), 14.
25 *Enriques/Nigro/Tröger*, Venture Capital (fn. 7), 15.
26 *Enriques/Nigro/Tröger*, Venture Capital (fn. 7), 15.

the margin, it can be expected to reduce the number and/or size of VC deals, which will lead to an overall thinner VC market with negative ramifications for innovation and economic growth.[27] The most recent high-level policy debate echoes these views.[28]

In the second of our companion papers, we conduct a comprehensive analysis of Italian corporate law governing both *società per azioni* (SpA) and *società a responsabilità limitata* (Srl) and assess the extent to which it impedes the transplant of US VC contracts.[29] We find that Italian corporate law includes both absolute and, to a greater extent, relative prohibitions that make, with one exception, all the arrangements that typically comprise US VC deals unviable, whether as such or as functionally equivalent solutions. More precisely, those arrangements: (a) are null and void; or (b) are valid only if relocated within shareholder agreements and/or contingent on being subject to either *ex ante* or *ex post* scrutiny regarding the fairness of their terms or the conduct of the party exercising the resulting rights; and/or (c) are subject to a high degree of uncertainty as to their validity or the conducts they permit.

Contracting parties have no better option than to replace those contractual provisions, to the extent possible, with alternative arrangements that, by definition,[30] entail higher costs or bring lower benefits to the parties. The bottom line is that contracts governing Italian VC deals prevent VCFs and entrepreneurs from defining the terms of their business relationship as they see fit.[31]

Importantly, our analysis reveals that the frictions between Italian corporate law and US VC contracting practices rarely stem from explicit blackletter corporate law provisions. Instead, they are more often the function of scholarly (and/or courts') interpretations. We now account for how internal legal culture shapes the way scholars construe the law.

---

[27] *Enriques/Nigro/Tröger*, Venture Capital (fn. 7), 17.

[28] The so-called "Draghi Report" stresses the importance of corporate law in supporting high-tech firms' access to capital across Europe and advocates a special pan-European corporate law regime for such firms. See European Commission, The Future of European Competitiveness – A Competitiveness Strategy for Europe, 9.9.2024, https://commission.europa.eu/topics/strengthening-european-competitiveness/eu-competitiveness-looking-ahead_en (15.6.2025), 29 f.

[29] *Enriques/Nigro/Tröger*, Can U.S. (fn. 7).

[30] See above, text preceding fn. 21.

[31] *Enriques/Nigro/Tröger*, Can U.S. (fn. 7), 23. See also *Nigro/Enriques*, Analisi Giuridica dell' Economia 2021, 149; *Giudici/Agstner*, European Business Organization Law Review 2019, 597; and *Agstner/Capizzi/Giudici*, Rivista Orizzonti del Diritto Commerciale 2020, 353. Giudici and his co-authors have more recently gathered empirical evidence that, as they claim, supports the view that Italian corporate law is more adequate than previously thought. See *Giudici/Agstner/Capizzi*, European Business Organization Law Review 2022, 787. We have argued elsewhere that their empirical evidence in fact confirms our findings, to the extent that functional equivalence is itself functionally defined. See *Enriques/Nigro*, Corporate Law and Venture Capital in Italy: What Does the Empirical Evidence (Really) Tell Us?, Oxford Business Law Blog, 16.11.2023, https://blogs.law.ox.ac.uk/oblb/blog-post/2023/11/corporate-law-and-venture-capital-italy-what-does-empirical-evidence-really (15.6.2025). See also *Enriques/Nigro*, Società 2023, 10.

III. How Internal Legal Culture Fosters "Über-Mandatory" Corporate Law

Italian corporate law's pronounced aversion to private ordering, which incidentally goes well beyond VC contracting,[32] may sound surprising and counterintuitive. After all, Italian corporate law on the books includes several elements that are consistent with the ambition of 21st century policymakers to increase corporate law's flexibility generally.[33] In 2003, the Italian Parliament delegated to the Italian Government the regime governing SpAs and Srls, instructing it to design corporate law rules that would be instrumental to "promoting the creation, growth, and competitiveness of businesses, including by facilitating their access to domestic and international capital markets".[34] Time and again, scholars have emphasized the pro-private ordering role of this directive and some of the provisions that the Government then enacted,[35] with many of them concluding that the reform had dismantled the rigidities that had until then characterised Italian corporate law.[36]

In addition, between 2012 and 2017 the regime governing Srls underwent further changes in the same direction.[37] Following these reforms, leading scholars concluded that private ordering is now virtually unlimited for Srls.[38]

While Italian corporate law on the books appears to be more respectful of contractual freedom today than at the start of this century, it is very far from the enabling model of corporate law that can be observed elsewhere.[39] If one redirects one's attention from blackletter corporate law to corporate law in action, the framework one observes becomes one of significant rigidity: as Giudici and his coauthors have poignantly put it, "Italian company law remains still a 'prisoner' of explicit or even more dangerous implicit prohibitions that limit economic development".[40]

The immediate cause of this persistent inflexibility lies in the country's internal legal culture, which enables scholars to elaborate, and practitioners and courts in

---

[32] For instance, under Italian corporate law, shareholders have a withdrawal right ("diritto di recesso"), a remedy that is similar to US appraisal rights. Many Italian legal scholars have argued against the legality of private ordering solutions aimed to expand its scope. See *Granelli*, Giurisprudenza Commerciale I 2013, 862, 870–875.

[33] For an overview of the relevant initiatives, see *Neville/Sørensen*, European Business Organization Law Review 2014, 545.

[34] Art. 2(1)(a) Legge 3.10.2001 no. 366. See also Arts. 3(1)(a)–(b) and 4(2)(a) Legge 3.10.2001 no. 366 (both stressing that the to-be-passed reform should expand the role of private ordering in defining the governance of SpA and Srl). Following this law, Italy's corporate law was profoundly reformed in 2003 with the declared intention of making it friendlier to private ordering. For details, see *Ferrarini/Giudici/Stella Richter jr.*, RabelsZ 2006, 658.

[35] See, eg, the contributions in Cian (ed.), Le grandi opzioni della riforma del diritto e del processo societario, 2004.

[36] See, eg, *d'Alessandro*, Rivista delle Società 2003, 34.

[37] For details, see *Giudici/Agstner* (fn. 31), 614–617.

[38] See, eg, *Zanarone*, La S.R.L. a vent'anni dalla riforma del diritto societario, 2023, 710.

[39] See *Giudici/Agstner* (fn. 31), 599.

[40] See *Giudici/Agstner* (fn. 31), 599.

their different capacities to apply, several implicit restrictive rules, concepts, and principles that hinder private ordering.

Italian statutory law's metarules are part of the story. In particular, the Italian Civil Code ("Codice Civile") provides that, if statutory law does not define explicitly the regime governing a specific set of facts (which may well include a contractual clause), then such regime must be determined by considering the legal provisions governing "similar cases" or "analogous matters" ("analogia legis").[41] In case no such provisions exist, account has to be taken of the "general principles of the legal system ("principi generali dell'ordinamento giuridico") ("analogia juris").[42] In addition, the Civil Code contains a broad anticircumvention rule, which declares null and void any agreement that is instrumental to evading a mandatory provision,[43] irrespective of the legal form of the transaction.[44]

However, Italy's metarules grant legal professionals discretion in interpreting the law, that goes well beyond the use of analogy and anti-avoidance rules. It is widely accepted that they may infer or deduce the existence of implicit, hitherto latent mandatory requirements from explicit rules, other implicit mandatory requirements, and even from abstract "concepts" and "categories" that may or may not be explicitly defined in legal sources. In fact, Italian legal scholars' core expertise lies in constructing a systematic framework from relevant legal sources, a skill deeply rooted in a robust legal tradition dating back to the late 19th century and heavily influenced by contemporary German legal scholarship.[45] This expertise involves isolating the building blocks of the legal system – rules, concepts/categories, and principles – to create a logically coherent theoretical structure.[46]

---

[41] Art. 12 Disposizioni sulla legge in generale. See *Enriques*, Mercato Concorrenza Regole 2005, 145, 173 (highlighting Italian courts' and scholars' inclination to apply other corporate law rules by analogy to fill supposed gaps in blackletter corporate law); and *Giudici/Agstner* (fn. 31), 626 (accounting for how legal rules applicable to SpA end up applying by analogy to Srl; and vice versa). One example is the commonly accepted interpretation of the regime governing the recharacterization as equity contributions of any loans that a shareholder may extend to the firm when it is under financial distress. See, for Srl only, Art. 2467 Codice Civile. With the support of scholars, courts have concluded time and again that this provision is the expression of a principle applying also to SpA. See, eg, *Tombari*, Rivista delle Società 2006, 201; Corte di Cassazione, 7.7.2015, no. 14056.

[42] See Art. 12 Disposizioni sulla legge in generale.

[43] See Art. 1344 Codice Civile.

[44] An example comes from the regime governing contractual arrangements that result in a waiver of the shareholder's withdrawal rights (see fn. 32 above). Such arrangements are null and void. See Art. 2437(6) Codice Civile. As to Srl, blackletter corporate law stipulates that in a number of instances shareholders can exercise their withdrawal rights "in any case". See Art. 2473 Codice Civile. While this regime may appear to apply only to arrangements outlined in the firm's constitutional documents, scholars argue, drawing, *inter alia*, from the supposedly broad scope of the prohibition on societas leonina (see below, fn. 51), that it extends to any private ordering solution that could effectively result in a waiver of withdrawal rights, including those located in shareholder agreements. See *Nigro/Maltese*, Rivista di Diritto Societario II 2022, 631.

[45] See, eg, *Grossi*, La cultura del civilista italiano, 2002, 15–23.

[46] cf *d'Alessandro*, Rivista Orizzonti del Diritto Commerciale 2019, 401, 401–412. This has always been part of Italian corporate law scholars' mindset. See *d'Alessandro*, in Bessone (ed.), Diritto

In the specific context of corporate law, scholars' "construction" of the system mainly relies on:

1. the rationale of statutory provisions (as identified by scholars themselves because Italian lawmakers are usually silent thereupon);[47]
2. explicit standards, such as equity ("equità"), fairness and good faith ("correttezza e buona fede"), and reasonableness ("ragionevolezza");[48]
3. provisions in the Italian Constitution ("Costituzione della Repubblica Italiana" or, simply, "Constitution");[49]
4. foundational legal concepts, including for example the idea of "property" as a fundamental component of private law relationships;[50]
5. foundational statutory provisions of the law of partnerships and companies,[51] which apply to any economic organization, irrespective of its legal form.[52]

---

giurisprudenziale, 1996, 221, 237 (flagging courts' pronounced tendency to extrapolate from black-letter corporate law, with the inputs of scholars, a variety of principles, generally with a wide-ranging scope, "aimed at protecting the most various interests") (our own translation).

[47] An example comes from scholarly work discussing the provision codifying the corporate opportunity doctrine. See Art. 2391(6) Codice Civile. Italian corporate law explicitly provides that creditors have the right to sue directors for failure to comply with their duties as regards the preservation of the firm's assets. See Artt. 2394 and 2476(6) Codice Civile, respectively for SpA and Srl. Drawing from this provision, which may be used also to sue a director who misappropriates a corporate opportunity, scholars conclude that the corporate opportunity doctrine protects (also) creditors and that, thus, the relevant provision is mandatory. See, eg, *Barachini*, in FS Gian Franco Campobasso, vol. 2, 2006, 603.

[48] cf *Enriques*, in Enciclopedia giuridica, vol. X, 2017, 958, 967.

[49] cf *Calvosa*, La clausola di riscatto nella società per azioni, 1995, 276–279 (arguing that, in light of Artt. 42 and 43 Costituzione della Repubblica Italiana, the shareholder whose shares are redeemed has the unwaivable right to receive their fair value and that this is key to prevent a shareholder from capturing part of the value of the shares of other shareholders). See also below, fn. 50.

[50] The emergence of principles derived from the constitutional provision protecting private property is a good example of how doctrinal constructs of the concept of property can be used to "find" additional principles that apply in the realm of corporate and contract laws. In brief, legal scholars seem to follow the following argumentative scheme. First, they reify company shares, making them the object of a property right; then, they notice that a shareholder's (economic) right is to a given fraction of the cash-flow rights of a firm. Second, they infer that any transaction (eg, a forced liquidation of the individual equity stake) at a price lower than the current value of the shares is an expropriation in the legal sense. Third, and conclusively, they address such expropriation by applying the relevant constitutional protection. See Art. 42(3) Costituzione della Repubblica Italiana. See, eg, *Salafia*, Le Società 2007, 1450, 1452; see also *Portale*, in FS Pietro Abbadessa, vol. 1, 2014, 107, 113 (stressing the importance of using the concept of property and the remedial apparatus that assists it under Italian (constitutional) law to address opportunism in the corporate context).

[51] The Italian term "società", which we usually translate as "company", is in fact used in a broader meaning in the Codice Civile, such that it comprises both partnerships and companies. See Art. 2247 Codice Civile.

[52] The prohibition on *societas leonina* as laid down in Art. 2265 Codice Civile is the most prominent example. That provision, on its face, only applies to partnerships. Legal scholars and courts have historically held, though, that it also applies to companies irrespective of their legal form and of whether the arrangement is located in the firm's constitutional documents or in shareholder agreements. The main rationales underlying this view are that the arrangements departing from it would make a shareholder insensitive to the firm's fate and thus create incentives to make irrespon-

The combination of *analogia legis* and *juris* and anti-avoidance rules with the sprawling number of implicit rules and broad principles elaborated by legal scholars (and courts), heavily encroaches on private ordering. This is also because seldom do corporate law scholars view cases that fall outside the scope of explicit provisions as unregulated[53] and therefore subject only to tort law and self-regulation via contracts.[54] As our findings show for VC contracting, such cases, when taking the form of contractual arrangements, are much more likely to be held to be inconsistent with one or more mandatory requirements,[55] whether explicit or, more often, implicit,[56] and therefore declared null and void.

As an outcome, contractual freedom is limited well beyond the boundaries that lawmakers may explicitly draw. Contractual practice reflects these constraints because of the influence thereupon of legal gatekeepers, namely attorneys, notaries, courts and arbitrators, all of which share scholars' legal culture.[57]

In performing their advisory function, attorneys may encourage contracting parties not to agree on arrangements that are clearly contrary to statutory or case law or even the implicit legal rules that predominant legal scholarship has identified as part of the system. Should borderline arrangements nonetheless slip through into the draft of the firm's constitutional documents, they may not pass notaries' scrutiny. Italian notaries operate under regulations providing that they must refuse to notarise a deed if its terms are against the law.[58] To support their members/affiliates in understanding what is against the law, notaries' local associations issue guidelines[59] that

sible decisions and that it would alter the logic (*causa negotii*) of the corporate contract. See, eg, *Abriani*, Il divieto del patto leonino. Vicende storiche e prospettive applicative, 1994, 41–51. Another example is the constraints that derive from the idea that the system requires interpreters to distinguish between equity and debt and hence to qualify a security as a share if and only if it exposes its holders to the firm's risk. See, eg, *de Luca/Stagno D'Alcontres*, *Manuale delle società*, 2nd ed., 2023, 188–195, 237–250.

[53] cf *Scano*, Rivista delle Società 2021, 1122, 1142–1153 (proposing a complex theory about how to fill regulatory gaps in which, owing to its autopoietic nature, corporate law, rather than tort law or contract, plays the most important role).

[54] For an application, see *Lamandini*, Banca Borsa Titoli di Credito I 2003, 519, 520 (making an example that shows that, under Italian corporate law, private ordering operates only within the space left empty by the system pieced together via interpretation).

[55] See Art. 1418 Codice Civile.

[56] See, eg, *Lamandini* (fn. 53), 520 (arguing that, in moulding the rights pertaining to a "share", private ordering is subject to the constraints stemming from the many principles that the corporate law system comprises).

[57] cf *Livingston/Monateri/Parisi*, The Italian Legal System. An Introduction, 2nd ed., 2015, 72–90 (discussing Italian legal professionals' education).

[58] See Art. 28 Legge 16.2.1913, no. 89. Case law endorses a broad interpretation of the statutory provisions defining that duty, finding that notaries breach it also in the event of deviations from the notarial best practices as enshrined in defining the requirements that contractual arrangements must meet to be valid. See *Enriques/Nigro/Tröger*, Mandatory (fn. 7), 18.

[59] See, eg, Consiglio Notarile dei Distretti Riuniti di Firenze/Pistoia/Prato, Indice sistematico delle massime in materia societaria, https://www.consiglionotarilefirenze.it/index.php/indice-sistematico-delle-massime.html (15.6.2025); and Consiglio Notarile di Milano, Massime notarili in

express their views on whether specific private ordering solutions are compliant with the law and, as the case may be, under what conditions and within what limits. Over time, these guidelines have become increasingly sensitive to private players' needs.[60] Yet, while attempting to cater such needs, those guidelines cannot overlook widely accepted scholarly interpretations of corporate law that embrace the existence of a specific implicit rule or general principle.[61] Thus, they often take a mixed approach: they allow for a specific private ordering solution, but only provided that it meets specific requirements and/or is designed in such a way as to be compliant with some "general principles".[62] Transactional practice regularly incorporates contractual arrangements that conform to such guidelines.[63]

Courts and arbitrators, in turn, hold scholarly interpretations in high regard.[64] Given scholars' general posture towards private ordering, courts and arbitrators unsurprisingly make decisions that curtail the exercise of contractual freedom.[65] Such a

---

materia societaria, https://www.consiglionotarilemilano.it/societa/massime-commissione-societa/ (15.6.2025).

[60] This applies particularly to those issued by the Milan notaries' association.

[61] See above, text preceding fn. 57.

[62] For instance, the Milan notaries association's guidelines qualify drag-along rights provisions as valid so long as they meet specific requirements. See Consiglio Notarile di Milano, Massima no. 88 of 22.11.2005, Clausole statutarie disciplinanti il diritto e l'obbligo di "covendita" delle partecipazioni (Artt. 2355-bis and 2469 Codice Civile), https://www.consiglionotarilemilano.it/massime-commissione-societa/88/ (15.6.2025). A second example is the Milan notaries association's guidelines on private ordering solutions to allocate the proceeds of so-called liquidity events. According to those guidelines, these private ordering solutions are valid provided that they are designed in such a way as to be compatible with two general principles of corporate law, namely, those resulting from the prohibition on *societas leonina* (see above, fn. 51) and the "principle of fair value" (according to which a shareholder who is forced to divest has the right to receive at least the fair value of their shares as determined by reference to the valuation criteria set in the corporate law rules on withdrawal rights [on which, see fn. 32]). See Consiglio Notarile di Milano, Massima no. 126 of 5.3.2013, Ripartizione non proporzionale del corrispettivo della vendita o del riscatto di partecipazioni sociali (Artt. 2348 and 2468 Codice Civile), https://www.consiglionotarilemilano.it/massime-commissione-societa/126/ (15.6.2025).

[63] See *Giudici/Agstner/Capizzi* (fn. 31), 811.

[64] See, eg, *Livingston/Monateri/Parisi* (fn. 57), 131–133. For instance, case law has recently confirmed the significance of the distinction between debt and equity theorized by scholars (see above, fn. 52). See Corte di Cassazione 4.7.2018, no. 17498. Likewise, courts have endorsed scholars' view that the concept of property has relevance in interpreting and applying corporate law when defining the regime applicable to drag-along rights provisions. See Tribunale di Milano 31.3.2008.

[65] One example concerns expulsion provisions included in the firm's constitutional documents under the regime governing Srls. According to the applicable statutory law, these provisions must be framed in such a way as to define "specific instances of cause" ("specifiche ipotesi di giusta causa") as trigger events of the expulsion. Art 2473-bis Codice Civile. Scholars have offered the most restrictive interpretation of this wording, construing it as requiring an analytical description of the facts that can trigger the expulsion of shareholders. Courts have promptly endorsed this interpretation and regularly apply it. For details and references, see *Nigro/Romano*, Diritto vivente e istituti morenti: l'esclusione del socio di s.r.l. (a vent'anni dalla riforma organica del diritto societario) (unpublished manuscript, on file with authors) 11–14. The most recent example comes from the case law that has invoked the principle of fair value (see above, fn. 62) to curtail contract-based caps on the price that a shareholder can obtain when exercising their withdrawal right (on which, see above,

stance also aligns with other deeply felt convictions of judges and arbitrators. First, they display a general tendency to sympathize with the (supposedly) "weak contracting party" ("il contraente debole").[66] Second, they typically have significant expertise in doctrinal interpretation but no business experience.[67] As a result, they have a strong inclination to protect the supposedly weaker party (in the VC setting, the entrepreneur) by declaring private agreements null and void. The nearly exclusive focus on the validity of the relevant arrangements has the significant advantage of allowing them to avoid a thorough examination of the facts of the case before them.[68] Finally, courts strive for fair outcomes *ex post*, without considering whether those outcomes are at all consistent with parties' reciprocal expectations *ex ante*[69] or could disrupt existing contractual practices and/or make certain private ordering solutions no longer viable, given the litigation risks they are revealed to entail.[70]

These three features (the inclination to protect weak contracting parties, the preference for legal analysis to fact-finding, and the tendency to look at cases only from an *ex post* perspective) contrive to make enforcement actors at least as alien as legal scholars to a deferential stance to private ordering.

In sum, Italian legal culture grants corporate law scholars' substantial freedom to shape the system governing the formation, governance, and management of corporations. This freedom contributes to the über-mandatory nature of Italian corporate law, which, through the involvement of lawyers, notaries, courts, and arbitrators, significantly influences everyday business practices.

---

fn. 32). For details, see *De Luca*, *Banca Borsa Titoli di Credito* II, 369. Courts' approach to drag-along rights provisions is another instructive example in this respect. See Tribunale di Milano 31.3.2008 (invalidating a drag-along rights provision granting one shareholder the right to co-sell the other shareholders' shares along with their own at any possible price for failing to include a proviso making reference to the principle of fair value [see above, fn. 62]). Arbitrators do not take a different approach. See also Lodo Arbitrale 29.7.2008 (reaching the same conclusion as to drag-along right provisions).

[66] See, eg, *Stabilini/Trapani*, Rivista di Diritto Commerciale I 2010, 949, 965 (making this point as they comment on the approach that an Italian court took in deciding on the validity of a drag-along rights provision).

[67] cf *Rordorf*, Le Società 2000, 152, 156 (stressing the problems associated with having judges with limited to no knowledge of economics).

[68] See, eg, *Perrone*, I soldi degli altri, 2008, 34–36 (discussing the private enforcement of financial services contracts under Italian law and showing that courts often declared the nullity of such contracts to quickly achieve the goal of protecting investors).

[69] See *Mosco/Nigro*, Analisi Giuridica dell'Economia 2021, 257, 275 (highlighting that Italian courts often adjudicate litigation based on the outcome of the litigated transaction while neglecting to consider the overall terms governing the business relationship between shareholders and the evolution of that relationship across time).

[70] On Italian courts' tendency not to consider the prospective impact of their decisions on the behaviour and incentives of market players more broadly, see *Enriques*, European Business Organization Law Review 2002, 765, 807–809.

IV. How External Legal Culture Affects the Italian Corporate Law Über-mandatory System

Having shown how internal legal culture works as a driver of Italian corporate law über-mandatory structure, it is now time to focus on what role *external* legal culture plays in shaping it.

The general premise here is that the rigidity or flexibility of any country's (corporate) law is the function of a variety of factors,[71] ranging from the relevant formal legal sources to the applicable metarules as well as culture (broadly conceived).[72] We focus here on four distinct elements of Italy's external legal culture, broadly defined as to encompass "the part of legal culture that is influenced by primarily non-legal actors and activities, such as politics, [economic forces], or communication technology".[73]

Let us first concede that legal sources themselves play a role in determining the law's rigidity. True, statutory corporate law has undergone several reforms meant, on their face, to broaden the scope for private ordering.[74]

Yet, as we reported in Part III, statutory metarules allowing for *analogia legis* and *juris* and providing for a general anti-avoidance rule push interpreters in the direction of interpretations unfavourable to private ordering. In addition, the law comprises broad standards of conduct ("clausole generali"), such as fairness and good faith,[75] that do apply to shareholders' and directors' behaviour and, hence, can be used creatively to restrict private ordering, especially in light of the incomplete nature of the arrangements governing the firm. At the same time, we should note that many of the corporate law constraints to private ordering are not derived from such explicit standards of conduct.

Similarly, constitutional principles, such as reasonableness and the references in the Italian Constitution to social utility as a constraint on freedom of enterprise ("libertà di iniziativa economica"),[76] as well as to the "social function" of property,[77] may offer additional tools for legal scholars' subtle crafting of limits to contractual freedom. Yet, to be fair, those constitutional principles are so broad that they cannot, per se, provide a strong argument in support of the conclusion that a given precept banning a particular contractual arrangement is part of the system. In addition, cor-

---

[71] cf *Dammann*, Hastings LJ 2014, 441.

[72] See *Roe*, University of Chicago Law Review 2002, 1251, 1253.

[73] *Sunde* (fn. 4), 24.

[74] See above, text accompanying fns. 34–38.

[75] See generally *Libertini*, Rivista Critica del Diritto Privato 2011, 345.

[76] Art. 41 Costituzione della Repubblica Italiana: "L'iniziativa economica privata è libera. Non può svolgersi in contrasto con l'utilità sociale o in modo da recare danno alla salute, all'ambiente, alla sicurezza, alla libertà, alla dignità umana" ("Private economic initiative is free. It may not be conducted in a manner that conflicts with social utility or causes harm to health, the environment, safety, freedom, or human dignity"; our own translation).

[77] Art. 42 Costituzione della Repubblica Italiana.

porate legal scholars display no tendency to refer to the Constitution's provisions on property rights to argue that specific proprietary rights should be curtailed in the interest of society as a whole. Rather, they use those provisions to advocate for solutions aimed to protect the individual interests of shareholders against the company and/or other shareholders.[78] In other words, they use these constitutional provisions to protect private property rather than to constrain it.

If legal sources provide at best a partial explanation for Italian corporate law's über-mandatory structure, what other forces are at play? We posit that four non-mutually exclusive factors also play a role. Two of them are economic in nature (path dependence relating to how companies are financed; legal professionals' self-interest), while two (the prevailing ideology about the role of markets and the state and "scholarly bravura", or how legal scholars prove their worth to peers) relate to legal culture more narrowly defined.

1. Path dependence. Decades-long patterns in corporate finance have acted as an external force indirectly shaping the system with the intermediation of lawmakers and scholars. Incumbent financiers, namely banks, had a strong preference for mandatory corporate law, while no other interest group has so far been able to push effectively in the opposite direction.

As a latecomer economy, Italy's economic development throughout the 20th century owes much to bank financing, with equity finance, let alone private equity, having had a much smaller role.[79] From a public choice perspective, banks' central role in the economy explains the pervasive presence of corporate law rules to protect creditor interests.[80] In general, creditors can be held to prefer rigid corporate law rules so as to economise on transaction costs: the more companies' constitutional documents look the same, the less will creditors need to gauge the effects of deviations from the default regime on creditworthiness and, as the case may be, to bargain for specific protections in loan covenants.[81] In short, a powerful interest group, banks, had a strong preference for rigid corporate law rules.[82]

---

[78] See above fns. 49–50 for instances of this use of constitutional provisions.

[79] See, eg, *Aganin/Volpin*, in Morck (ed.), A History of Corporate Governance around the World, 2005, 325, 328. Private equity and VC markets only took off at the turn of the century in Italy. See *Bentivogli et al.*, Il private equity in Italia, Banca d'Italia Occasional Paper No. 41, 2009, https://www.bancaditalia.it/pubblicazioni/qef/2009-0041/index.html?com.dotmarketing.htmlpage.language=1&dotcache=refresh (15.6.2025), 7.

[80] On the centrality of creditor protection in Italian corporate law see, eg, *Nieddu Arrica*, I principi di corretta gestione societaria e imprenditoriale nella prospettiva della tutela dei creditori, 2016, 5–32. No one doubts that corporate law rules aiming to protect creditors are mandatory. See, eg, *Rivolta*, Diritto delle società. Profili generali, 2015, 149.

[81] See *Strampelli*, Distribuzioni ai soci e tutela dei creditori. L'effetto degli IAS/IFRS, 2009, 38.

[82] cf *Enriques/Macey*, Cornell Law Review 2001, 1165, 1203 (stressing banks' interest in preserving the regime on legal capital).

At the same time, because VC, like private equity more broadly, is such a recent phenomenon in Italy,[83] for decades and decades no interest group was there to push back on the pervasiveness of mandatory rules. Shareholdings in private companies have traditionally been in the hands of families,[84] meaning that shareholders relied on informal arrangements based on trust, rather than explicit contracts, to define their mutual expectations.[85]

How these market dynamics had an impact not just on the relevant legal sources but also crept into the system with the intermediation of legal scholars and courts is harder to pinpoint. But one channel may well be the fact that litigation over corporate law questions has traditionally arisen in the context of bankrupt companies, where the interest of creditors looms large, while shareholders are out of the picture (and are often the villains in the story).

2. Self-interest. The über-mandatory model of corporate law is intuitively consistent with the private interests of legal practitioners (among whom most corporate law scholars must also be counted[86]).[87] Demand for their services is bound to stay high in a setting where practically nothing can be done without legal advice, given the complexity of finding alternative arrangements in such a sprawling system of implicit mandatory principles and the ensuing uncertainty as to the applicable regime.[88] Note that the legal advice required in such a legal environment is not the transaction cost engineering work typical of US corporate lawyers, who sharply focus on finding solutions that maximize the joint welfare of contracting parties[89] under virtually no legal constraints.[90] Rather, it takes the form of guidance on how to shape private ordering in a way consistent with the strictures of the system,[91] with demand therefor being ultimately created by the crafters of the system themselves.

At the same time, the system empowers judges with greater discretion in deciding (corporate law) cases, because every private ordering exercise becomes subject to their scrutiny.[92]

---

[83] See *Bentivogli et al.*, Il private equity (n 79).

[84] *Bianchi/Bianco/Giacomelli/Pacces/Trento*, Proprietà e controllo delle imprese in Italia. Alle radici delle difficoltà competitive della nostra industria, 2005, 90–92.

[85] On the significance of trust in private companies, see generally *Easterbrook/Fischel*, Stanford Law Review 1986, 271, 274.

[86] *Libertini*, Quaderni fiorentini per la storia del pensiero giuridico moderno 2020, 735, 764.

[87] cf *Enriques* (fn. 41), 145.

[88] Italian corporate law also entails widespread uncertainty as to the validity of the arrangements used in VC deals or the way in which contracting parties can exercise the ensuing rights. See *Enriques/Nigro/Tröger*, Venture Capital (fn. 7), 43–46 (discussing this point and providing examples).

[89] See *Gilson*, Yale Law Journal 1984, 239.

[90] At least so long as the transaction only involves privately held companies as is the case with VC-backed firms.

[91] cf *Nigro/Romano* (fn. 65), 33 (providing an example).

[92] *Enriques* (fn. 41), 170–171.

Far be it from us to claim that a desire to keep demand for legal services high and to grant judges greater power over corporations *motivates* scholars in articulating, and other corporate law professionals to apply, restrictive interpretations of existing legal texts. Scholars and judges are most likely not even aware of the intuitive correlation between über-mandatory corporate law and legal professionals' rents. But it is fair to argue that, had a laissez-faire approach to private ordering better served the legal profession's interests, the state of affairs we have shed light on would have been less likely to emerge.

3. Ideology. It is only reasonable to surmise that an ideology contrary to private ordering, markets, and free enterprise also contributes to the über-mandatory structure of Italian corporate law.

To be sure, evidence of such an ideology is hard to find in Italian corporate law scholars' works. Particularly telling is the fact that they seldom refer to the Constitution to substantiate mandatory interpretations of the law;[93] and when they do refer to it, they do so out of the concern of protecting some shareholders against other shareholders.[94] In other words, they build upon the "liberal" provisions protecting private property rather than using the Constitution's references to the social function of property and the social limits to economic freedoms to constrain shareholders' and managers' freedom. This attitude starkly contrasts with the systematic use of the Constitution that many prominent Italian private law scholars – some responding to Marxist views and some inspired by social-catholic doctrines – have made since long to, in short, socialise private law.[95]

Unlike private law scholars, corporate law academics, especially since the decade in which progressive, constitutionally based private law scholarship set sail (the 1970s), have tended "to retreat within the golden cage of technicality and specialization", as a leading business law scholar, Mario Libertini, has recently put it.[96] Scholars' arguments in favour of interpretations that invalidate private ordering solutions are in fact rather technical in character. And when scholars do refer to the interests underlying the principles they elaborate, they draw from generic rationales, like creditor protection, the need to curb abuse of power, whether by majority or minority shareholders, and even a "technocratic", efficiency-based rationale, namely the idea that constraining contractual freedom is conducive to firms' higher profitability.[97]

---

93 See *Cariello*, Il Codice di Corporate Governance. Da soluzione a problema, 2024, 223–224.

94 See above, fns. 49–50 and the text corresponding to fn. 78.

95 See, eg, *Grossi* (fn. 45), 155–158; *Rescigno/Resta/Zoppini*, Diritto privato. Una conversazione, 2017, 163–165; *Perlingieri*, Il diritto civile nella legalità costituzionale, vol. II, 2020.

96 *Libertini*, Rivista Orizzonti del Diritto Commerciale 2020, 291, 291–292 (our own translation) (the entire sentence is as follows: "[dopo la morte di Ascarelli e Bigiavi], la disciplina [del diritto commerciale], pur mantenendo una produzione dottrinale di qualità, è apparsa incline a ripiegare entro la gabbia dorata del tecnicismo e dello specialismo").

97 See, eg, *Libertini*, Rivista Orizzonti del Diritto Commerciale 2018, 1, 9 (reporting as commonly held the view that "a rich set of mandatory and default rules is functional to a greater degree of

Ironically, in the second half of the 20th century, some of the best and most highly regarded corporate law scholars took a Marxist perspective on capitalism and its institutions, chief among them the corporation. However, as recently noted by Floriano d'Alessandro, "in an apparent paradox, what happened was that those scholars would put forward the most conservative and even reactionary interpretations of the law: such interpretations were meant to demonstrate how backward and inimical to the working classes the capitalist system was".[98]

It would be wrong to conclude, though, that ideology has had no role to play. While an overtly anti-market, private-ordering-averse ideology may have exerted minimal discernible influence on Italian corporate scholars' ostensibly technocratic and politically neutral interpretations, think of it this way: *the absence of a pro-market, pro-private-ordering vision* has facilitated the emergence of the über-mandatory system of corporate law we have described. If any attention had been given to the legislative intent of the reforms adopted in the past three decades,[99] the legal sources of Italian corporate law would have lent themselves to interpretations favourable to private ordering rather than to ones curtailing it. But that fell on deaf ears: legal scholars harbouring a benign view of private ordering were a small minority twenty years ago and dwindled even further over time.[100]

Second, and related to this, leaving aside the individual and, if there is one, the collective ideology of corporate law scholars, Italy as a country clearly stands out as a coordinated economy within the "variety of capitalism" framework.[101] That implies a broader political culture which, owing much to socialist and social-catholic ideologies, clearly considers collective, centralized tools to allocate resources as preferable to markets.[102] The dominant political *Zeitgeist* inevitably moulds the attitude towards markets of corporate law scholars, reticent as they may mostly be about their own views on markets and state intervention.[103]

efficiency for the private sector as a whole" [our own translation; emphasis added]); *Notari*, in Sacchi/Toffoletto (eds.), Esiste uno "stile giuridico" neoliberale?, 2019, 85, 100.

98 *d'Alessandro*, Rivista Orizzonti del Diritto Commerciale 2019 (fn. 46), 416 (our own translation).

99 See the text accompanying fns. 34–37. See especially Legge 3 October 2001 no. 366, which, as noted above, delegated the government to reform the law of SpAs and Srls in its entirety with the primary objective of "promoting the creation, growth, and competitiveness of businesses, including by facilitating their access to domestic and international capital markets". It is fair to say that the view that this provision should be used as a key metarule to interpret the reformed law (as argued by *Enriques* [fn. 48], 958) has never gained any traction.

100 *Libertini* (fn. 97), 9: "[the] strand of research [opposing the use of standards and, conversely, expressing favour for statutory autonomy] has remained […] rather weak and the ideological stance of exalting contractual freedom in corporate law has faded considerably" (our own translation).

101 See, eg, *Crouch*, in Hancké (ed.), Debating Varieties of Capitalism: A Reader, 2009, 75, 84.

102 See, eg, *Mingardi*, The Independent Review 2021, 593.

103 A prominent exception is *Denozza*, in Sacchi/Toffoletto (eds.), Esiste uno "stile giuridico" neoliberale? (fn. 97), 1, whose extremely critical stance on what he calls the neoliberal legal style – which is ultimately a critique of a neoclassical economic approach to policy questions – has gone virtually unquestioned within the circle of Italian business law scholars.

4. Bravura. One final element to consider for the understanding of our findings relates to one peculiar feature of doctrinal legal scholarship: doctrinal scholars' skills are best tested on their ability to "find" new rules and principles from both the available legal sources and the principles and concepts that are already part of the system.[104] Each new concept and principle a scholar can find is a brick the scholar adds to the system edifice, and one that, by definition, eats into the territory of private ordering.[105] Adding a "negative brick", that is, holding that there is no brick that constrains a given private ordering arrangement, is awkward to say the least. It is almost an admission that one lacks the modicum amount of creativity that is needed to infer new principles from the system or, worse, the knowledge of the literature required to find the one principle among the many that legal scholarship has already found, that applies to that specific arrangement. In fact, the thesis that a given private ordering arrangement (such as a specific clause in the corporate charter) should be considered valid rests on two assertions: (1) no overriding principles challenge the validity of the arrangement and, therefore, (2) the principle of contractual autonomy applies. Assertion (1) is painstakingly hard to demonstrate analytically because it requires proving a negative. In contrast, assertion (2) relies on one centuries-old principle, namely that contractual freedom rules in the absence of mandatory requirements.

In short, in a community of scholars almost entirely dominated by doctrinarism, there is no prestige to be gained from exercising self-restraint in the collective endeavour of building the system. If you want to be part of that community and gain the respect of its most prominent members, you add your brick and worry not about the negative consequences of adding that bring, if any, on the dynamism of your country's economy. After all, you can always assert, as Italian legal scholars in fact do,[106] that a system that heavily constrains private ordering is welfare-enhancing because it prevents private parties from choosing suboptimal solutions, if not for themselves then for society.[107]

---

[104] We draw inspiration for this intuition from a comment by Paolo Giudici, who, in orally discussing one of our papers (namely, *Enriques/Nigro/Tröger*, Venture Capital, fn. 7), argued that a prospective legal scholar whose career progress depends on the ability to impress senior scholars has an incentive to adapt to the mainstream and write articles and monographs where new legal concepts and principles are found.

[105] See *Libertini* (fn. 97), 20 ("i principi si realizzano mediante regole di rango inferiore: essi sono norme rivolte ai produttori di norme di livello più basso tra i quali, secondo la dottrina più plausibile, si pongono anche gli autori di atti di autonomia privata").

[106] See above, fn. 97 and accompanying text.

[107] Rigorous economic analysis of law has seldom been part of the Italian corporate law scholar's toolkit. cf *Libertini*, Passato e presente del diritto commerciale, 2023, 67–68. Generic (supposedly) efficiency-based arguments in favour of one pro-regulatory solution or the other are relatively common, though, especially drawing from asymmetric information and market power, rarely matched by considerations of government failures or unintended consequences (in other words, when economic arguments are used, they fall prey to the nirvana fallacy. See generally *Demsetz*, Journal of Law & Economics 1969, 1, 1–2).

V. Conclusion

Our companion papers with Tobias Tröger show that Italian corporate law hinders the transplant of virtually all the clauses of US VC contracts due to a plethora of mainly implicit requirements to be found in the system of rules that doctrinal legal scholarship moulds. This system imbues Italian corporate law with its rigid mandatory structure, which subsequently permeates everyday transactional practice with the intermediation of lawyers, notaries, courts, and arbitrators. VC contracting is, however, just one major example of how Italian corporate law stands in the way of private ordering more broadly.

Our essay builds on those findings to account for the proximate and ultimate causes of that state of affairs. The proximate cause of the burgeoning number of constraints on private ordering under Italian corporate law is Italy's internal legal culture, including its metarules. The ultimate causes lie instead with external legal culture. We have speculated that four factors can be singled out as having mainly contributed to the über-mandatory structure of Italian corporate law. First, the traditionally central role of banks in financing Italian firms and the only recent growth of private equity explain the strong role creditor protection plays in shaping corporate law and its aversion to flexible solutions. Second, legal professionals' ability to extract rents from a highly mandatory structure of corporate law favours its persistence. Third, the absence of a pro-contractual freedom mindset among the (legal) elites and, more generally, an ideology consistent with Italy's characterization as a coordinated economy are the cultural preconditions for the state of affairs we have spotlighted. Finally, (legal) academics' ultimate goal as such is to establish themselves as reputed scholars within their field. For this purpose, using the doctrinal legal scholarship's toolkit to "find" new principles eroding private ordering's turf is a much better strategy than advocating that, in the absence of explicit statutory prohibitions, contractual freedom should prevail.

Shareholders' agreements and sustainable governance

Maria Elisabete Ramos

Abstract: Under the context of the CSDD framework, the paper addresses four research questions: *a*) the meaning of due diligence and its contribution to the 'economic and social transition to sustainability'; *b*) who is responsible for due diligence governance under the Portuguese law?; *c*) are shareholders' agreements the suitable instrument to accommodate or "expand" the "voice" of shareholders in matters of environmental sustainability and human rights? *d*) agreements between shareholders and stakeholders are the appropriate legal tool to empower stakeholders? The paper highlights that CS3D addresses the enterprise due diligence as a policy and a process that meet the interests of stakeholders. The paper concludes that under Portuguese law atypical shareholders' agreements may bring together shareholders and stakeholders. Shareholder agreements cannot force directors to take business decisions aimed at sustainability neither to take decisions aimed at respecting human rights. Shareholder agreements that issue orders or instructions to directors or supervisors on due diligence measures are void and null. But there are grey areas. Shareholder agreements are not enforceable against company and are therefore not the best tool for empowering stakeholders in terms of human rights and the environment. The contribution of shareholder agreements to sustainable corporate governance is limited, precarious and circumstantial. They are not the right substitute for the (non-existent) legal duty of directors to make sustainable business decisions.

I. Context in a nutshell

In USA "eighty-one percent of DuPont shareholders approved a proposal requiring the company to disclose how much plastic the company releases into the environment each year and to assess the effectiveness of DuPont's pollution policies. Sixty-four percent of ExxonMobil shareholders approved a proposal requiring the company to describe "if, and how, ExxonMobil's lobbying activities (direct and through trade associations) align with the goal of limiting average global warming to well below 2 degrees Celsius (the Paris Climate agreement's goal)". [1] These examples, gathered from the experience of the United States of America, suggest, according to some views, "a dramatic increase in shareholder engagement on environmental and social issues". [2] Providing a divergent analysis, recent research, also concerning the US ex-

[1] See Hart/Zingales, "The new corporate governance", in Enriques et al. (eds.), *Board-shareholder dialogue. Policy debate, legal constraints and best practices* (Cambridge University Press, 2024), 24.

[2] Ibid.

perience, suggests the decline of the "shareholder support for environmental and social (E&S) proposals".[3]

It is undisputed that encouraging or guiding companies towards environmentally and socially sustainable activities is the purpose of different international soft law instruments that recommend "ethical guidelines".[4]/[5] For example, in the context of the United Nations, the Global Compact[6], the UN Guiding Principles on Business and Human Rights.[7] Within the OECD, we can mention the Guidelines for Multinational Enterprises on Responsible Business Conduct with their system of National Contact Points.[8]

Recognising the weakness of voluntary (or market) actions dependent on company decisions to achieve sustainability objectives, the European Union is moving towards *hard law* regulatory tools.[9] This regulatory shift is visible in the incorporation of due diligence into companies' risk management. The Corporate Sustainability Due Diligence Directive (hereafter, CS3D) turns the due diligence recommendations issued by the OECD into mandatory and harmonized sustainability due diligence rules in EU.[10]

CS3D "aims to ensure that companies active in the internal market contribute to sustainable development and the sustainability transition of economies and societies".[11]

---

[3] See Khoo/Tallarita, *Expanding Shareholder Voice: The Impact of SEC Guidance on Environmental and Social Proposals* (Law Working Paper No. 822/2025, February 2025), 1, http://ssrn.com/abstract_id=4913660 (access 12th February 2025).

[4] Sjåfjell, "Achieving Corporate Sustainability: What is the Role of the Shareholder?", in Birkmose, *Shareholders' Duties in Europe* (Kluwer Law International, 2017), Chapter 18 , University of Oslo Faculty of Law, Research Paper No. 2016-10, Nordic & European Company Law Working Paper No. 18-07, https://ssrn.com/abstract=2828573, p. 397.

[5] See Hösli/Weber, "Climate change reporting and due diligence frontiers of corporate climate responsibility", (2021) European Company and Financial Law Review 948; Chamorro Domínguez, "La influencia de los socios en la consecución de la sostenibilidad corporativa", in Chamorro Domínguez et al. (eds.) *Derecho de sociedades y sostenibilidad* (La Ley 2023) 267. See also Libertini, "Sulla proposta di Direttiva UE su "Dovere di diligenza e reponsabilità delle impresa" (2021), Rivista delle società, 66, 325.

[6] United Nations, Who Cares Wins. Connecting Financial Markets to a Changing World, Recommendations by the financial industry to better integrate environmental, social and governance issues in analysis, asset management and securities brokerage, 2004. https://www.unglobalcompact.org/docs/issues_doc/Financial_markets/who_cares_who_wins.pdf.

[7] Guiding Principles on Business and Human Rights. Implementing the United Nations "Protect, Respect and Remedy" Framework, 2011.

[8] *OECD Guidelines for Multinational Enterprises on Responsible Business Conduct*, OECD Publishing, Paris, 2023, https://doi.org/10.1787/81f92357-en., https://mneguidelines.oecd.org/mneguidelines/ (access 28th December 2024).

[9] See Sjåfjell, "Reforming EU company law to secure the future of European business", in Câmara et al. (eds.), *The Palgrave Handbook of ESG and Corporate Governance* (Palgrave Macmillan, 2022), 71, on the main EU initiatives oriented to sustainability.

[10] Directive (EU) 2024/1760 of the European Parliament and of the Council of 13 June 2024 on corporate sustainability due diligence and amending Directive (EU) 2019/1937 and Regulation (EU) 2023/2859. See Ferrarini, "Sustainable governance and corporate due diligence: the shifting balance between soft law and hard law", in *Câmara* et al. (eds.), The Palgrave Handbook of ESG and Corporate Governance (Palgrave Macmillan, 2022), 51.

[11] See Recital 16 of CS3D.

Companies covered by CS3D are required to comply with "the identification, and where necessary, prioritisation, prevention and mitigation, bringing to an end, minimisation and remediation of actual or potential adverse human rights and environmental impacts connected with companies' own operations, operations of their subsidiaries and of their business partners in the chains of activities of the companies, and ensuring that those affected by a failure to respect this duty have access to justice and legal remedies"[12].

This brings up the question of the meaning of due diligence and its contribution to the economic and social transition to sustainability[13].

Differing from OECD Guidelines for Multinational Enterprises on Responsible Business Conduct, CS3D does not provide any rules regarding *due diligence governance*. And this is a significant development, given the CS3D legislative process. In 2020, the European Commission launched the "initiative on sustainable corporate governance" that "would enable companies to focus on long-term sustainable value creation rather than short-term benefits. It aims to better align the interests of companies, their shareholders, managers, stakeholders and society. It would help companies to better manage sustainability-related matters in their own operations and value chains as regards social and human rights, climate change, environment, etc".[14] In 2022, the Commission's proposal shifted in the other direction towards the "corporate sustainability due diligence".[15] The proposal to harmonise the duties or responsibilities of the board of directors has been dropped.

Which leads us to the second question: who is responsible for due diligence governance under the Portuguese law?

The CS3D is silent on the role of shareholders in implementing the objectives of "sustainable development and the sustainability transition of economies and societies". [16] In 2020, the "study on directors' duties and sustainable corporate governance" "had put a very strong focus on the role of shareholders and the perceived negative, short-termist pressure the capital markets put on companies".[17]

The silence on the role of shareholders leads us to the third question. Where are the shareholders in the due diligence process? Are shareholders' agreements the right instrument to accommodate or "expand" the "voice" of shareholders in matters of environmental sustainability and human rights?[18]

---

[12] See Recital 16 of CS3D. See art. 2, 2, of CS3D.

[13] See Recital 16 of CS3D.

[14] See https://ec.europa.eu/info/law/better-regulation/have-your-say/initiatives/12548-Sustainable-corporate-governance_en (access 28th December 2024).

[15] Proposal for a Directive of the European Parliament and of the Council on Corporate Sustainability Due Diligence and amending Directive (EU) 2019/1937, COM(2022) 71 final, 2022/0051(COD), Brussels, 23.2.2022..

[16] Recital 16 of CS3D. See *Och*, The Case of the Missing Shareholders in the Proposed Corporate Sustainability Due Diligence Directive, https://www.ecgi.global/publications/blog/the-case-of-the-missing-shareholders-in-the-proposed-corporate-sustainability-due (access 12th February 2025).

[17] See *Roe/Spamann/Fried/Wang*, "The European Commission's Sustainable Corporate Governance Report: A Critique", European Corporate Governance Institute (Law Working Paper 553/2020).

[18] See *Khoo/Tallarita* (n 3).

CS3D gives "voice" to stakeholders in the context of due diligence process.[19] For the purposes of "Meaningful engagement with stakeholders", art. 13 of CS3D requires that "Member States shall ensure that companies take appropriate measures to carry out effective engagement with stakeholders".

This leads us to the question of whether agreements between shareholders and stakeholders are the appropriate legal tool to empower stakeholders.

II. Due diligence as a mandatory corporate process

1. From soft law to hard law regulatory approach

Due diligence is a *polysemic* expression. Etymologically, "the term due diligence means reasonable care of appropriate carefulness and refers to the level of attention required by circumstances in order to avoid liability and negligence" (Barron's Dictionary of Legal Terms, 5th ed. 2016).[20] Legally speaking, due diligence is, on the one hand, a "regulatory tool" at the service of sustainable development and the economic and social transition to sustainability. And on the other, due diligence is a corporate policy and a *corporate process.*[21]

As a regulatory tool, due diligence was first designed as soft law in various international instruments.[22] In 2011, due diligence was incorporated into the Guiding Principles on Business and Human Rights (UNGP) which described it "as a *process* by which companies identify, prevent, mitigate, and account for how they address their actual and potential adverse impacts on human rights".[23]

Again in 2011, risk-driven due diligence is one of the key elements of the revision of the OECD Guidelines, "and extended beyond human rights to encompass all areas covered by the guidelines that relate to business impacts, including the environment,

---

[19] See Article 3, *n*), of CS3D. See also the Proposal for a Directive of the European Parliament and of the Council amending Directives 2006/43/EC, 2013/34/EU, (EU) 2022/2464 and (EU) 2024/1760 as regards certain corporate sustainability reporting and due diligence requirements, on stakeholders' definition.

[20] On the differences between "due diligence" and "Sorgfaltspflicht" under German Law or vigilance under French Law, *Hösli/Weber* (n 5) 969.

[21] *Hösli/Weber* (n 5) 951.

[22] *Bright*, "Corporate due diligence: history and future prospects", in Abreu et al. (eds.), Dever de diligência das empresas e responsabilidade Empresarial (Faculdade de Direito/Instituto Jurídico, 2022), regarding the evolution from soft law to "mandatory human rights and environmental due diligence". See also Abreu, "Dever de diligência das empresas e responsabilidade civil (a propósito do projeto de diretiva do parlamento europeu de 10/3/2021)", in Abreu et al. (eds.), Dever de diligência das empresas e responsabilidade Empresarial (Faculdade de Direito/Instituto Jurídico, 2022), 30.

[23] Guiding Principles on Business and Human Rights: Implementing the United Nations "Protect, Respect and Remedy, Annex to UNHRC, Report of the Special Representative of the Secretary-General on the Issue of Human Rights and Transnational Corporations and Other Business Enterprises, John Ruggie (21 March 2011), UN Doc A/ HRC/17/31 ("UNGP").

bribery, consumer rights, etc".[24] In 2018, a OECD publishes its Due Diligence Guidance for Responsible Business Conduct "with the aim of promoting a common understanding of due diligence among governments and stakeholders across sectors".[25]

Recently, there has been a trend towards *due diligence hard law rules*. At the level of European Union member states, several national jurisdictions have opted to incorporate hard law rules on due diligence. These are the examples of French *Loi de Vigilance* (2017), of Dutch Child Labour Duty of Care Act (2019) and of German *Lieferkettengesetzes* (2023).[26] At the level of the European Union, the due diligence standards previously drafted as international non-binding standards become mandatory under CS3D.

As a regulatory tool, due diligence interacts with other models that are also orientated towards sustainability. SRD II, in terms of "engagement policy" of institutional investors and asset managers[27], applies the comply or explain approach.[28] According to article 3 g), 1, of SRDII, "institutional investors and asset managers either comply with the requirements set out in points (a) and (b) or publicly disclose a clear and reasoned explanation why they have chosen not to comply with one or more of those requirements". The engagement policy shall describe "how they monitor investee companies on relevant matters", including "social and environmental impact and corporate governance, conduct dialogues with investee companies, exercise voting rights and other rights attached to shares, cooperate with other shareholders, communicate with relevant stakeholders of the investee companies"[29].

---

[24] Hösli/Weber (n 5) 970.

[25] On other documents regarding due diligence, see Hösli/Weber (n 5) 970.

[26] Loi n° 2017-399 du 27 mars 2017 relative au devoir de vigilance des sociétés mères et des entreprises donneuses d'ordre. See Magnier, "Old-Fashioned yet Innovative. Corporate Law, Corporate Governance and Sustainability in France", in Sjåfjell et al. (eds.), Cambridge Handbook of Corporate Law, Corporate Governance and Sustainability (Cambridge University Press, 2019), 276, 281–282. Wet van 24 oktober 2019 houdende de invoering van een zorgplicht ter voorkoming van de levering van goederen en diensten die met behulp van kinderarbeid tot stand zijn gekomen (Wet zorgplicht kinderarbeid). See Act on Corporate Due Diligence Obligations in Supply Chains (Lieferkettensorgfaltspflichtengesetz, LkSG) (Lieferkettengesetzes ou LkSG). See Guidance on conducting a risk analysis as required by the German Supply Chain Due Diligence Act 'Lieferkettensorgfaltspflichtengesetz' or 'LkSG'.

[27] See Article 3, g), titled "Engagement policy" of the Directive (EU) 2017/828 of the European Parliament and of the Council of 17 May 2017 amending Directive 2007/36/EC as regards the encouragement of long-term shareholder engagement. On engagement policy, see Birkmose, "Article 3G: Engagement policy", in *Birkmose* et al. (eds.*), The Shareholder Rights Directive II (Elgar,* 2021), 143; *Enriques/Strampelli*, "The dialogue between corporations and institutional investors. An introduction", in *Enriques* et al. (eds.), Board-shareholder dialogue. Policy debate, legal constraints and best practices (Cambridge University Press, 2024), 2; *Chamorro Domínguez* (n 5) 289.

[28] Directive (EU) 2017/828 of the European Parliament and of the Council of 17 May 2017 amending Directive 2007/36/EC as regards the encouragement of long-term shareholder engagement.

[29] See article 3, *g*), 1, *a*), of SRDII. Gatti/Strampelli/Tonello, "How does board-shareholder Engagement really work", in *Enriques* et al. (eds.), Board-Shareholder dialogue. Policy debate, legal constraints and best practices (Cambridge University Press, 2024), 361, argue that institutional investors also engage with smaller companies and usually with ESG issues.

The mandatory due diligence rules incorporated in the CS3D are coexistent with the regulatory model of reporting sustainability information used by the non-financial reporting directives or, in the most recent version, "corporate sustainability reporting".[30]/[31]

2. Due diligence policy and due diligence process

Companies covered by the CS3D must implement risk-based due diligence in the fields of human rights and the environment. Among other measures, companies must integrate due diligence into their policies and risk management systems. In addition, companies must design a due *diligence policy* that guarantees risk-based due diligence.

CS3D refrains from defining the concept of due diligence, opting instead to receive/refer to international standards "specified and further developed in the Guidelines for Multinational Enterprises (MNE Guidelines) of the Organisation for Economic Co-operation and Development (OECD) which extended the application of due diligence to environmental and governance topics. The OECD Due Diligence Guidance for Responsible Business Conduct (Guidance for Responsible Business Conduct) and sectoral guidance are internationally recognised frameworks setting out practical due diligence steps to help companies identify, prevent, mitigate and account for how they address actual and potential impacts in their operations, supply chains and other business relationships. The concept of due diligence is also embedded in the recommendations of the International Labour Organization's (ILO) Tripartite Declaration of Principles concerning Multinational Enterprises and Social Policy".[32]

According to CS3D, "Member States shall ensure that companies integrate due diligence into all their relevant policies and risk management systems and have in place a due *diligence policy* that ensures risk-based due diligence".[33] The due diligence *policy* covers three elements: *a)* description of the company's approach, including in

[30] See Article 19a of Directive 2014/95/EU of the European Parliament and of the Council of 22 October 2014 amending Directive 2013/34/EU as regards disclosure of non-financial and diversity information by certain large undertakings and groups. On "non-financial" reporting and "sustainability reporting", *Hösli/Weber* (n 5) 960. On the non-coordination between CS3D and the Non-Financial Reporting Directive, *Sjåfdell*, "Time to get real: a general corporate law duty to act sustainability", in *Chamorro Domínguez* et al. (eds.), Derecho de las sociedades y sostenibilidad (La Ley 2023) 109.

[31] Directive (EU) 2022/2464 of the European Parliament and of the Council of 14 December 2022 amending Regulation (EU) n. ° 537/2014, Directive 2004/109/EC, Directive 2006/43/EC and Directive 2013/34/EU, as regards corporate sustainability reporting.

[32] See Recital 6 of CS3D. See *Ferrarini* (n 10) 47. *Pargendler*, The rise of International Corporate Law, (European Corporate Governance Institute, Law Working paper 555/2020), based on the dissemination of guidelines issued by international organisations, identifies the emergence of International Corporate Law (ICL) which, in part, reacts to the "interjurisdictional externalities and nationalist bias of domestic regimes".

[33] See article 7 of CS3D. On due diligence regarding conflict-affected and high-risk areas, as defined in accordance with Regulation (EU) 2017/821, see Recital 40 of CS3D.

the long term, to due diligence; *b*) code of conduct; *c*) description of the processes put in place to integrate due diligence into the company's relevant policies and to implement due diligence.[34]

A clear distinction must be made between *due diligence policy* and *due diligence process*.[35] This due diligence process "should cover the six steps defined by the Guidance for Responsible Business Conduct, which include due diligence measures for companies to identify and address adverse human rights and environmental impacts. That process encompasses the following steps: (1) integrating due diligence into policies and management systems; (2) identifying and assessing adverse human rights and environmental impacts; (3) preventing, ceasing or minimising actual and potential adverse human rights and environmental impacts; (4) monitoring and assessing the effectiveness of measures; (5) communicating and (6) providing remediation".[36]

3. *Due diligence governance in the context of Portuguese law*

CS3D does not follow the academic proposal to incorporate sustainability into corporate governance through the legislative enactment of a sustainability oriented "duty of care" designed not for profit maximisation, but for the "sustainable value creation".[37] That academic proposal advocates for "creating value for the undertaking, while respecting the rights of its members, investors, employees, and other contractual parties, and promoting good governance, decent work and equality, and the human rights of its workers and affected communities and peoples[38]. "Environmental, social and governance aspects, together form the core of the sustainable value creation."[39]

Back at the time the Portuguese Commercial Companies Code (hereinafter referred to as CSC) was published, the prevailing opinion was that the purpose of corporate governance was to increase profits to be shared with shareholders. Saving the planet for future generations while respecting the "planet boundaries" or safeguarding the interests of stakeholders affected by the company's economic activity were seen as issues outside company law.[40] Labour, social and environmental issues were regulated by other branches of law (labour law, consumer law, environmental law, etc.).[41]

---

[34] See Recital 39 and article 7, 2, of CS3D. On monitoring the due diligence policy, see article 15 of the Directive: "Where appropriate, the due diligence policy, the adverse impacts identified and the appropriate measures that derived shall be updated in accordance with the outcome of such assessments and with due consideration of relevant information from stakeholders".

[35] See ISO 9000:2015, 3.5.8. See ISO 9000:2015, 3.4.1.

[36] See Recital 20. See article 13 of CS3D.

[37] *Sjåfdell* (n 30) 95, 98.

[38] *Sjåfdell* (n 30) 102.

[39] *Sjåfdell* (n 30) 104. See also *Sjåfjell* (n 9).

[40] *Sjåfdell* (n 30) 97.

[41] On corporate sustainability definition, see. *Sjåfjell* (n 4). This Author argues that corporate sustainability is "when businesses (or more broadly, economic actors) in aggregate create value in manner that is: (a) *environmentally* sustainable in the sense that it ensures the long-term stability

This framework did not change significantly in 2006, when the reform of article 64, 1, *b*) of the CSC incorporated the express reference to the 'sustainability of the company' and the balancing of the interests of other subjects relevant to the company's sustainability, such as its employees, clients and creditors. Firstly, the sustainability referred to in this precept is essentially what is known as 'internal sustainability', which is about the "outside-in risks" which refers to risks to which the company is exposed and impacts its business.[42] The reference to the interests of stakeholders relevant to society indicates, to a lesser extent, "in-outside risks" that cover risks related to the social and environmental impacts of economic activity on the entire value chain of the company.

Article 64, 1, *b*), of the CSC does not bring any significant changes. It embraces a 'moderate and inconsequential institutionalism', an 'instrumental stakeholderism' or 'democratic' or 'functional nature' almost without sanction, which, strictly speaking, is compatible with business discretion orientated towards the pursuit of profit.[43] It will be up to business decisions to grant workers more favourable conditions than those resulting from the law or market practices (for example, to attract and retain talent), to respect the environment to a greater extent than is required by law to increase reputational gains with consumers, to adopt stricter and more demanding governance practices than competitors, etc.[44] All these business decisions are, on the one hand, compatible with the profit and, on the other, with the duty of loyalty of directors. To summarise: article 64, 1, *b*), of the CSC does not lay down the duty of directors to orientate business discretion towards sustainability or respect for human rights.

According to article 7.º, 1, of CS3D, "Member States shall ensure that companies integrate due diligence into all their relevant policies and risk management systems and have in place a due diligence policy that ensures risk-based due diligence". It is up to national laws to define the rules on due diligence governance.

According to the OECD Due Diligence Guidance for Responsible Business Conduct, "given the wide range of topics covered by the OECD Guidelines for MNEs and the cross-functional nature of implementing due diligence across an enterprise's varied operations and business relationships, there are likely to be a number of different business units, functional areas and individuals responsible for implementing

---

and resilience of the ecosystems that support human life, (b) *socially* sustainable in the sense that it facilitates the respect and promotion of human rights, and (c) *economically* sustainable in the sense that it satisfies the economic needs necessary to stable and resilient societies" – Ibid, 378.

[42] See *Richter jr.*, "Corporate Sustainability Due Diligence: noterelle semiserie su problemi serissimi" (2022), Rivista delle Società 67 722.

[43] See *Abreu*, Curso de direito comercial. Vol. II. *Das Sociedades* (8th ed., Almedina, 2024), 308. See Barcelona, "La sustainable governance nellae proposte di reforma del diritto europeo: a propósito dei limiti struturali del c.d. stakeholderism" (2022), Rivista delle Società 67 3; Hopt/Veil, "Gli stakeholders nel diritto azionario tedesco: il concetto e l'applicazione. Spunti comparatistici di diritto europeo e statunitense" (2020), Rivista delle Società 927.

[44] Barcelona (n 43) 4.

due diligence".[45] The OECD Due Diligence Guidance recommends that companies should "assign oversight and responsibility for due diligence to relevant senior management and assign board level responsibilities for RBC more broadly".

In order to "embed responsible business conduct into policies and management systems", OECD Due Diligence Guidance recommends companies to "Seek to embed the enterprise's policies on RBC issues into the enterprise's oversight bodies. Embed the enterprise's policies on RBC issues into management systems so that they are implemented as part of the regular business processes, taking into account the potential independence, autonomy and legal structure of these bodies that may be foreseen in domestic law and regulations". This requires, among other measures "practical actions", to "Assign oversight and responsibility for due diligence to relevant senior management and assign board level responsibilities for RBC more broadly".[46]

OECD Due Diligence Guidance adopts a "one size doesn't fit all" approach. "What alignment across teams and business units will look like in practice will depend heavily on an enterprise's specific characteristics such as the nature of its activities, size, and the nature of the specific risks it faces. Enterprises can consider which units of their business operations could impact observance of its RBC policies to identify which must be considered in ensuring aligned objectives. These may include *a)* Those making high-level decisions about the enterprise (e.g. boards and high-level management). *b)* Those in charge of compliance (e.g. legal, compliance, human resources, environment departments, on the ground management). *c)* Those making decisions about new business relationships (e.g. sourcing departments, procurement departments, sales departments, investment fund managers. Those in charge of development or oversight of products and operations linked to risk (e.g. product designers, operational and technical leads). Those responsible for sales and marketing of products or services".[47]

According to article 5 of CS3D, "Member States shall ensure that companies conduct risk-based human rights and environmental due diligence as laid down in Articles 7 to 16 ('due diligence')". CS3D does not identify the bodies responsible for drafting the due diligence policy and for applying, monitoring and evaluating the due diligence process. This is appropriate as there is no harmonisation of corporate governance structures at EU level. The political-legislative option of the CS3D is therefore compatible with the diversity of national governance of companies incorporated in the EU. Moreover, the CS3D also applies to companies incorporated under the law of a third country (art. 3, 2, CS3D).

Under Portuguese law, the due diligence policy that ensures risk-based due diligence (article 7 of CS3D) and the due diligence process must be managed by the board or by the high-level management. The supervisory body and compliance struc-

---

[45] OECD Due Diligence Guidance for Responsible Business Conduct, 2018, p. 10. See Ferrarini (n 10) 45.

[46] See OECD Due Diligence Guidance for Responsible Business Conduct, 2018, p. 23.

[47] OECD Due Diligence Guidance for Responsible Business Conduct, 2018, Q. 16, p. 59. Table 5.

tures will perform a crucial role in assessing the effectiveness of the due diligence measures implemented. This is also highlighted by OECD Due Diligence Guidance: "Boards will generally be involved in approving an enterprise's RBC policies. They may also be involved in taking decisions about a business strategy which may have implications for RBC. Additionally, they may intervene in instances where the RBC policies are not being implemented and request management to take action. It can be useful to appoint board member(s) with expertise on and responsibility for RBC issues. In this respect the G20/OECD Principles of Corporate Governance recognised that an important responsibility of the board of public enterprises is to oversee the risk management system and systems designed to ensure that the corporation obeys applicable laws, including tax, competition, labour, environmental, equal opportunity, anticorruption, and health and safety laws (OECD, 2015a, Ch.VI). Management, on the other hand, will be responsible for developing a strategy to ensure the RBC policy is implemented. While the role of boards and management is distinct, in practice high-level management personnel may sit on enterprise boards and thus play a dual role.".[48]

Under Portuguese law, the board of directors is responsible for the 'various corporate policies', which also includes the due diligence policy.[49] As part of the directors' duty of care, the "duty of organisational-functional control and vigilance" includes, among other things, "availability" and "knowledge of the company's activity".[50] On the other hand, the board of directors is responsible for deciding on any matter relating to the management of the company (article 406 of the CSC, applicable ex vi 431, 3 of the CSC to the executive board of directors).

Portuguese corporate governance is consistent with OECD Due Diligence Guidance recommendations. Board and senior management perform a leading role in due diligence process, mainly drafting the due diligence policy. Supervisory board has a leading role on monitoring the compliance due diligence policy.

III. Shareholders agreements and sustainability

1. Shareholder voting, sustainability and human rights

CS3D does not address the rights of shareholders, nor does it impose any duty on them to take the interests of stakeholders into account when exercising their voting rights. It is silent on the role of shareholder-owners in achieving the objectives of "sustainable development and the sustainability transition of economies and societies through the identification, and where necessary, prioritisation, prevention and

[48] OECD Due Diligence Guidance for Responsible Business Conduct, 2018, p. 62.

[49] See *Abreu*, Governação das sociedades comerciais (2nd ed. Almedina, 2010), 40.

[50] See *Abreu*, 'Deveres de cuidado e de lealdade dos administradores e interesse social', in Abreu (ed.), Reformas do Código das Sociedades (Almedina, 2007), 20.

mitigation, bringing to an end, minimisation and remediation of actual or potential adverse human rights and environmental impacts connected with companies' own operations, operations of their subsidiaries and of their business partners in the chains of activities of the companies, and ensuring that those affected by a failure to respect this duty have access to justice and legal remedies".[51]

CS3D does not follow the academic proposal advocating 'investor social responsibility', which calls for a change that "could be initiated by shareholders who use their shareholder rights to urge corporate behavior that is consistent with public interests, most especially as related to long-term sustainability".[52]

The recent study carried out by Khoo and Tallarita on the US experience suggests the "decline" of "shareholder support for environmental and social (E&S) proposals".[53] This study analyses shareholder preferences ("investor's pecuniary and non-pecuniary preferences"), particularly institutional investors, given their ideological perspective on E&S issues on the one hand and the financial costs incurred on the other.[54] The study carried out by Khoo and Tallarita reaches some findings that "are consistent with the hypothesis that many institutional investors do not "walk the talk" when E&S concerns conflict with pecuniary maximization objectives (...). Indeed, while substantial emphasis has been placed on the importance of pro-social preferences in mitigating environmental and social externalities (...), our findings suggest that, for the vast majority of funds, the financial costs of prescriptive proposals often outweigh the intensity of E&S preferences".[55] The most recent research suggests that the "most investors are primarily driven by financially-oriented objectives, though their responses are moderated by ideological preferences regarding E&S issues".[56]

Although the experiences and regulatory mechanisms aimed at sustainability are different in the US and the EU, the preferences of shareholders (particularly institutional investors) are very relevant, given that corporate measures aimed at sustainability have financial costs that affect distributable profits. And therefore, the 'voice' of shareholders (whether in support or rejection) is relevant when it comes to the company's sustainability policies.[57] We cannot ignore the fact that directors are elected and dismissed by the shareholders and, furthermore, it is up to the shareholders, at each annual general meeting, to 'carry out a general appraisal of the company's management and supervise the company' (art. 376.º, 1, *c*), do CSC)

---

[51] See Recital 16 of CS3D. Och (n 16); Chamorro Domínguez (n 5) 269.

[52] *Sjåfjell* (n 4) 378.

[53] *Khoo/Tallarita* (n 3).

[54] *Khoo/Tallarita* (n 3).

[55] *Khoo/Tallarita* (n 3) 5.

[56] *Khoo/Tallarita* (n 3).

[57] *Racugno/Scano*, "Il dovere di diligenza delle empresa ai fini delle sostenibilità: verso un Green Deal europeo" (2022), Rivista delle società 740, identify the concentration of shareholder control in a few shareholders (characteristic of the European market and also of Italy) as one of the obstacles to the virtuous impulse of institutional shareholders/investors.

In its Green Papers, 'Corporate governance in financial institutions and remuneration policies' and 'The EU corporate governance framework' the "European Commission identified shareholders as one of the factors contributing to the failure of corporate governance of not only financial institutions but also listed companies in general"[58]. Later, Shareholder Rights Directive ('SRD II') includes specific considerations on sustainability, requiring institutional investors and asset managers to develop an engagement policy including, inter alia, social and environmental impact and corporate governance aspects.[59]

The topic of the role of shareholders is disputed. The Ernst and Young study that based the first CS3D proposal concluded that shareholders, subject to short-term pressures in the capital market, have a negative influence on sustainability because they favour short-term profits.[60] Those who argue that shareholders generally have a positive influence on the company and that the accountability of directors can mitigate the short-term tendencies of directors disagree with the above view.[61]

Given that the rules on the role of shareholders to sustainable development and the economic and social transition to sustainability have not been harmonised, this topic is regulated by national rules on the rights and duties of shareholders. Under Portuguese law, there is no duty for shareholders to align the exercise of their voting rights with sustainability requirements or respect for human rights. We can say that the right to vote essentially serves the interests of its holder. As a rule, shareholders are free to decide how they vote. This principle is not contradicted by Article 58(3) of the CSC or by the essentially 'negative' nature of the duty of loyalty of shareholders.

This principle of freedom to vote is not affected by the CS3D rules, which are addressed to certain 'companies' and not to their shareholders. To sum up: under Portuguese law, shareholders are not bound to align their vote with respect for human rights or compliance with the prohibitions and obligations included in international environmental instruments.[62]

---

[58] Green Paper *The EU corporate governance framework, Brussels, 5.4.2011 COM (2011) 164 final. Green Paper Corporate governance in financial institutions and remuneration policies, Brussels, 2.6.2010 COM (2010) 284 final. Birkmose (n 27) 144; Birkmose, "From shareholder rights to* shareholder duties – a transformation of EU corporate governance in a sustainable direction?" (2018), InterEULawEast journal for the international and european law economics and market integrations 78. See also Birkmose, "The Transformation of Passive Institutional Investors into Active Owners: "Mission Impossible"?", in *Birkmose* et al. (eds.) The European Financial Market in Transition (Wolters Kluwer, 2012).

[59] See Article 3g SRD II. See supra.

[60] European Commission: Directorate-General for Justice and Consumers, Study on directors' duties and sustainable corporate governance – Final report, Publications Office, 2020, drafted in 2020 by EY for the European Commission. On the "private dialogue with corporate directors that takes place "behind scenes"", see Gatti/Strampelli/Tonello (n 29) 382.

[61] See *Bebchuk*, "The Case for Increasing Shareholder Power", available at https://papers.ssrn.com/sol3/papers.cfm?abstract_id=387940 (access 19th December 2024); Edmans, "Why shareholder capitalism benefits wider society", https://cepr.org/voxeu/columns/why-shareholder-capitalism-benefits-wider-society (access 19th December 2024).

[62] See list of international instruments identified in Part II of the Annex to CS3D.

Bearing in mind that the (controversial) duty of loyalty of shareholders is not the appropriate legal instrument to align the vote of shareholders with the cause of sustainability and respect for human rights and the environment, the question arises as to whether shareholders' agreements dedicated to corporate sustainability are suitable to promote such alignment.[63] This raises the question of whether shareholders' agreements are the right instrument to accommodate or expand shareholders' 'voice' on sustainability in terms of the environment and human rights.

2. Green shareholders' agreements

Approaching sustainability and due diligence with shareholders' agreements makes sense because these legal agreements can have as their object the "modulation of certain aspects relating to the organisation of the company" and can be aimed at "stabilising multi-annual management policies".[64] Shareholders' agreements can deal, among other issues, with the composition of corporate boards, instrumental or procedural aspects, structure or the conduct of corporate policy, if the limits of typicality are respected.[65] Think, for example, of the creation of advisory bodies or the formation of qualified majorities to amend the articles of association.[66]

Shareholders' agreements are a non-harmonised legal figure whose legal regime is governed by national law. In Portugal, shareholders' agreements are regulated by Article 17 of CSC, and are referred to in Article 83(1), (3) and (4) of the same Code, and are the subject of rules spread throughout the Portuguese legal system, for instance, the rules incorporated into the Securities Code (Articles 19(1), 29h(1)(g), 176a(1)(o), 182a(1)(a)(b)(4)), on publicising shareholders' agreements and public offers.

It is clear from article 17, 1, of the CSC that shareholders' agreements are concluded between all or some shareholders; in their capacity as shareholders, they are obliged to engage in conduct(s) not prohibited by law; with effects between the parties involved; on the basis of these agreements, acts of the company or of the shareholders towards the company cannot be challenged.[67] Through shareholders' agreements, shareholders aim to "regulate their behaviour in the company, in their capacity as shareholders".[68]

Shareholder agreements are not enforceable against the company or third parties. Consequently, 'neither the non-fulfilment of a valid shareholders' agreement nor the fulfilment of an invalid shareholders' agreement can have consequences that affect the company'.[69] And, in principle, this insensitivity towards the company should also

---

[63] See *Sjåfjell* (n 4) 393.

[64] *Cordeiro/Reis*, "Artigo 17.º (Acordos parassociais)", Código das Sociedades Comerciais anotado, in Cordeiro (ed.) (5th ed., Almedina, 2022) 158.

[65] See *Cordeiro/Reis* (n 64) 161.

[66] See *Cordeiro/Reis* (n 64) 161.

[67] See *Abreu* (n 43) 159–160.

[68] *Vasconcelos*, A participação social nas sociedades comerciais (2nd ed., Almedina, 2006), 63.

[69] Considering the situation in which the company is not a party to the shareholders' agreement.

be advocated in the case of so-called "omnilateral" shareholders' agreements (which involve all the shareholders). However, shareholders' agreements are intended to have effects that "will have repercussions in the company sphere".[70]

Under Article 17 of the CSC, in abstract terms, matters relating to companies' due diligence – identifying, preventing and mitigating the real or potential effects associated with their operations, supply chains and other business relationships, and accounting for how they correct these effects – can be the subjects of shareholders agreements. We can label them 'green shareholders agreements' and characterise them as contracts concluded between all or some shareholders, but also between shareholders and stakeholders who produce effects relating to sustainability-related matters in companies own operations and value chains as regards social and human rights, climate change, environment.

Approaching shareholders' agreements to the policy and process of due diligence strengthens the legal relevance of "atypical shareholders" agreements' – agreements between shareholders and third parties concerning the 'regulation of corporate legal situations'.[71] Following the recommendations of the OECD, the compliance with the duty of diligence in terms of human rights and the environment requires a "meaningful engagement with stakeholders" (art. 13 of CS3D).[72]

In this context, it is possible to conceive of shareholders' agreements between shareholders and stakeholders or organisations representing stakeholders (consumers, workers, affected communities, business partners) which allow for collaboration in good faith in order to hear from stakeholders about the profile of the management team in terms of sustainability, or to find out about the real and potential impacts that the company's activity may have on a given community and to enable shareholders committed to sustainability to assess the company's management in general (art. 376, 1, c) of the CSC), namely whether the board of directors has designed the appropriate "engagement with stakeholders" (art. 13 of CS3D).[73]

A different question is whether a company can be party to a shareholders' agreement in which its partner(s) are the shareholders. In fact, the question is not unexpected, given that in other countries it is common practice for companies to take part in shareholders' agreements. In Portugal, the doctrine has accepted the company's

---

Cunha, "Artigo 17.º – Acordos parassociais", in *Abreu* (ed.), Código das Sociedades Comerciais em Comentário (vol. I, 2nd ed. Almedina, 2017), 316.

70 *Cunha* (n 69) 305.

71 *Cordeiro/Reis* (n 64) 155.

72 OECD Due Diligence Guidance for Responsible Business Conduct recommends that "Consultation with relevant stakeholders may be useful in developing RBC policy. This may be particularly relevant in contexts in which strong model policies do not already exist. Guidance from employer organisations, industry associations, relevant NGOs, or multi-stakeholder initiatives can also be helpful in developing policy approaches". See Q 15, p. 58. See recital 65 of CSD3.

73 See recital 65 of CSD3. See Opinion of the European Economic and Social Committee on the Proposal for a Directive of the European Parliament and of the Council on Corporate Sustainability, Due Diligence and amending Directive (EU) 2019/1937 (COM (2022) 71 final) (2022/C 443/11), 3.6., Rapporteur: Antje Gerstein.

participation in shareholders' agreements that concern it. This judgement of lawfulness has been made in the context of qualifying a particular agreement as a shareholder agreement.[74] The question of the competence of the board of directors to participate in such an agreement is not discussed with the same depth, nor is the question of the effects of such an intervention.[75]

Considering that these atypical shareholders' agreements "are not (necessarily) null and void", they may be important for aligning the company and shareholders in terms of, for example, the design of the due diligence policy.[76] Imagine that the participating shareholders oblige themselves to support the management body's long-term policies or vote in favour of changes to the articles of association to incorporate targets for reducing water consumption, management strategies for energy transition with the adoption of renewable energy sources or circular economy policies.

Under Portuguese law, shareholders' agreements can govern the exercise of voting rights and the appointment of members of governing bodies, but they can also concern matters relating to the organisation of the company, the assumption of responsibilities by certain shareholders or even be purely prospective, in relation to the possibility of opening up the company to new capital, even in terms of mere financing (e.g. whenever the subscribing shareholder wishes to be heard on the matter).[77] In this regard, let's suppose that the participating shareholders agree to support the management body's long-term policies or vote in favour of changes to the articles of association to incorporate targets for reducing water consumption, management strategies for energy transition with the adoption of renewable energy sources or circular economy policies. Or, in the case of amendments to the articles of association, support the creation of statutory bodies to assist the management body in preparing strategic decisions on sustainability.

Or let's imagine that the group of shareholders who are part of the shareholders' agreement perceive the rule of distributing half of the distributable profit for the year (art. 294 of CSC) as contrary to a long-term vision and not in harmony with the objective of financing the decarbonisation of the company's activity, the improvement of working conditions for employees and the energy transition. And, consequently, through the shareholders' agreement, they will be able to contribute either to promoting changes to the articles of association that imply, for example, the non-distribution of distributable profit for the year (maintaining the distribution of balance sheet profit and final profits).

---

[74] See *Santos*, Contratos parassociais e acordos de voto nas sociedades anónimas (Edições Cosmo 1996) 7; *Trigo*, Os acordos parassociais sobre o exercício do direito de voto (Universidade Católica Editora 1998), 147; *Cunha* (n 69) 306, 307, 315; *Morais*, Acordos parassociais – restrições em matéria da administração das sociedades (Almedina, 2014), 16, n 2.

[75] See *Duarte*, "A regulação contratual (entre sociedade e "investidor externo") da subscrição de aumentos de capital", in *Martins* et al. (eds.) Diálogos com Coutinho de Abreu. Estudos oferecidos no aniversário do Professor (Almedina, 2020), 920.

[76] See *Cordeiro/Reis* (n 64) 161.

[77] See *Cunha*, Direito das sociedades comerciais (8th ed. Almedina, 2025), 218; Cunha (n 69) 313.

The aim of this shareholder strategy would be to keep in the company the financial assets needed to fund the energy or social transition. Or by agreeing to vote against the proposal to dismiss the directors at the 'annual general meeting' (article 376, 1, c) of the CSC), because their 'general appraisal of the management' shows that the poorer company performance can be explained by the investments needed to decarbonise the company's activity, the energy transition or the mitigation of impacts on human rights.

In a nutshell: Atypical shareholders' agreements can foster sustainability in several ways. Firstly, the negotiation of shareholders' agreements fuels the debate about sustainability issues, which helps to ensure that values and sustainability goals of the parties are aligned.

Secondly, the shareholders' agreement can frame shareholder voting on sustainability-related questions.

A few examples:

a) Modification of the articles of incorporation to update the sustainability oriented corporate purpose;

b) Mix of sustainability skills that board members should meet;[78]

c) Profile of the Chief Sustainability Officer;

d) ESG Key performance indicators (KPIs) that can shape the vote of shareholders when they make a general appreciation of the management of the company;

e) Election or dismissal of directors or supervisors;

f) Deliberations on the allocation of profits driven by sustainability criteria.

Thirdly, shareholders' agreements can cover the transfer of shares, for example by requiring "green transfers".

Assuming that the general meeting is called upon to vote on the due diligence policy – let's say at the 'request of the board of directors' (article 373, 3, of the CSC) – the shareholders' agreement that binds the parties to vote in a certain way on such a resolution will not be null and void, given that the due diligence policy will be carried out not by the general meeting, but by other company bodies and structures.[79]

IV. "Meaningful engagement with stakeholders" and shareholders agreements

According to art. 13 of CS3D, "Member States shall ensure that companies take appropriate measures to carry out effective engagement with stakeholders".[80] For the

[78] See *Demirtașa/Strengera/Trögerb*, Sustainability skills disclosure for boards: an essential prerequisite for assessing sustainability competence (SAFE Working Paper nº. 427 August 2024), 2.

[79] See *Abreu* (n 43) 165.

[80] The Proposal for a Directive of the European Parliament and of the Council amending Directives 2006/43/EC, 2013/34/EU, (EU) 2022/2464 and (EU) 2024/1760 as regards certain corporate

purposes of the "Meaningful engagement with stakeholders", the company must promote the consultation of stakeholders at various stages of the due diligence process, in accordance with Article 13(3). Let's highlight, for example, the consultation of stakeholders at the time of the decision to terminate or suspend a business relationship under the terms of Articles 10(6) and 11(7), or when the company adopts appropriate measures to remedy negative effects under the terms of Article 12 of CS3D

What role do shareholders' agreements play for the purpose of "Meaningful engagement with stakeholders"? May shareholders' agreements drive company management towards business decisions that benefit the interests of stakeholders? Are shareholders' agreements the right tool to empower stakeholders? Through participation in shareholders' agreements, can stakeholders force company management to interrupt a business relationship that has negative effects on the environment?

In abstract terms, Portuguese law does not prevent shareholders and stakeholders from participating in a due diligence agreement. Some examples: *a*) shareholders and stakeholders agree on mutual consultation to identify current or potential risks arising from the company's activity; *b*) Input from stakeholders on measures needed to cease or mitigate negative impacts on human rights or environment; *c*) Shareholders are bound to consult stakeholders prior to certain resolutions (e. g. election of directors).

However, the 'design' of the specific shareholders' agreement cannot ignore the imperative limits that article 17, 2, 3 of the CSC sets on the parties' freedom to stipulate. Under Article 17(2) of the CSC, shareholders' agreements (both typical and atypical) may not govern the conduct of parties involved or other persons exercising management or supervisory functions.[81]

This legal limit on shareholders' agreements is intended to preserve the typical nature of the company, in terms of the distribution of competences between the governing bodies and, at the same time, to preserve the freedom of action of the members of the management and supervisory bodies.[82] The rule that shareholders' agreements may not interfere in the supervision of the company aims to safeguard the independence of the exercise of this function.

According to Portuguese law, due diligence shareholders agreements may not cover the conduct of persons performing management or supervisory functions.

sustainability reporting and due diligence requirements, Brussels, 26.2.2025 COM(2025) 81 final 2025/0045 (COD), clarifies that "companies are only required to engage with "relevant" stakeholders, thereby underlining that companies do not have to consult every possible stakeholder group but may limit themselves to those stakeholders that have a link to the specific stage of the due diligence process being carried out (e. g., affected individuals when designing a remediation measure). In addition, the proposed amendments further limit the stages of the due diligence process at which companies are required to engage with stakeholders" (p. 18).

81 Atypical shareholders' agreements are lawful, and, by analogy, the regulatory limits set out in articles 17(2) and 17(3) of the CSC apply to them. Accordingly, see *Trigo* (n 74) 147; *Abreu* (n 43) 160; *Cordeiro/Reis* (n 64) 161; *Cunha* (69) 306.

82 Accordingly, *Trigo* (n 74) 162; *Cunha* (n 69) 325; *Cordeiro/Reis*, (n 64) 162, 163.

Article 17(2) of the CSC rules that shareholders' agreements "may not concern the conduct of the parties involved or other persons in the exercise of management or supervisory functions". Consequently, shareholders' agreements or clauses in shareholders' agreements that contain directives or orders for the management and supervisory bodies (in terms of powers, duties or responsibilities); or grant the parties the right to issue such directives or orders by non-organic-corporate means; or bind the parties to vote in favour of corporate resolutions containing directives or orders on matters within the exclusive competence of the other bodies' will be *null and void*.[83]

In addition to this limit, we must also consider the legal limits set out in Article 17(3) of the CSC, the violation of which renders the shareholders' agreement null and void. Agreements by which the shareholder undertakes to vote: *a*) always following the instructions of the company or one of its bodies, *b*) always approving the proposals made by the latter; *c*) exercising the right to vote or abstaining from exercising it in return for special advantages, are null and void. The nullity of shareholder agreements sub *a*) and *b*) pursues the interest of preserving the distribution of competences between company bodies, 'it not being lawful for the internal decision-making body to be commanded by others'.[84]

Shareholders' agreements (or certain clauses) which, regarding due diligence matters, issue instructions to the management or supervisory body will therefore be void, whether or not the members of the management or supervisory body are party to these agreements. It is through voting that the shareholders may legally have a say in the activities of the board of directors. It is through general meeting resolutions that shareholders can legitimately influence the organisation and operation of management and supervisory board.[85]

But there are grey areas. The line between lawful and unlawful "say" is fuzzy. Some Portuguese Authors accept that, through the shareholders' agreement, shareholders can exercise a de facto influence which, however, does not trigger legal obligations for directors or supervisors.[86]

To sum up: shareholders' agreements (whether typical or atypical) are not the appropriate legal instrument for shaping the directors' sustainability-oriented duty of care.

V. Key findings

Under Portuguese law, atypical shareholders' agreements can bring together shareholders and stakeholders. The rules in Article 17(1) and (2) of CSC are applicable to

[83] *Abreu* (n 43) 165.

[84] *Abreu* (n 43) 166.

[85] *Abreu* (n 43) 165.

[86] *Cunha*, "Acordos parassociais e conduta dos administradores", in Congresso comemorativo dos 30 anos do Código das Sociedades Comerciais (2017), 339.

these agreements by analogy. It is controversial whether the company can be a counterparty to the shareholders' agreement. Sustainability and, in particular, human rights or environmental due diligence issues may be the scope of atypical shareholders' agreements.

The final version of the CS3D refused the 'Directors' duty of care' on sustainability and did not accept the academic proposal of the "corporate duty to act sustainably".

Shareholder agreements cannot force directors to take business decisions aimed at sustainability neither to take decisions aimed at respecting human rights.

Shareholder agreements that issue orders or instructions to directors or supervisors on due diligence measures are void and null.

But there are grey areas.

Shareholder agreements are not enforceable against company and are therefore not the best tool for empowering stakeholders in terms of human rights and the environment.

Within the legal limits, shareholders' agreements "relating to the exercise of voting rights" (Art. 17, 2) are lawful. But they are a contractual instrument of limited scope: a) in the event of non-compliance with the agreement regarding the exercise of voting rights by any of the parties, 'no acts of the company or of the shareholders towards the company may be challenged'; b) the voting agreements (of the shareholders) may not govern the exercise of directors' voting rights; c) they are of a circumstantial and voluntary nature, serving the interests of the parties, and are therefore not the appropriate instrument to ensure the transition to the new legal system of sustainable corporate governance.

The contribution of shareholder agreements to sustainable corporate governance is limited, precarious and circumstantial. They are not the right substitute for the (non-existent) legal duty of directors to make sustainable business decisions.

Bearing in mind that big and very big companies impact significantly on the planet and on human rights, respect for human rights and the environment cannot be achieved without a strong commitment from States. The European Economic and Social Committee stresses that "companies have a clear responsibility to respect human rights, but they cannot replace the critical role and proper functioning of the State, particularly the State duty to protect against human rights abuse within their territory and jurisdiction by taking appropriate steps to prevent, investigate, punish and redress human rights abuses through effective policies, legislation, regulations and adjudication".[87]

---

[87] Opinion of the European Economic and Social Committee on the proposal for a Directive of the European Parliament and of the Council on Corporate Sustainability, Due Diligence and amending Directive (EU) 2019/1937 (COM[2022] 71 final) (2022/C 443/11), nº 3.3., Rapporteur: Antje Gerstein.

Shareholders' agreements and board independence: can we bring theory and practice together? Reflections from a roundtable discussion

Carolina Cunha

Abstract: This article explores some aspects of the complex interplay between shareholders' agreements and the principle of board independence under Portuguese law. It begins by examining the explicit prohibition against agreements interfering with management. Drawing on doctrinal debates and the practical realities of corporate governance, it highlights the tension between shareholders' legitimate influence and the need to preserve directors' fiduciary autonomy. The discussion extends to omnilateral agreements, the distinct features of *sociedades por quotas* and *sociedades anónimas*, and briefly considers the impact of covenants in financing and M&A contexts. By comparing the Portuguese framework with recent developments in other jurisdictions, the article questions whether greater flexibility could be introduced without undermining core principles of company law. Ultimately, it argues that while certain shareholder influences are unavoidable and even beneficial, they should remain subject to transparent processes that do not undermine the legal separation of corporate organs.

I. Portuguese Law and the Ban on Management Agreements: Between Principle and Practice

The question at the heart of this roundtable presents a significant challenge: can we reconcile theory and practice when it comes to shareholders' agreements and board independence? It is, in every sense, the proverbial million-euro question.

We should perhaps begin by acknowledging what the legal framework actually establishes. Although the general validity of shareholders' agreements is clearly settled under Portuguese law – Article 17(1) of the Portuguese Commercial Companies Code (PCCC)[1] –, there is nonetheless a specific provision that prohibits such agreements from directing the conduct of parties or other persons involved in the management of companies (Article 17(2) of the Portuguese Commercial Companies Code – PCCC).

[1] For an overview of shareholders' agreements in Portuguese law, see Carolina Cunha, 'Comentário ao art. 17.º (Acordos parassociais)' in J. M. Coutinho de Abreu (ed.), *Código das Sociedades Comerciais em Comentário*, vol. I (2nd edn Almedina 2017) .

The rationale usually invoked for this prohibition lies in a foundational principle of company law: the principle of typicity (princípio da tipicidade), enshrined in Article 1(3) of the PCCC. According to this principle, the legal system provides a closed list of corporate forms, each defined by a set of core structural and mandatory features. These features include, crucially, the degree of independence attributed to each corporate body as well as the exclusive powers conferred upon it. The compulsory nature of this typology is said to safeguard not only public interests but also the interests of shareholders and company creditors, since it provides a stable legal architecture – the rules of the game – upon which all stakeholders must be able to rely.[2]

If a shareholders' agreement were to grant certain shareholders a contractually enforceable power to determine management decisions – whether by issuing instructions to individual directors or to the board as a whole – it would constitute a violation of the board's independence. Such interference would effectively allow shareholders to hijack management powers, undermining the legislative framework that assigns distinct and exclusive roles to corporate bodies.[3]

Moreover, it is necessary to ensure that the influence of shareholders, even when legally permissible, is exercised through proper institutional channels, specifically through resolutions of the general meeting.[4]

A further rationale for the prohibition lies in the potential breach of directors' fiduciary duties. The logic is that, since directors are personally accountable for acting in the best interest of the company and may incur liability if they fail to discharge their duty, their decision-making autonomy must be shielded from shareholder interference.[5] It is also essential to uphold the principle of the non-waivability of man-

---

[2] J. M. Coutinho de Abreu, *Curso de Direito Comercial*, vol. II, "Das Sociedades" (8th edn Almedina 2024), 87.

[3] The relevance of this issue has been consistently underlined in the literature – see Galvão Telles, 'União de contratos e contratos parasociais' (1951) 11 Revista da Ordem dos Advogados 37, 102; J. Oliveira Ascensão, *Direito Comercial – Sociedades comerciais*, vol IV (Faculdade de Direito de Lisboa 2000), 297; M. Pupo Correia, *Direito Comercial. Direito da Empresa*, (11th edn Ediforum 2009), 188; Ana Filipa Leal, 'Algumas notas sobre a parassocialidade no Direito português' (2009) 1 Revista de Direito das Sociedades 135, 162; António Menezes Cordeiro, *Direito das Sociedades*, vol. I – Parte geral (4th edn Almedina 2020), 630; Adelaide Menezes Leitão, 'Acordos Parassociais e Corporate Governance' in *Estudos em Homenagem a Miguel Galvão Teles*, vol II (Almedina 2012) , 577, 586.

[4] Placing particular emphasis on this argument when dealing with sociedades por quotas (sociedades por quotas), Ana Perestrelo de Oliveira, *Acordos parassociais*, (Almedina 2025), 118: a group of shareholders outside the general meeting should not be able to constrain or influence the exercise of a director's duties.

[5] The issue has also been addressed by numerous commentators – J. Calvão da Silva, 'Pacto parassocial, defesas anti-OPA e OPA concorrente' in *Estudos de Direito Comercial (Pareceres)*, (Almedina 1996) 249; M. Leite Santos, *Contratos parassociais e acordos de voto nas sociedades anónimas*, (Edições Cosmos 1996), 221; Pedro Pais de Vasconcelos, *A participação social nas sociedades comerciais*, (2nd edn Almedina 2006), 64; Maria Graça Trigo, 'Acordos parassociais – síntese das questões jurídicas mais relevantes' in *Problemas do direito das sociedades*, (IDET/Almedina 2002) , 175; Leal, (n 4) 'Algumas notas sobre a parassocialidade no Direito português', 162–163; Paulo Olavo Cunha, *Direito das Sociedades Comerciais*, (7th edn Almedina 2019), 191.

agerial duties, which would be undermined if management were entrusted to a group of shareholders or a third party.[6]

Furthermore, preserving the free formation of the will of the management body in the pursuit of the company's interest requires recognising that this entails not only serving the interests of the shareholders as a collective, but also considering the interests of other stakeholders, in accordance with Article 64 of the PCCC.[7]

This seemingly clear-cut regulatory framework is, however, less sharp than it may initially appear.

In fact, the broader legal framework also explicitly acknowledges – and clearly accepts – the connection between shareholders and directors as it arises from several standard clauses frequently found in shareholders' agreements – namely, clauses granting each contracting party the right to appoint one or more directors, and clauses conferring on each party the power to remove the directors they had previously appointed. In both cases, the agreement typically requires the other parties to vote in favour of the proposed appointment or removal, thereby pooling their votes to secure the required majority.

These arrangements are widely considered unproblematic. Indeed, such clauses are often regarded as a straightforward expression of company law in practice: after all, shareholders are legally entitled to elect and remove directors[8], and Article 17 of the PCCC expressly allows them to coordinate their votes as they see fit.

But is it really that simple? That depends on whether one is willing to confront the elephant in the room. The connection thus established between shareholder and director often extends well beyond a simple expression of confidence in the director's judgment, competence, or alignment with the shareholder's interests on the board.

In practice, this relationship frequently entails a much closer bond – one that can manifest in recommendations and even direct instructions concerning matters of company management. At that point, the line separating influence from interference is crossed, and the principle of board independence is placed in serious jeopardy[9].

This dynamic arises from a well-known dilemma faced by directors: either they comply with shareholder instructions and secure their position, or they refuse and risk being removed from office. It is important to recall that Portuguese law – like the laws of many other jurisdictions – allows directors to be removed at any time, with-

---

6 Oliveira, (n 4) *Acordos parassociais*, 119–120.

7 See Oliveira, (n 4) *Acordos parassociais*, 118–119.

8 See PCCC Articles 252(2) and 391(1) – directors' appointment; Articles 257(1), 403(1) and 430º(1) – directors' removal without cause.

9 For further discussion, see Carolina Cunha, 'Acordos parassociais e relações dos sócios com os administradores: análise de algumas cláusulas frequentes' (2015) ano III AB INSTANTIA – Revista do Instituto de Conhecimento AB 45; and Carolina Cunha, 'Acordos parassociais e conduta dos administradores: um difícil equilíbrio' in Paulo de Tarso Domingues (ed.), *Congresso comemorativo dos 30 anos do Código das Sociedades Comerciais*, (Almedina 2017).

out cause. This legal mechanism places considerable pressure on directors to conform to the expectations of those who control the voting majority.[10]

The legislative stance on this is largely one of turning a blind eye – a pragmatic, and characteristically Portuguese, approach.

For the sake of clarity, it should be acknowledged that the ability to remove directors at will grants majority shareholders – whether acting individually or in concert – a very real de facto influence over them. In practice, it reduces the so-called red line of board independence to a largely symbolic safeguard.

And the Portuguese legislator is fully aware of this reality, as evidenced by the contents of Article 83 of the PCCC. Particularly telling is paragraph 4, which explicitly connects the shareholder's power to remove directors – via voting rights – to the exercise of decisive influence over the director's conduct.[11]

This recognition has prompted several scholars – myself included – to argue that there is no general prohibition on shareholder influence over directors, or, at the very least, that not all forms of such influence are unlawful.[12]

Indeed, the only consequence foreseen in Article 83 is the joint liability of the influencing shareholder in cases where the director causes harm to the company or to other shareholders. Influence, therefore, is not prohibited per se, but rather regulated through the imposition of liability for its improper exercise.

Finally, one may ask what happens if a shareholders' agreement goes beyond regulating the election or removal of directors and, for instance, explicitly grants shareholders the power to issue direct instructions to individual directors or to the board as a whole.

Such powers would not be contractually enforceable, as any clause to that effect would be deemed null and void in light of the mandatory rule set forth in Article 17(2)

---

[10] Abreu, (n 2) *Curso de Direito Comercial*, 623–624.

[11] Article 83(4) reads as follows: "A shareholder who, either by virtue of contractual provisions or by the number of votes held – alone or together with persons with whom they are bound by shareholders' agreements – is in a position to remove or cause the removal of a manager, director, or member of the supervisory body and uses their influence to induce that person to perform or omit an act, shall be jointly liable with them if, as a result of such act or omission, that person incurs liability towards the company or the shareholders under the terms of this law.".

[12] See Teresa Anselmo Vaz, 'A responsabilidade do accionista controlador' (1996) III-IV O Direito 329, 395; M. Carneiro da Frada, 'Acordos parassociais 'omnilaterais' – Um novo caso de 'desconsideração' da personalidade jurídica?' (2009) I Direito das Sociedades em Revista 97, 117; Rui Pinto Duarte, 'Formas jurídicas da cooperação entre empresas' in *Escritos Jurídicos Vários 2000–2015*, (Almedina 2015) , 449–451; Rui Pereira Dias, 'Comentário ao art. 83º (Responsabilidade solidária do sócio)' in *Código das Sociedades Comerciais em Comentário*, vol I (Almedina 2017) , 1038; Helena Silva Morais, *Acordos parassociais – Restrições em matéria de administração das sociedades*, (Almedina 2014), 68, n 76; Cunha, (n 9) 'Acordos parassociais e relações dos sócios com os administradores: análise de algumas cláusulas frequentes', 82–86; Oliveira, (n 4) *Acordos parassociais*, p. 127 (adding that company law does not censure influence over the management body; on the contrary, it provides a legal framework for it and, in certain circumstances, expressly qualifies it as a relationship of control, as set out in Article 486 of the PCCC).

of the PCCC. This provision leaves little room for doubt: it clearly prohibits interference by shareholders' agreements in matters reserved to management[13].

Nevertheless, such clauses may still operate as a kind of "de facto gentleman's agreement", with all parties informally complying: shareholders issue instructions, and directors carry them out – even in the absence of any contractual obligation to do so[14]. In any event, contractual enforcement becomes largely unnecessary when the nuclear option of removing non-compliant directors without cause remains legally available.

Two further nuances should not be overlooked in this discussion.

First, the picture outlined above applies primarily to the sociedade anónima, where the separation of powers between shareholders and the board is structurally embedded. In the sociedade por quotas, by contrast, this separation is far more blurred, and the proximity between ownership and management is often a defining feature[15].

Second, and more broadly, regardless of the corporate form: what about the interests of shareholders who are not parties to the agreement? Do these non-signatory shareholders require special protection? If so, what justifies such protection, and through what legal mechanisms should it be ensured?

II. Admissibility of Shareholders' Management Agreements Across Company Types

When considering the relevance of the differences between the sociedade por quotas (SQ) and the sociedade anónima (SA), it becomes evident that each corporate form is grounded in a distinct underlying philosophy that shapes the internal distribution of powers.

In the SQ model, shareholders are typically fewer in number and more actively engaged in the company's day-to-day affairs. By contrast, in the SA structure, the shareholder base is generally broader and more fragmented – often marked by a structural divide between passive, absentee investors and controlling, invested shareholders.

This fundamental distinction underpins the different legal approaches found in the PCCC, with Article 259 imposing a duty on directors in SQs to comply with shareholders' resolutions, whereas Article 373(3) provides that in SAs shareholders may only adopt resolutions on management matters at the express request of the

---

13 Cunha, (n 9) 'Acordos parassociais e relações dos sócios com os administradores: análise de algumas cláusulas frequentes', 85–86.

14 Cunha, (n 9) 'Acordos parassociais e relações dos sócios com os administradores: análise de algumas cláusulas frequentes', 58.

15 Raúl Ventura, 'Acordos de voto: algumas questões depois do Código das Sociedades Comerciais' (1992) ano 124.º O Direito 17, 62–63; Leal, (n 3) 'Algumas notas sobre a parassocialidade no Direito português', 161.

board. These provisions reflect the differing assumptions about the appropriate balance of power between shareholders and directors in each corporate form.

It is worth recalling that, historically – particularly in the 19th century – it was common for company law to vest all powers, including those related to management, in the general meeting of shareholders.

According to some scholars, the subsequent shift of management powers to the board, thereby excluding the shareholders in plenary from direct decision-making authority, served two apparent purposes. First, to ensure that managerial decisions would be taken by a body composed of individuals selected (and removable) by the controlling shareholders. Second, to prevent minority shareholders from raising questions or objections that could interfere with the decision-making process – something that would be far more likely if management matters were subject to deliberation in the general meeting[16].

According to other scholars, the imposition of a domain of autonomy for the board of directors, under its own responsibility, free from instructions from shareholders or other corporate bodies, was aimed to ensure the promotion of the best interests of the company as a whole, safeguarding its self-determination in pursuit of its own purposes.[17]

From yet another perspective, the emancipation of the management body from the general meeting and the expansion of its powers do not result from any devaluation of the latter's role, but rather from its practical limitations in handling day-to-day business decisions and the need to professionalise and streamline management.[18]

Against this background, the interplay between Article 373 and Article 405 of the PCCC has been extensively analysed in Portuguese scholarship, revealing a diversity of interpretative approaches.[19] Article 405 assigns the board the exclusive power to manage the company, requiring it to comply with shareholders' resolutions only where such compliance is expressly mandated by law or the company's bylaws.[20] On this basis, some authors accept that the bylaws may validly allocate certain management powers to the shareholders.

This approach appears to me to be, at least in principle, acceptable, although it raises delicate questions of liability.[21] While directors' liability towards the company

---

[16] This account draws primarily on the framework advanced by Abreu, (n 2) *Curso de Direito Comercial*, 93–94.

[17] José Ferreira Gomes, 'A eficácia dos acordos parassociais (incluindo ominilaterais)' in Carlos Osório de Castro (ed.), *Estudos em Honra de João Soares da Silva* (Almedina 2021).

[18] Oliveira, (n 4) *Acordos parassociais*, 121.

[19] For a comprehensive overview of the relevant doctrinal approaches, J. M. Coutinho de Abreu, 'Comentário ao art. 373º (Forma e âmbito das deliberações)' in *Código das Sociedades Comerciais em Comentário*, vol VI (Almedina 2019) , 21 ff.

[20] Article 405(3) reads: "The board of directors is responsible for managing the company's activities and shall be bound by the resolutions of the shareholders [...] only in cases where this is required by law or by the company's articles of association".

[21] As noted by Alexandre Soveral Martins, 'Comentário ao art. 405º (Competência do conselho

might be excluded in cases where they act in accordance with shareholder instructions, their liability towards the company's creditors remains unaffected.

That said, I believe that allowing the bylaws to allocate certain management powers to the shareholders as a collective body – such as requiring the board to obtain prior approval, through a shareholders' resolution, for the performance of specific categories of acts – may be beneficial from a broader governance perspective. For one thing, it brings all shareholders – including minorities – into the conversation, giving them at least the opportunity to participate in the deliberative process. Moreover, it enhances transparency and accountability: any instructions issued to the board will be formally recorded, accessible to all, and traceable to the shareholders who endorsed them.

A final remark on the distinction between sociedade por quotas (SQ) and sociedade anónima (SA): there is a curious bias in Portuguese practice that discourages the adoption of the SQ model purely on its functional merits. What I mean is that companies with a small number of shareholders – where individual qualities and trust relationships matter, and which could genuinely benefit from the greater flexibility offered by the SQ form – often opt instead for the SA structure, simply to avoid the perception of being less important or less powerful.[22]

III. A closer look at Omnilateral Shareholders' Agreements

There is undeniably a different quality to shareholders' agreements that involve all shareholders. For one thing, concerns over minority discrimination largely disappear: the risk of disenfranchising minority shareholders is effectively neutralised.

The relevant question then becomes: why not simply use the bylaws to achieve the same result? If the answer lies in the fact that agreements are more flexible and easier to amend than bylaws – and provided that no third-party interests are adversely affected – then I see no objection, in principle, to granting such omnilateral agreements a particular degree of enforceability, approaching that of the bylaws themselves[23].

---

de administração)' in *Código das Sociedades Comerciais em Comentário*, vol VI (Almedina 2019) , 427.

[22] No such bias appears to exist, for instance, with respect to the GmbH in Germany. This may well be one of those uniquely Portuguese idiosyncrasies – akin, perhaps, to the cultural habit of referring to every university-educated person as "doctor.".

[23] Advocating this position under Portuguese law, Trigo, (n 5) 'Acordos parassociais – síntese das questões jurídicas mais relevantes', 178; Frada, (n 12) 'Acordos parassociais 'omnilaterais' – Um novo caso de 'desconsideração' da personalidade jurídica?', 100, 108, 113; and Gomes, (n 17) 'A eficácia dos acordos parassociais (incluindo omnilaterais)', 378 ff., 386 (clarifying that "Future shareholders are likewise safeguarded: if they adhere to the shareholders' agreement, they accept its specific shaping of the corporate framework; if they do not adhere, the agreement is no longer omnilateral, and the general rules apply").

However, the argument of greater flexibility as a justification for resorting to shareholders' agreements instead of the bylaws is not entirely convincing. Note that, in the case of an omnilateral shareholders' agreement, its amendment is (in theory) more difficult than an amendment to the bylaws (at least in sociedades por quotas and sociedaes anónimas), since it requires unanimity under contract law (Article 406 of the Civil Code), rather than the qualified majority applicable in company law. Nonetheless, the argument concerning the lower financial cost and reduced bureaucratic burden associated with amending a shareholders' agreement remains valid.

That said, when the choice to use a shareholders' agreement rather than the bylaws is motivated by a desire to avoid disclosure, a transparency issue arises. Bylaws are public by nature: they are subject to registration and thereby serve to inform all interested stakeholders of the rules governing the company. This function would be undermined if similar rules were instead codified in private agreements – even when signed by all shareholders.

Another important question concerning agreements involving all shareholders is whether they can legitimately alter the duties of care expected of directors – or whether such modifications would constitute an inappropriate attempt to undermine mandatory standards by indirect means. For instance, can an omnilateral shareholders' agreement establishing a specific commercial policy for the company shape the conduct of board members in a binding manner? [24]

Delving too deeply into the nature of directors' duties would take us beyond the scope of this discussion. I would merely note that, when it comes to limiting directors' personal liability towards he company for breaches of the duty of care – as addressed in Article 72(5) of the PCCC – , it is debatable whether to treat instructions issued pursuant to a shareholders' agreement involving all shareholders as equivalent to a formal shareholders' resolution[25]. The two differ substantially in terms of transparency, disclosure, and even accountability.

[24] See Frada, (n 12) 'Acordos parassociais 'omnilaterais' – Um novo caso de 'desconsideração' da personalidade jurídica?', 111–112: relying on a teleological interpretation of Article 17(2), and further supported by Article 83 of the PCCC, the author argues that an omnilateral shareholders' agreement that imposes a certain commercial policy on the company by subjecting the directors to the shareholders' instructions becomes binding on those directors, provided that third-party interests are not affected (which will normally not be the case). Also Gomes, (n 17) 'A eficácia dos acordos parassociais (incluindo ominilaterais)', 388: if all shareholders participate in the agreement, shaping the conduct of the company's directors in the manner they deem most appropriate for the development of their business project, the rationale underlying the validity rule set out in Article 17(2) of the PCCC is lost. However, in my view, when SAs are concerned, the obstacle arising from Articles 373 and 405 of the PCCC (the definition of the company's business strategy falls within the exclusive competence of the board of directors) would still persist. The issue lies less with the principle of separation between the corporate and parasocial dimensions, and more with the principle of typicity. Therefore, when public or third-party interests are at stake, it is no longer a matter of shareholders – even if all of them are in agreement – contractually governing their own interests.

[25] Arguing that directors who align their conduct with the omnilateral shareholders' agreement cannot be held liable for any damage arising to the company as a result, applying Article 72(5) of the

That being said, it is not impossible for an omnilateral shareholders' agreement, reduced to writing and signed by all shareholders, to be legally treated as a unanimous written resolution, valid under Article 54(1) of the PCCC. Let us not forget, however, that in SQs directors are required to comply with shareholders' resolutions (Article 259), whereas in SAs shareholders may only adopt resolutions on management matters at the express request of the board (Article 373(3)).

As for the definition of the 'company's interest' (particularly as framed in Article 64) when pursued through a shareholders' agreement, it continues to pose significant challenges. If one adopts the view that the company's interest corresponds to the common interest of the shareholders, linked to the company's stated lucrative purpose, it is highly questionable whether that interest can be redefined by a group of shareholders through a contractual arrangement.[26] However, when that group comprises the entire shareholder base, the answer can be more nuanced.[27] Yet even in such cases, it is important not to overlook the need for directors to take into account the interests of all stakeholders, and not merely those of the shareholders, while preserving their managerial discretion.[28]

IV. Covenants, M&A and management independence

In financing contracts, covenants are frequently used by lenders to impose restrictions or obligations on borrowers and their management, with the aim of ensuring financial stability and safeguarding the lender's interests. Similarly, in the context of mergers and acquisitions, it is common to find agreements in which a shareholder undertakes certain behaviours in exchange for commitments concerning future

PCCC a fortiori see Gomes, (n 17) 'A eficácia dos acordos parassociais (incluindo ominilaterais)', 388.

[26] Defending this view, Ascensão, (n 3) *Direito Comercial – Sociedades comerciais*, 294; (it is necessary to verify whether the agreement at least upholds 'a permissible understanding of the corporate interest'); (n 4) *Direito Comercial. Direito da Empresa* 188 (agreements cannot contradict the corporate interest, which acts as a limit to the shareholders' interests); António Pereira Almeida, *Sociedades comerciais*, (Coimbra Editora 2006) 296 (the corporate interest constitutes a limit to the validity of agreements).

[27] See Frada, (n 12) 'Acordos parassociais 'omnilaterais' – Um novo caso de 'desconsideração' da personalidade jurídica?'116–118: the definition and implementation of the corporate interest belongs to the shareholders, and that it may be shaped through an omnilateral shareholders' agreement; it is not possible to exonerate a party from breaching such an agreement by invoking an extrinsic conception of the corporate interest that conflicts with what they have unanimously agreed upon.

[28] As noted by Oliveira, (n 4) *Acordos parassociais*. The author nonetheless attaches significance to the existence of an omnilateral shareholders' agreement addressing management matters, considering that the board breaches its duty of loyalty if, in the course of the required balancing of interests – and in the absence of other competing interests – it fails to take into account the interests expressed in the shareholders' agreement.

management decisions. This raises an important question: how do such arrangements align with the principle of management independence?[29]

As far as financing contracts are concerned, it is important to recognise that covenants are typically imposed on the company as a legal person – in its capacity as borrower. It is thus more a matter of general company law than of the specific regime governing shareholders' agreements Naturally, since the board is the corporate body entrusted with management, the imposition of covenants inevitably places limits on the board's discretion. The key issue is whether this partial restriction of managerial autonomy constitutes a reasonable trade-off for access to capital. This is ultimately a judgment to be made ex ante, when negotiating the financing agreement.

In the context of mergers and acquisitions, the analysis becomes more complex. There may be a direct correlation between a shareholder's commitment to act in a certain way and corresponding commitments regarding future managerial decisions. In such cases, the compatibility of these arrangements with the principle of board independence largely depends on the content and scope of the commitments undertaken. A careful examination of the specific terms is therefore essential.

V. Shareholders agreements' and other stakeholders

Since the current legislative framework emphasises the role of directors in serving the interests of all stakeholders, and not merely those of the shareholders, one may question whether this should influence our treatment of shareholders' agreements concerning management, potentially reinforcing arguments in favour of their inadmissibility.

The most immediate answer would appear to be yes: the current emphasis on ESG considerations and the recognition of fiduciary duties extending beyond shareholders to include other stakeholders surely casts additional doubt on the admissibility of shareholders' agreements that interfere with management functions.

That being said, the reference in Article 64 of the PCCC to those involved in the company's sustainability – such as employees, customers, and creditors – appears to be ranked below the duty to serve shareholders' interests. Some authors have even argued that this reference is largely symbolic, if not toothless, given that the sacrifice of stakeholder interests in favour of shareholder benefit rarely triggers significant consequences for directors.[30]

In practice, these broader interests are often invoked more as justifications for controversial management decisions than as binding constraints. For this reason, I am

---

[29] For an extensive treatment of these topics, see Oliveira, (n 4) *Acordos parassociais*, 127 ff., 131 ff.

[30] In this sense, see Abreu, (n 2) *Curso de Direito Comercial*, 300 ff. But see Oliveira, (n 4) *Acordos parassociais*, 81.

not entirely persuaded that stakeholder considerations will have a meaningful impact on the legal assessment of shareholder agreements concerning management.

VI. Foreign Experiences and the Case for (or Against) Reform

Some jurisdictions display greater legal flexibility in accommodating shareholder agreements involving company management. For example, the Delaware General Corporation Law (DGCL) was recently amended to allow certain shareholder agreements involving company management, in response to prior judicial invalidations. One may debate whether adopting a similar approach would enrich our legal framework without compromising its internal coherence, or whether such developments would risk unsettling the current equilibrium of Portuguese company law.

Of course, the answer ultimately depends on what we want our system to be. The State of Delaware has long demonstrated its ambition to preserve a leading role in the field of corporate law. What remains to be seen is the cost at which such ambition will be pursued. In the United States, a vigorous debate continues over the risks associated with allowing significant shareholders to exert influence over corporate management without adequate board oversight.

It should be noted, however, that what the recent Delaware amendments introduced was a default rule – meaning it may be set aside by the certificate of incorporation – explicitly authorising a corporation to enter into certain contractual arrangements with its shareholders or beneficial owners. Included are arrangements requiring the approval or consent of one or more persons or bodies before the corporation may take specific actions, as well as covenants by which the corporation, or its governing bodies, commits to taking (or refraining from taking) specified actions in the future. In any case, such agreements must be approved by the board of directors.[31]

What emerges, then, is a structure in which it is the corporation itself, as a legal person, that voluntarily binds itself to accept the influence of certain shareholders. In my view, this model is somewhat more transparent and openly formalised than influence exercised through undisclosed shareholders' agreements – and this is, in itself, a positive feature.

Could such a model be adopted in our Portuguese system? In practice, I have come across numerous shareholders' agreements in which the company itself is indeed a contractual party.

The implications of such an arrangement may differ significantly.[32] Where the company merely assumes the role of a creditor, objections are generally unlikely. This

---

[31] See § 122(18) and § 147 of the Delaware Code.

[32] This leads Cordeiro, (n 3) *Direito das Sociedades*, 633, to argue that shareholders' agreements which bind the company itself constitute atypical instruments, whose validity must be assessed on a case-by-case basis, balancing the freedom enshrined in Article 405 of the Civil Code against the binding force of mandatory rules.

is typically the case when shareholders undertake specific obligations in favour of the company that are not provided for in the bylaws – for example, committing, through a shareholders' agreement, not to compete with the company even after ceasing to hold shares.[33]

However, it is often the case that the company becomes a party to the agreement not merely as a passive participant, but in order to acknowledge its existence and to undertake any actions necessary for its effective implementation. Under the current legal framework, the validity – or, at least, the enforceability – of such commitments is highly questionable. One must bear in mind that Article 17(1) of the PCCC explicitly states that the company's acts cannot be challenged on the basis of a shareholders' agreement.[34] To accept a binding commitment by the company in this context would mean effacing that boundary: the internal operation of the company would not remain undisturbed by the shareholders' agreement.[35]

Thus, adopting a model similar to Delaware's would indeed disrupt two core pillars of the current system – namely, the rule in Article 17(1) and the equally central rule in Article 17(2), which prohibits shareholder interference in management.

That said, the law is not immutable – and this is all the more true in the field of company law, which is a particularly dynamic and adaptable body of rules. As a legal construct, the corporation – like other legal persons – can, in principle, be reshaped in multiple ways. Whether we should pursue such a transformation, however, is an altogether different and far more complex question.[36]

33 This position has long been supported by authors like Telles, (n 3) 'União de contratos e contratos para-sociais', 73–74, 76–77, 80–81, with the general agreement of subsequent legal scholarship.

34 As a consequence of the so-called principle of the separation between the company and its members arising from the collective legal personality, which creates a sharp divide between the corporate dimension, shaped by the company's articles of association, and the parasocial dimension, which governs the specific relationships between the parties to the shareholders' agreement – see Gomes, (n 17) 'A eficácia dos acordos parassociais (incluindo ominilaterais)', 348 ff.

35 Nevertheless, some authors question the rigidity of the separation principle as applied to omnilateral shareholders' agreements when no rules safeguarding third parties are involved, recalling that the company is ultimately a legal instrument for the implementation of the shareholders' business project – namely Gomes, (n 17) 'A eficácia dos acordos parassociais (incluindo ominilaterais)', 350–351, 367 ff.

36 Favouring a reconsideration of the existing stance on shareholders' agreements and managerial authority, with particular regard to the realities faced by Portuguese enterprises, Cordeiro, (n 3) *Direito das Sociedades*, 630; Vaz, 'A responsabilidade do accionista controlador', 401.

Shareholders' agreements and boards' independence: can we bring theory and practice together?[1]

Paulo Olavo Cunha

Abstract: This paper reflects on the tension that exists between the necessary independence of company management and the agreements made by shareholders and set out in shareholders' agreements, demonstrating that interference by shareholders in company management through an instrument of this nature is prohibited, and therefore any clause that constitutes such a situation is null and void, pursuant to the general regime of invalidity of legal transactions in Portuguese law, enshrined in Article 294 of the Civil Code.

I. Framework

The issue we must deal with concerns the tension that exists between the necessary independence of company management and the arrangements made by shareholders and reflected in shareholders' agreements.

As we all know, in Portugal, shareholders' agreements cannot stipulate the conduct of the board of directors, and any clauses that stipulate this and determine how the board of directors should conduct itself in the management and representation of the company are null and void (see article 17, no. 2 of the Companies Code[2]).

In fact, all the clauses in a shareholders' agreement that violate a mandatory legal provision will be null and void, due to the application of the general rules on the invalidity of legal transactions (cf. article 294 of the Portuguese Civil Code)[3] . The generic solution is therefore not to be found in the Companies Code, and the invalidity of a contractual or statutory provision cannot be confused with the invalidity of a company resolution, although it is common to try to determine the invalidity of a

[1] Bearing in mind that our communication and (oral) intervention – made impromptu – was essentially a sharing of personal reflections on this subject, we chose to present a text, in the form of an essay, with practical examples, without any bibliographical reference. Naturally, we cannot forget the various authors, particularly the Portuguese, who have studied this topic and whom we consider and cite in our book on Direito das Sociedades Comerciais (Company Law), 7th edition, Almedina, Coimbra, 2019 (I–XX, 1353 pp.) (and in the 8th edition, in press).

[2] Portuguese Companies Code (PCC) to which all provisions not specifically referenced relate.

[3] Agreements that require shareholders to assume company debts up to a certain amount are not null and void – as they do not violate articles 197 and 198 of the PCC. In this regard, see the Oporto Court of Appeal Judgement (Acórdão da Relação do Porto) of 30 June 2011 (Deolinda Varão), *CJ*, ano XXXVI, t. III, 2011, pp. 204–206.

statutory clause or a contractual provision (of a shareholders' agreement, for example), using the rules governing the invalidation of company resolutions.

II. Article 17, no. 2 (PCC) and directors' main duties

Having done this, let's return to the legal rule in question (Article 17), under which shareholders' agreements cannot relate to "the conduct of stakeholders or other persons in the exercise of management functions" (no. 2, in fine).[4]

Therefore, if such clauses are included in company contracts (or articles of association), they will be null and void because they violate a mandatory legal provision (Article 294 of the Civil Code).

The board of directors must therefore act in the best interests of the company it manages, and not in the interests of its main *stakeholders*, which are its shareholders. The confluence of the fundamental duties of directors established by company law in Article 64 points to this need: the duties of care and loyalty.

It is clear from the specific limitation on shareholders' agreements – which is that "agreements concerning the conduct (actions) of the respective parties or other persons in the exercise of management or supervisory functions are null and void (cf. Article 17(2) in fine of the CSC and article 294 of the CC)" – that persons cannot be conditioned in their actions to the detriment of the company[5]. Their duties must be carried out with care and loyalty, in a judicious and diligent manner (see Article 64).

The first duty requires directors to have the appropriate technical knowledge to carry out their duties – in other words, to have the *know-how* compatible with the complexity of the company's activity – and to carry them out in a judicious and orderly manner (cf. Article 64(1), *point a))*, making their decisions, which must not involve their own or personal interests, in full knowledge of their purpose, i.e. duly informed, and according to criteria of business rationality (cf. Article 72, no. 2).

[4] Article 17, which reads as follows, is supplemented by paragraphs 1 and 3:

1. The shareholder agreements entered between all or some shareholders under which, in this quality, they are bound to a conduct not prohibited by law, has effects between the parties, but cannot constitute the basis to impugn the acts of the companies or of the shareholders for the company.
2. The agreements mentioned on the previous number may regard the exercise of the voting right, but not the conduct of the parties or other individuals in the exercise of the administrative or supervisory functions.
3. As void are deemed the agreements through which a shareholder is bound to vote:
   a) Always following the company's or its bodies' instructions;
   b) Always approving the proposals submitted by them;
   c) Exercising the voting right or abstaining from exercising it in return of special advantages.

[5] For this reason, "in the event of a shareholders' agreement imposing behaviour on the board of directors that is not in line with the company's interests, not only is such behaviour unenforceable, but there is a real duty on the part of the directors not to comply with it, as they are primarily bound by the pursuit of the company's interests" [Judgement of the Oporto Court of Appeal of 30 June 2011 (Teresa Santos), *CJ*, year XXXVI, t. III, 2011, pp. 206–209].

This means that the scope and reach of the duty of care must be tempered by the *business judgement rule*, which is accepted (positively) in civil liability, but as a way of excluding the presumption of guilt that falls on directors when the company suffers damage as a result of their actions.

In turn, in the exercise of their duties and in the acts and omissions that materialise them, directors must take into account the interests of the company's *stakeholders*, and in their universe, although investors or shareholders are at the top, workers – who correspond to the institutional component of the company –, suppliers and creditors, clients (see Article 64(1), *b*)) and all those whose personal legal sphere may be affected by the company's activity,[6] even if they are not the company's business counterparties, are also included.

However, the correct exercise of management and representation of the company is only done in the interests of the company being managed and should not consider the personal interests of the managers, as has been pointed out, nor the interests of a category of *stakeholders*, such as the partners or shareholders, to whom the constitution of the company is owed.

That is why shareholders (or partners) are prevented from interfering with company management, and it is not acceptable for directors to be subordinated to their command, beyond what results from the company's purpose and the resolutions that the partners may take; and which have a different scope and reach in the various types of company.

In this paper, we will try to look at the issue from a theoretical point of view, within the framework of Portuguese law, but without ruling out solutions from other jurisdictions, and we will see how practice responds to shareholder pressure in the construction of shareholders' agreements.

III. The *praxis*

Let's start by pointing out that shareholders' agreements are often chosen to include rules of dubious legality, which by the nature of the business are beyond the control of the central authorities.

Almost all the matters that are typically the subject of a shareholders' agreement can be covered by the articles of association (or the by-laws), especially when they are common to all the shareholders.

But when some of the shareholders – and not all – want to agree on aspects of company life, or when those partners, or even all of them, agree on solutions that may conflict with mandatory legal rules, the use of a shareholders' agreement may be the appropriate solution that the articles of association do not allow.

[6] This is why the law stipulates that the guarantee that directors must provide to perform their duties – when it is not dispensed with (by resolution or by law) (see Article 396(3) *in fine* and (5)) or is not dispensable (Article 396(3)) – is intended to guarantee "indemnity holders" (see Article 396(2)).

Moreover, shareholders' agreements may involve all the shareholders, but they may believe that they should not include future shareholders, so including the matter in the articles of association may not be a valid option.

1. Company's management

Among the clauses that usually form part of shareholders' agreements are those relating to the management of the company.

These include rules aimed at ensuring the appointment of a director, i.e. which materialise the commitment of certain shareholders to vote for the appointment of a shareholder, or whoever they appoint, as a director, or which grant a shareholder the power to veto the appointment of company directors, such as the following clause:

"Second
(Board of Directors)

1. The Company's board of directors shall initially be composed of three members, the chairman of which shall be the First Contracting Party, and the remaining directors shall be appointed by the Second and Third Contracting Parties.
2. As long as the current shareholdings are maintained, the three Contracting Parties shall each have the right to appoint at least one director of the Company.
3. The director proposed by one of the Contracting Parties must have the agreement of the others, who may veto a maximum of one name nominated by each of them.
4. For the purposes of the preceding paragraphs, and at least fifteen days prior to the election of a director, the aforementioned shareholders must provide each other with the name and CV of the person they intend to propose as a director.
5. In the absence of the disclosure referred to in the previous paragraph, the contracting shareholder shall be deemed to have waived the right granted to him by this rule.
6. Within five days of the deadline referred to in paragraph 4, i.e. up to the tenth day prior to the elective general meeting, any Contractor may veto the name(s) of the candidate(s) proposed by the others.
7. If the second candidate nominated is vetoed by the Contractor who did not oppose the first nominee, the proposing shareholder has two days to nominate a new candidate and is deemed to have waived his right if he does not do so within this period.
8. The Contractor who did not object to the first name proposed has three days to object to the second name and is deemed not to intend to exercise the veto if he does not do so.
9. If the second name proposed is validly vetoed by the Contractor who did not oppose the first, the proposing shareholder has three days to nominate a third candidate, who must be accepted by the others and form part of the overall list.
10. The list of candidates shall be completed at least by the day before the elective meeting.
11. If there is no consensus on the candidate for director who should be elected chairman of the board of directors, the candidate proposed by the First Contracting Party shall be appointed to that position.
12. The Contracting shareholders to this agreement undertake to vote in favour of the appointment or removal of the directors proposed by the Contracting Parties under this Agreement, as well as to withdraw the proposal of a candidate for the board of directors who is vetoed under the terms of the previous paragraphs and to nominate new name(s)."

The above clause appears to be perfectly valid and likely to be fully complied with, as we have always understood that the advance notice for submitting a list of candidates for the governing bodies, and in particular for the board of directors, provided for in Article 289(1)*(d)* is not mandatory, but merely indicative, as this legal provision deals with the obligations of the management and not of the shareholders, who do not have the duty to submit a list of candidates more than a fortnight in advance.

Along the lines of the previous clause, we also accept as possible a contractual rule that allows a shareholder proposing a director to propose that the director be removed from office and that the other subscribers to the shareholders' agreement be obliged to vote on the (unjustified) removal of that director. In this case, the biggest objection lies in the effects that such a dismissal could have on the company, since it will formally bear any compensation for the lack of grounds for the dismissal; and it is not easy to see how it could be compensated by the shareholder proposing the dismissal.

The clauses to which we have alluded so far do not relate to the conduct of directors, but rather to the shareholders' vote to elect or dismiss them.

2. *Interference with management freedom*

About clauses that constitute interference in corporate governance, we have serious doubts about their legality and validity.

We therefore consider *agreements that restrict management freedom*, which materialise in a clause such as the one reproduced below, to be void or ineffective.

"Third
(Management)

1. The company must be managed by consensus and considering the strategic objectives of the Group of which the company is a part.
2. In decisions involving share capital increases, shareholder loans (in whatever form, including shareholder loans) or indebtedness to third parties, namely credit institutions, in the overall amount exceeding € 500,000.00 (five hundred thousand euros), the board of directors must first consult the shareholders who hold or represent more than 15 % (fifteen per cent) of the company's capital and must take the respective decision by an absolute majority of its members in office."

The clause is ineffective, since failure to comply with it cannot lead to any consequences for directors who do not respect its content. Directors must always consider the company's objectives – and not those of the Group in which the company is integrated – unless it is under total control or is part of a subordination contract.

As for the content of number 2, it corresponds to reality in most companies but does not constitute a valid obligation of the board of directors, namely because it violates the principle of equality.

For the same reason, rules imposing so-called proactive information, which takes the form of an obligation to inform certain shareholders or to disclose documents and share information with certain specific shareholders or those with a percentage of share capital above a certain amount, should be ruled out.

Regarding clauses concerning the formation of directors' resolutions and their conduct, these are totally invalid (null and void) and have no effect whatsoever.

Clauses that require the *shareholders general meeting* to approve certain decisions or proposals by the board of directors on matters that fall within its exclusive remit, or that require the vote of certain director(s), or that impose a qualified quorum on management matters, are not acceptable.

Let's see what is at stake in these situations.

IV. Shareholders resolutions on management matters

Shareholders in general and, consequently, the general meeting can only decide on management matters when requested to do so by the board of directors. This limitation results from the combination of Articles 405(1), on the competence of the board of directors, and 373(3) on the extraordinary competence of the general meeting.

If the latter legal rule is enlightening, as it states that "on matters of company management, shareholders may only pass resolutions at the request of the management body", Article 405(1) is perfectly in line with it, as it states that the board of directors "shall be bound by the resolutions of the shareholders only in cases where the law or the articles of association so determine" (emphasis added); and consequently not when such imposition arises from a different instrument, namely of a shareholder nature.

In these terms, it is possible for the articles of association (the by-laws) to contain a specific clause which, by introducing a specific deviation from the rule of the board's competence, gives the collective of shareholders the power to decide on matters for which it would not have the competence, for example, deciding on the acquisition of a certain property or certain shareholdings. In this case, the provisions of Article 373(3) are not at issue, but rather Article 373(2), insofar as it refers to the specific (contractual) competence of the general meeting.

What is not acceptable is for another contractual instrument to determine that certain matters within the legal and statutory competence of the board of directors must be submitted to the general meeting on the initiative of the directors. In other words, contractual commands addressed to the company's management, outside the company's articles of association, are null and void, as they constitute interference in management and violate the provisions of Article 17(2).

Therefore, if the shareholders' agreement provides, for example, that the board of directors must submit to the general meeting acquisitions above a certain amount or the disposal of certain assets that do not jeopardise the company's business,[7] the shareholders' clause is invalid and should be considered unwritten.

---

[7] If the Shareholders' Agreement provided that the sale of assets that jeopardise a substantial

But we also consider null and void, because they would be null and void in the context of the articles of association, provisions that make a certain resolution of the board of directors' dependent on the favourable vote or agreement of certain directors.

In fact, the legal rule on board resolutions (Article 410(7)) is imperative and constitutes a provision with a mixed character, given that it must be understood as injunctive in current board resolutions on the company's business – imposing that they must be taken by majority vote only and cannot be subject to an aggravated qualified quorum that could lead to a deadlock -, but does not prevent the articles of association from subjecting decisions on matters that do not fall within the original remit of the management body or that are only attributed to it by express provision in the articles of association to a qualified majority of the directors. In this context, the authorisation of the board of directors for the transfer of shareholdings which is subject to the company's consent (see Article 328(1)(*a*)), the increase in share capital by new cash contributions (see articles 456, 406(*l*) and 85(1) *in* fine), the delegation of management powers and, *in* the context of this, the creation of an executive committee or managing director (see Article 407(3)) or the distribution of early dividends (see Article 297) may be statutorily dependent on a qualified quorum or even unanimity.

However, if we look at the provisions of Article 410(7), and its proper interpretation, shareholders may seek to avoid a provision in the articles of association that is null and void and replace it with a shareholders' clause with less visibility, but which is supposed to be binding.

Here is an example of a rule with this purpose and object.

"Fourth

(Board resolutions)

1. The company's board of directors must pass resolutions by two thirds of its members on the following matters:
   a) Approval of the company budget;
   b) Opening and closing commercial establishments;
   c) Acquisitions of more than € 10,000.00 and disposals of more than € 2,000,000.00;
   d) Long-term financing, i. e. for five or more years; and
   e) Granting of guarantees.
2. Prior to the board's resolutions, the partners who signed this agreement shall meet to determine amongst themselves, by majority vote, how the board should conduct itself in all the matters set out in the previous paragraph.
3. The shareholders undertake to instruct the directors they propose to vote in accordance with the will of the majority and to ensure that these directors make company decisions in accordance with the rules set out in this article.
4. Failure to comply with the provisions of the previous paragraphs shall be penalised by a penalty clause of € 1,000,000.00."

---

part of the company's business should be the subject of a resolution at the general meeting, it could be admitted that this clause was valid if it was understood that it did not alter the normal and natural competence of the general meeting on such matters; and that, consequently, the Shareholders' Agreement would not be imposing any obligation on the board of directors that did not already derive from the law.

The clause we have just listed is, in our opinion, null and void because it is a prime example of interference in the management of the company, in breach of Article 17(2).

Let's move on to another clause whose content may merit some discussion.

"Tenth
(Strategic decisions)

1. Regardless of which body within the company is competent to take the strategic decisions set out in the following paragraph, the Contracting Parties undertake to approve such decisions only by a majority at least corresponding to the combined votes of three of them, but never less than 50 per cent of the share capital.
2. The following shall constitute strategic decisions for the purposes of the preceding paragraph:
   a) The internationalisation of the Company, including the export of goods and/or services;
   b) The opening of commercial establishments;
   c) The creation of partnerships with entities outside the Group and the creation of new entities with third parties, when such participation corresponds to a percentage greater than 10 per cent of the capital of the new entity;
   d) The merger, demerger, transformation or dissolution of the Company or any of the companies that make up the Group;
   e) The indebtedness of the Company in an amount that annually exceeds twice the share capital;
   f) Investments which, in cash or in instalments, involve a cost of more than € 1,000,000.00 (one million euros).
3. The admission of new shareholders with an individual or global stake of more than 10 per cent must be approved by the Contracting Parties."

This clause – which apparently deals with the strategic decisions of a given company – contains some rules of dubious validity in the context of a public limited company, perhaps partially null and void, and others that are valid.

Thus, number one – in conjunction with the various points of number two (in particular *b), e)* and *f)*, since the others correspond to the typical competence of the general meeting) – is not acceptable in the context of the board of directors, constitutes an inadmissible interference by the shareholders in the management of the company and is therefore partially null and void, and should be reduced (cf. Article 292 of the Portuguese Civil Code) and be deemed to apply exclusively to the decisions of the shareholders or the general meeting.

With regard to the internationalisation of the company (*point a)*), partnerships with other entities (*point c)*) and structural changes to the company (*point d)*), these matters are usually of the competence of the shareholders, so it is not unreasonable to accept that decisions on them are subject to a voting syndicate, and therefore have no immediate impact in the context of company management and are therefore valid.

We do not believe that it is necessary to distinguish how different types of agreements can affect company management, based solely on their specific content, because the problem lies in the clauses themselves, and not in the type of agreement.

While it is true that shareholders can always bind themselves in a way that is consistent with their status as shareholders and their articles of association, refraining from constructing and formalising instruments that materialise gross violations of the law – even if they are not subject to a specific duty of loyalty – the dividing line between a shareholders' agreement and the articles of association exists, with the shareholders' agreement limiting itself to disciplining shareholders' rights without seeking to put pressure on directors; and, consequently, limiting itself to interfering with the powers and competence of the body that brings the shareholders together: the general meeting.

We may also wonder whether it is relevant to analyse the rigidity of the legal framework – such as the Portuguese Companies Code – regarding the distribution of authority between the (main) shareholders and the governing bodies.

We do not think so.

The separation of powers within the company is an expression of a classic principle of democracy that exists in legal persons such as (commercial) companies, at the level of their organisation, leading these entities to act independently and autonomously from their investors, if they are plural in number.

However, it is important to note that there are substantial differences between the main types of Portuguese companies.

Thus, while the private limited company (PLC) is a personalised and subjective company, which recognises subjective rights for all its *quota holders* (shareholders), but accepts that the interests of the shareholders may constrain the actions of the management (see Article 259),[8] in the public limited company – whether private or public – the shareholders cannot interfere in management (see Article 373(3)), and the directors must act exclusively in the interests of the company, never following instructions from the shareholders who are responsible for appointing them to the Board.

Shareholders can decide on matters that fall within the board's remit in two different situations:

- when the articles of association recognise this competence (within the framework of the provisions of Article 373(2)), provided that this attribution of powers does not de-characterise the competence of the board; and
- in cases where it is the board of directors that questions them (which happens from time to time), in which case the management body does not lose its competence.

---

[8] See *Cunha*, in Viera González/Teichmann (eds.), Private Company Law Reform in Europe: The Race for Flexibility, 2023, 461–569, 526–537, in particular, 527.

V. Creditors interference and interaction between articles of association and shareholders agreements

Regarding limitations and obligations in financing agreements, used by creditors to impose restrictions or obligations on borrowers and their management, with the aim of ensuring financial stability and protecting creditors' interests, such agreements should not be considered shareholders' agreements in the technical sense, but financing agreements, even if they are structured agreements.

Creditors (lenders) are not restricted to negotiating with the management of the financed company.

The situation is different when it comes to forcing or compelling shareholders to make changes to the company's articles of association.

The directors of the borrower can adapt their behaviour and the management of the company to the demands of the lenders, but they must also do so in the exclusive interest of the company.

The legal flexibility seen in other jurisdictions – such as those of the United States (notably Delaware) and Italy – where shareholders' agreements are allowed to cover management acts if they comply with the articles of association and the law, could cause disruption in the Portuguese legal system.

This type of contractual provision would allow investors (shareholders) in the Portuguese ecosystem to interfere in the functions and decisions of directors, who are usually already willing and receptive to carrying out surreptitious instructions passed on to them by the main shareholders.

We should also bear in mind that the principle of equal treatment of partners (or shareholders) can be seriously jeopardised by a shareholders' agreement signed by the largest shareholders that grants them prerogatives in their dealings with the company's management and guarantees them an influence that subverts the legal-corporate system.

But above all, we do not see any advantage in admitting this interference, nor any reason to support it and legalise a solution of this nature.

Let us also raise a question, considering the Italian system: who determines the red line between respect for the articles of association and the law by the shareholders' agreement once the interference has been materialised?

Notwithstanding what we have just said, we do not believe that the system would be jeopardised by the adoption of legal provisions that would relax the (direct) interference of shareholders in company management, because there are other safeguards, which we have pointed out as scrupulous respect for the fundamental (legal) duties enshrined in Article 64, and read in the light of the provisions of Article 72(2), as we explained above. But a solution of this nature would not fail to be an opening to allow an action to which the main door is closed to enter through the back yard.

In addition, it does not seem appropriate to introduce a differentiation in cases where the shareholders' agreement is signed by all the partners (or shareholders), since we do not know whether those who are already shareholders will remain, nor do we know whether future partners will want to join the solution and be willing to accept it to the natural detriment of the company's interests (social interest).

For this reason, we cannot declare that omnilateral agreements (i.e. those that include all the shareholders) are any different from other shareholders' agreements, since they are contracts that do not bind third parties, but only those who enter them.

In fact, the legal and corporate framework is increasingly recognising the importance of other *stakeholders* – other than the shareholders themselves – and so we must consider the interests of everyone (the *stakeholders*) and not just the interests of the shareholders, even though they are undoubtedly the main *stakeholders*. This is why shareholders who participate in company management cannot influence management decisions or the behaviour of the other members of the Board of Directors.

This reading is the most appropriate and is a corollary of the fundamental legal duties of directors.

However, practice tries to find a way to overcome the legal limitations, creating rules that are positioned on the borderline of legality and which it is difficult to consider outside it.

An example of this is the following clause:

"When exercising their nomination rights pursuant to this Agreement, the relevant Shareholder:

(a) shall ensure that the individuals being nominated by it as Directors or members of governance bodies of the Company and/or Group Companies (but excluding any independent non-executive Directors) acknowledge, accept, and agree to be bound and to approve the provisions and rules set out in this Agreement, subject always to their statutory and fiduciary duties from time to time; and
(b) acknowledges, accepts, and agrees that a breach of this Agreement caused by the conduct of such an individual shall be deemed to be a breach by the Shareholder who indicated such member, irrespective of whether the relevant member was specifically instructed by the Shareholder to perform the act that caused the relevant breach."

VI. Summary

To summarise, having gone through the various possible situations and cases in the context of a shareholder agreement, we have come to the conclusion that the interference of shareholders in company management, and in the way it is carried out, through an instrument of this nature is prohibited (by Article 17(2) *in fine*), so that any clause that sets up a situation of this kind is null and void, by application of the general regime for the invalidity of legal transactions in Portuguese law, enshrined in Article 294 of the Civil Code.

Thus, unlike in other legal systems, agreements that affect the management of the company are prohibited in Portugal and must remain independent from the influence of the shareholders, unless the company is wholly owned by its (sole) shareholder.

This limitation, legally established in the rule governing shareholders' agreements (Article 17), protects the independence of the board of directors and the authority of management, allowing directors to act exclusively to fulfil the company's interests.

Shareholders' agreements, private equity and venture capital

Alexandre de Soveral Martins

Abstract: This text will call the readers' attention to some practical issues that should be taken into consideration when dealing with investments in companies subject to Portuguese company law when investors want to conclude shareholders' agreements. Many investors are used to the common law world, and sometimes it is difficult to explain the differences found in Portuguese Company Law with regard to shareholders' agreements. Also, this essay will highlight some aspects that should receive special attention when negotiating one of those agreements in order not to be surprised by unexpected consequences.

I. Private Equity vs. Venture Capital?

Darryl Cooke[1] wrote that "private equity and venture capital describe equity investment in unquoted companies", adding that "the term 'private equity' is the term generally used in the UK to cover the industry as a whole including buy-outs and venture capital. 'Venture capital' is a sub-category covering the start-up to expansion stages of investment".[2] The same view is shared by Feldhaus: "[...] Venture capital is a subsector of the private equity industry and comprises the business of investment companies that primarily invest in young companies, mainly in high-tech industries".[3]

The AIFM Directive,[4] in its Recital 78, distinguishes Private Equity from Venture Capital, but does not provide any criteria for the distinction ("In particular for private equity and venture capital funds [...]").

---

[1] *Cooke*, Private Equity: Law and Practice, 2018, 1. See, on the origins of the Private Equity Structure, Davidoff, South California Law Review, 82 (2009) 82, 481, 489.

[2] *Fenwick/Vermeulen*, in Zetzsche (ed.), The Alternative Investment Fund Managers Directive, 2020, 161, wrote that Venture Capital "is in the business of changing the world".

[3] The translation is of our own responsibility. The original text reads that "[...] bezeichnet Venture Capital einen Teilbereich der Private Equity-Branche und umfasst das Geschäft von Beteiligungsgeselschaften, die vorwiegend in junge Unternehmen – vorzungsweise in High-Tech-Branchen – investieren". See *Feldhaus*, in Feldhaus/Veith (eds.), Frankfurter Kommentar zu Private Equity, 2010, 4.

[4] Directive 2011/61/EU of the European Parliament and of the Council of 8 June 2011 on Alternative Investment Fund Managers and amending Directives 2003/41/EC and 2009/65/EC and Regulations (EC) No 1060/2009 and (EU) No 1095/2010.

Portuguese law on Asset Management[5] describes what is known as "risk" capital investment as the acquisition of equity instruments and debt capital instruments in companies with high development potential, as a way of benefiting from the respective increase in value.[6] The description is so broad that it includes what is usually known as Private Equity and Venture Capital.[7]

Quoted companies may also be investees when the investment is used to delist firms ("public to private"). But attention must be paid to statutory limitations.

Private Equity investments include MBOs, MBIs, BIMBOs (buy-in/management buy-out), rescues, sec-pur (secondary purchases), PPEs (Purchasing from a Private Equity house), PES (Purchasing from Existing Shareholders), Expansion capital (Development or Growth capital), Early-Stage investment, and start-ups investment.[8] Venture capital investors will be particularly interested in start-ups. The operation may be prepared looking forward to a future possible sell to a Private Equity investor who is not interested in investing in Venture Capital.

Private Equity and Venture Capital investments are very useful when the investee has no means of providing enough security to a bank. Factoring and invoice discounting may also not be enough when the company does not own other relevant assets.

Private Equity or Venture Capital investors will probably want to negotiate a shareholders' agreement (*acordos parassociais, Gesellschaftervereinbarungen, patti parasociali, pactes d'actionnaires*). Those agreements may deal with all the most important issues usually included in that kind of agreements. They will probably include clauses concerning share transfers, share acquisition rights, voting, information rights and duties, new investments to be made by the company and stabilization agreements.[9]

Particular attention must be given on how the shareholders' agreement will interact with the investment contract and the articles of association. If the investor is an AIF, its manager needs to pay attention to all the rules concerning how it may act. The rules dealing with asset stripping, for instance, are very important.[10] And if the Por-

---

[5] Approved by Decree-Law 27/2023 of 28 April 2023.

[6] Art. 227 (1): 'Considera-se investimento em capital de risco a aquisição de instrumentos de capital próprio e de instrumentos em capital alheio em sociedades com elevado potencial de desenvolvimento, como forma de beneficiar da respetiva valorização'.

[7] However, *Oliveira*, Acordos Parassociais, 2025, 19, links Venture Capital to start-ups and Private Equity to restructuring. In Desvinculação Programada do Contrato, 2022 – reimp., *Oliveira* accepts that "risk" capital may include Venture Capital and Private Equity investments. In the Portuguese translation of the European Venture Capital Fund Regulation – Regulation (EU) No. 345/2013 of the European Parliament and of the Council of 17 April 2013 on European venture capital funds –, venture capital is considered to be "risk capital".

[8] See *Cooke* (fn. 1), 2, *Oliveira*, Desvinculação Programada do Contrato, 392.

[9] See, for a global overview, *Napokoj/Pelinka*, Der Beteiligungsvertrag. Venture-Capital-Finanzierung, 2017, 24.

[10] See AIFMD, Art. 30, on asset stripping. See also Arts. 219 and 227 (2) of the Portuguese Asset Management Law. On AIFMD, Art. 30, and asset stripping, see *Martins*, in Martins et al. (coord.),

tuguese Company Law applies to the shareholders' agreement, it is crucial to see how the former establishes the perimeter of the admissible clauses.

The content of the clauses will depend on the strategies of the parties. Private Equity investors are usually interested in having some influence on the members of the board of directors, but many times they do not wish to manage the investee.

Private Equity and Venture Capital investments are intended to be limited in time. Exit strategies usually are, therefore, of utmost importance[11], and the shareholders' agreement will probably have clauses on that. On the other hand, it is also important to limit the exit of those who have all the know-how, making leaver (Good-Leaver and Bad-Leaver clauses) and vesting clauses very important.[12]

But, on the other side, the Private Equity or Venture Capital investor may be using resources made available by its own investors. That will also have influence on the clauses related to the duration of the investment and with what is expected to happen during that time.

II. And the trigger is...

Shareholders' agreements must be negotiated with a clear understanding of what will trigger what. Therefore, it is also important to have clear definitions.

If, for instance, the agreement contains clauses on future financing (v. g. because new investments will be necessary or because the company is in distress[13]), it is important to pay attention to how the applicable law and the articles of association divide power between the board of directors and the shareholders' meeting. Identifying the applicable law is, of course, very important.[14]

If new financing is a consequence of a board of directors' decision, clauses of the shareholders' agreement concerning voting majorities required for shareholders' resolutions lose much of its practical importance. One of those clauses may rule that resolutions on new investments require a special majority of votes, but that clause

---

Diálogos com Coutinho de Abreu, 2020, 23, 31, *Boogard/Mullmaier* and *Clerc/Eckner*, in Zetzsche (ed.), The Alternative Investment Fund Managers Directive, 654 and 665, and *Schröter*, Der Geltungsbereich und die inhaltliche Ausgestaltung des Asset-Stripping-Verbots in § 292 KAGB sowie seine Anwendung auf Private Equity-Fonds, 2019, 31.

[11] See *Oliveira* (fn. 8), 388, 391.

[12] See, on both problems, *Oliveira*, in 20 Anos do Código dos Valores Mobiliários, 2021, *Oliveira* (fn. 8), 462, *Napokoj/Pelinka* (fn. 9), 25, *Hornung*, Leaver-, Vesting und Shoot-Out-Klauseln, 2018, 31.

[13] See, on shareholders' agreements with clauses concerning extra contributions in case of distress, *Havel*, in Mock/Csach/Havel (eds.), International Handbook on Shareholders' Agreements, 2018, 103. The author also calls the attention to shareholders' agreements that may be considered executory contracts and to the consequences of the opening of insolvency when the company is a party to the agreement. The latter problem will be addressed in point VII.

[14] See, on the issue, *Csach*, in Mock/Csach/Havel (fn. 13), 83, and *Laimer*, in Kindler et al. (eds.), Gesellschaftsrechtliche Nebenvereinbarungen in Europa. Handbuch, 2024, 29, (the author also highlights the fact that it might be difficult to solve the 'qualification' problem – 31).

may be circumvented by a board of directors' decision if the latter is competent to decide on the issue.

The board of directors' resolutions may have consequences for what each party must do. If the board of directors decides to develop a certain project, the company may need more resources. A start-up frequently depends on several financing rounds. If one of the parties in the agreement is not able to participate in the new financing round, it is crucial to have a clear view on what will happen next. Will that be considered an infringement of the agreement? If that is the case, what are the consequences? Is there a call option in the agreement? If such an option exists, the shareholder incapable of financing the company may have to give away its shares. Was he counting on that? Probably not.

III. Deadlocks and compulsory transfer clauses: be afraid! Be very afraid!!!

When shareholders take decisions on new financing, the shareholders' agreement may require a special majority or a unanimous vote for the resolution. Shareholders may think that this will give them a veto power.

However, that can backfire. It may be seen as a deadlock situation according to the definitions included in the agreement. Deadlocks may work as the trigger for an auction or for setting in motion other types of clauses (v. g. "Russian Roulette" or "Texan Shoot-Out" clauses[15]) benefiting the party with more money available.

It is also important to see who will have to participate in the auction. Only those who voted *against* a certain proposal? Or also some of those who voted *for* the proposal? If the latter must participate, they may also end the day without their shares… That could be a surprise for them.

Clauses like those may be very useful to solve problems caused by deadlocks. However, it is important to have in mind that the deadlock situation may have been caused as part of a strategy to squeeze-out a particular shareholder. This is especially dangerous when the investee had access to Venture Capital, and its initial shareholders have good ideas but no cash.

Special attention must also be paid to what is considered a breach of the agreement, or a serious breach of the agreement. Once again, if there is a decision of the board of directors requiring new financing, and refusing to participate in the new round is seen as a breach or a serious breach of the agreement, that may act as a trigger for compulsory transfers clauses.

---

[15] See *Schulte*, NZG (2005), 24–31, *Fleischer/Schneider*, European Company and Financial Law Review (2012), 35, *Oliveira* (fn. 8), 449.

IV. Don't trust on special majorities clauses

Special majorities clauses may give a wrong idea to the parties. If those clauses concern shareholders' resolutions, one must see if those resolutions are the only way to decide on a certain subject. As we have seen before, if the shareholder has a veto power on a shareholders' resolution, but the decision on a particular subject may also be taken by the board of directors, the veto power may not be very effective.

The articles of association have a role to play there, and the same may be said about shareholders' agreements. Therefore, it may be useful to use the articles of association to establish that certain issues should be always decided by a shareholders' resolution. But that will depend on the applicable law for the type of company in question. In Portugal, it is not clear how far it is possible to go with regard to companies by shares.

It is also important to underline that, in Portugal, special majorities clauses in a shareholders' agreement may not be used as grounds to call into question a shareholders' resolution.[16]

V. Too much is too much

Investors often want to know how far they may go if they want to try to influence the board of directors. Equity funds managers and Venture Capital funds managers have duties towards their investors. That may cause some pressure on them to have a say on how the board of directors of the company where the money is invested will act because that may be seen as a way of assuring good management or of focusing on a purpose, sustainability or ESG issues.[17] In other cases, the investor may be looking for an opportunity to conclude contracts with the company (with all the dangers that come with it). For instance, as supplier of the company or as manager of one of the company's assets.

Shareholders' agreements could be seen as a tool to achieve those objectives. However, in Portugal that kind of approach is dangerous. Portuguese Company Law forbids clauses concerning the conduct of the parties or other persons in the exercise of management or supervisory functions.[18] That is particularly relevant when there is

---

[16] See Portuguese Company Law, Art. 17 (1), *Oliveira*, (fn. 7), 8.

[17] See *Afsharipour*, in Enriques/Strampelli (eds.), Board-Shareholder Dialogue, 2024, 297, 299.

[18] See Portuguese Company Law, art. 17 (2). However, the provision has been interpreted in different ways: see, for an overview of different perspectives, *Silva*, in Silva, Estudos jurídicos (Pareceres), 2001, 233, *Leitão*, in Miranda et al. (org.), Estudos em Homenagem a Miguel Galvão Teles II, 2012, 586, *Frada*, Direito das Sociedades em Revista 2 (2009), 97, 111, *Morais*, Acordos Parassociais. Restrições em Matéria de Administração das Sociedades, 2014, 33, *Almeida*, Scientia Iuridica LXIV 33 (2015), 375, *Duarte*, Formas Jurídicas de Cooperação Entre Empresas, 2022, *Cunha*, in Abreu (coord.), Código das Sociedades Comerciais em comentário, vol. I, 2nd. ed. 2017, 325, *Oliveira*, (fn. 7), 114.

a business plan that the parties want to be followed by the company or when shareholders' agreements are used to improve the Board-Shareholders dialogue.[19]

In Portuguese limited liability companies ("sociedades por quotas"), shareholders' resolutions on management issues are generally admissible, and the board of directors will have to respect them. The shareholders' agreement may have clauses on how to vote in those shareholders' meetings.

Companies by shares have a different legal environment. It is debatable if the articles of association may require a shareholders' resolution about management issues. It seems that the articles of association may impose on the board of directors the duty to ask for a shareholders' resolution in what concerns some management issues. In that case, the shareholders' agreement could also have clauses on how to vote. The same may be said with regard to voting on a proposal to change the articles of association to include the duty to ask for a shareholders' resolution.

Sometimes, the parties want to include clauses related to the delegation of powers by members of the board of directors. In Portugal, the board member of a limited liability company or of a company by shares is not allowed to delegate his powers on someone who is not already a member of the board. Even in the case of delegation to a member or the board, this usually depends on a decision of the board itself.

Investors wanting to have the power to choose one member of the board of directors will probably wish to include clauses about it in the shareholders' agreement. However, according to Portuguese Company Law, the shareholders' agreement is not the appropriate way to provide that kind of powers to the parties.[20] Therefore, the parties should think about including clauses on how to vote when the issue being discussed in the shareholders' meeting is the appointment of directors.

The articles of association of a Portuguese limited liability company may give a shareholder the special right to appoint one or more directors.[21] The shareholders' agreement may also have clauses concerning voting on changes to be introduced in the articles of association related to those special rights.

Portuguese companies by shares, on the other hand, have very different rules. Individual shareholders may not have special rights because those rights must always be connected to a class of shares, but even that is not allowed in what concerns the right to appoint directors.[22] However, AIFMs have a different regime: the manager of a risk capital fund may be appointed for the board of directors of the investees.[23]

---

[19] See, on the latter issue, *Gatti/Strampelli/Tonello*, in Enriques/Strampelli (fn. 17), 325, 326.

[20] The right to appoint a member of the board would be considered a 'special right' (art. 24 of the Portuguese Company Law). For Private Limited Companies, special rights must be included in the articles of association: see art. 252 (2) of the Portuguese Company Law. The special right to appoint a director is not available for Public Limited Companies: see art. 39 (3), final part, of the Portuguese Company Law.

[21] See Portuguese Company Law, art. 252 (2).

[22] See Portuguese Company Law, art. 391 (3).

[23] See the Portuguese Asset Management Law, Art. 228 (2) (a).

VI. The exit

Private Equity and Venture Capital firms are usually very concerned about the exit moment. As Oliveira wrote, risk capital investment is geared towards a profitable exit.[24] Usual alternatives are IPOs, Trade Sales, Secondary Buy-Outs and Buy-backs.[25] Private Equity and Venture Capital firms will try to coordinate the exit moment with the commitments they have towards their own investors.

Drag-along clauses may be very helpful. When they are included in shareholders' agreements, they will increase the chances of finding someone interested in buying the shares. Once again, the trigger must be well identified.[26] Clauses concerning how to vote when shareholders' resolutions are necessary to sell the shares are also very useful.

Venture Capital investors may also be interested in tag along clauses.[27] They will count on them when shareholders with the know-how want to leave. But clauses limiting the freedom of the latter to exit the company are also very common.

Sometimes, the shareholders' agreement will have clauses connecting the effects of the agreement to the maintenance of a certain shareholder in the company or to the number or importance of his shares. Once again, the end of the story will depend on the triggers.

VII. The end is near…

Portuguese Civil Code rules on contracts containing clauses in favour of a third party.[28] At least in some cases, clauses like those may be enforced by the company against the parties to the agreement. This may be particularly dangerous when the shareholders' agreement has clauses imposing duties related to financing. The danger is clear in case of the opening of an insolvency procedure concerning the investee if the insolvency practitioner may choose to enforce those clauses.

Sometimes, the company is also a party to the shareholders' agreement. However, Portuguese Company Law is not clear on how those agreements must be treated, and the authors do not have one unanimous opinion on them.[29]

---

24 See *Oliveira*, (fn. 7), 28.

25 See, for Private Equity investments, *Feldhaus* (fn. 3), 102, *Cooke* (fn. 1), 343. The "certifying agent" role of Venture Capital companies may bring with it some risks: see *Lee*, Venture Capital and Firm Performance. The Korean Experience in a Global Perspective, 2018, 3, and *Oliveira* (fn. 8), 397.

26 Drag-along clauses may be linked to call options or discount call options: *Oliveira* (fn. 8), 422.

27 See *Maidl*, NZG (2003), 1091, 1095, *Sáez/Bermejo*, European Business Organization Law Review 11 (2010), 423, *Oliveira* (fn. 8), 440.

28 See Portuguese Civil Code, Arts. 443, and *Oliveira*, (fn. 7), 31.

29 *Ventura*, Estudos Vários Sobre Sociedades Anónimas, 1992, 13, writes that Portuguese Company Law Art. 17 (1) does not apply; *Trigo*, Os Acordos Parassociais Sobre o Exercício do Direito de Voto, 1998, 147, and *Leal*, Revista de Direito das Sociedades 1 (2009), 135, 148, accept that Art. 17

VIII. To conclude

Shareholders' agreements must be drafted carefully to avoid surprises at the end of the day. In the previous lines, a few examples were used to show precisely that.

This text also endeavoured to draw the attention to the fact that foreign Private Equity and Venture Capital investors may be counting on a flexible legal regime in Portugal: a regime that allows more freedom in the drafting of shareholders' agreements. However, the Portuguese Company Law, Art. 17, presents several limitations to what may considered legal, and it is dangerous to take things for granted in what concerns some practical issues. It's time to start thinking about how the wording of Art. 17 of the Portuguese Company Law should be changed to make it more investor-friendly without affecting other relevant interests. Specially, when so many limitations were already identified with regard to the shareholder meeting as an "engagement mechanism".[30]

applies to those agreements, and *Oliveira*, (fn. 7), 31, seems to have the same opinion; *Duarte*, in Martins et al. (org.), Diálogos com Coutinho de Abreu, 2020, 909, 920, doubts of the validity of such kind of agreements; *Cunha*, Direito das Sociedades Comerciais, 2019, 186 writes that only agreements between shareholders may be considered shareholders' agreements.

[30] See *Bowley/Hill/Kourabas*, in Enriques/Strampelli (fn. 17), 368, 380.

Shareholders' Agreements, contractual remedies and the limits of contractualism in Company Law

Francisco Mendes Correia

Abstract: This article aims to contribute to the identification of suitable grounds for the principle of separation between shareholders' agreements and articles of association, in line with the principle of privity of contracts. An adequate foundation for the principle will make it possible to more rigorously establish its limits and the secondary rules that can be drawn from it, especially with regard to the enforcement of obligations emerging from shareholders' agreements.

I. Introduction

Shareholders' agreements are contracts between two or more shareholders, that create obligations the object of which is the exercise of rights and the performance of duties of the parties as shareholders.[1] Therefore, from the perspective of its legal consequences, a shareholders' agreement is an obligational contract, in that it creates new obligations: to act or abstain from acting in a certain way; from the perspective of its object, a shareholders' agreement disciplines the way in which the rights/duties of the parties *as shareholders* will be exercised/performed.

The most common objects of regulation through shareholders' agreements are the transferability of shares, the exercise of voting rights, corporate financing and the involvement of shareholders in the management of the company (e.g., know-how contribution obligations) but, with limited exceptions, the exercise of all rights/performance of duties of a shareholder as such can be regulated via such agreements.

Different criteria are used to distinguish between a shareholders' agreement and the articles of association of a company. A fruitful approach combines distinctions based on formal, material and intentional aspects: on the one hand, shareholders' agreements tend to be formalized in separate documents, that are not subject to the formal requirements set out in Company Law; on the other hand, shareholders' agreements do not cover "constitutional" aspects of the company, that are set out in the articles of association (e.g. the creation of the company in itself); additionally,

[1] *Mock/Csach/Havel*, in Mock/Csach/Havel (eds.), International Handbook of Shareholders' Agreements, 2018, 3 ff., for an alternative definition: "A shareholders' agreement is an agreement of at least two shareholders establishing a contractual link in regard to their position as shareholder".

a contractual intention to create obligations that are *not* subject to Company Law but to Contract Law is usually discernible. However, some of these distinctions can be hard to draw,[2] especially in those cases where all shareholders are parties to the shareholders' agreement.

There are several reasons why shareholders may recur to a shareholders' agreement, as a complement for the regulation of corporate rights and duties emerging from the articles of association. Some of these reasons relate to the subjective scope of both agreements: shareholders' agreements can be used if the personal scope of the obligations that are being created is narrower or wider that the scope of the articles of association. It can be the case that only some (but not all) shareholders are parties to the agreement, that the agreement differentiates between different groups of shareholders as to the obligations it creates, or that third parties are also involved in the agreement. In other cases, shareholders' agreements are used for its confidentiality (or absence of publicity), in contrast with the articles of association, that must be entered in the commercial registry. Among other additional reasons, the flexibility regarding amendments of the initial contractual arrangement and the availability of different remedies in case of non-performance, other than the limited remedies offered by Company Law or envisaged in corporate documents (articles of association), can also explain the option for shareholders' agreements.

In any case, a more general reason explains *all* shareholders' agreements: the parties' intention to create obligations regarding the exercise/performance of corporate rights/duties that are *not* subject to general Company Law and to the rules set out in the articles of association, either because they *want* to subject those obligations to a different (merely contractual) regime, or because they *cannot* subject them to general Company Law, due to imperative rules.

The limits of Contract Law in the enforcement of obligations arising from a shareholders' agreement is a commonly discussed topic. Among other rules and principles, the so-called principle of separation is usually invoked, to ground and explain certain limitations to such enforcement.

However, if shareholders' agreements have been described as a "puzzling phenomenon of corporate law" or as being shrouded "in mystery",[3] the same can be said of the principle of separation, to the extent that it is sometimes invoked with something of a mystical aura, by which legal consequences are extracted without a sufficient justification of law or principle.

In very broad terms, the principle of separation is generally invoked to argue that the binding effect of shareholders' agreements is exclusively contractual and thus cannot have legal effects vis-à-vis the company. In this context it is often said, as gen

[2] *Mock/Csach/Havel* (fn. 1), 5.

[3] *Mock*, in Fleischer/Recalde/Spindler (eds.), Family Firms and Closed Companies in Germany and Spain, 2021, 205 ff. (205).

eral rule, that shareholders' agreement cannot have *erga omnes* legal consequences. This general principle is then used to derive some specific rules.

Although the principle of separation expresses some useful and well-founded normative content, it is often invoked to express legal consequences that are not founded in law, or in principles of Contract Law or Company Law. Throughout this article I will try to provide some contribution to the adequate foundation and scope of the principle of separation, and to its main consequences, in what concerns the enforcement of the obligations emerging from shareholders' agreements.

I will begin by briefly describing the principle of separation and by enunciating some consequences often derived from it. Afterwards, I will briefly analyze some general principles and rules regarding the legal consequences an obligational contract – i. e., a contract creating obligations – can have vis-à-vis third parties. Finally, I will try to assert whether those contractual rules and principles can shed some light on debated issues on the enforcement of obligations emerging from shareholders' agreements.

I will not analyze issues regarding the *validity* of the provisions of a shareholders' agreement, which raise important and complex questions regarding the relations between this kind of agreements and mandatory Company law provisions.[4]

Throughout the rest of the analysis, I will adopt a Portuguese law perspective, but whenever possible and appropriate, I will draw some parallels with German or English law.

II. The Principle of Separation

In Portuguese law, as in other jurisdictions, shareholders' agreements are generally admissible, pursuant to the principle of freedom of contract. Shareholders are, thus, generally allowed to enter into agreements with the purpose of governing the way they will exercise their rights and perform their duties as shareholders, on a contractual level, distinct from the articles of association.

However, a principle of separation (*Princípio da separação,* in Portuguese; *Trennungsprinzip,* in German) is generally affirmed in this context, to explain that articles of association and shareholders' agreements should be strictly distinguished, and to affirm the different binding effects of a shareholders' agreement, when compared with the articles of association. According to this principle, the binding effects of a shareholders' agreement should be strictly limited to the contracting parties whereas the articles of association and the corporate deliberations made in accordance with them are binding to all present and future shareholders, to the corporate bodies and to third parties.[5]

---

[4] *Mock/Csach/Havel* (fn. 1), 13 ff.

[5] *Mock/Csach/Havel* (fn. 1), 15 ff.

Or, to put if differently, "[a]lthough shareholders can arrange or coordinate their interests by concluding a shareholders' agreement, such an agreement cannot change the unarranged structure of the interests of the shareholders in the corporation itself. Therefore, a shareholders' agreement cannot have a binding effect on the corporation and its bodies".[6]

1. Normative content of the principle of separation

In a first dimension, very basic but essential, the principle of separation calls for the idea of differentiation and autonomy between the statutes and the shareholders' agreement. This is an important fact, since for some reason – which should, as a rule, be determined for interpretative purposes – the shareholders did not want to establish in the articles of association the obligations provided for in the shareholders' agreement. This first dimension is particularly important when interpreting the shareholders' agreement and the articles of association.

On a second level, the principle of separation calls for differentiation between the set of rules that the parties have chosen for each group of rights and obligations: Company law or Contract law. In this second dimension, the confrontation between the solutions contained in the shareholders' agreement and the mandatory rules of Company Law (but also the mandatory rules of Contract Law) is particularly relevant. The principle of separation will have in this context mainly a *negative* effect, setting the mandatory boundaries for the rights and obligations created pursuant to the shareholders' agreement.

On a third level, the principle of separation calls for a distinction in terms of legal effects. In this light, it is stated that the constitution of obligations through the shareholders' agreement has no legal effects on the rights and obligations constituted under the articles of association and that the voluntary (or forced) performance of these obligations cannot determine changes in the corporate positions of the parties involved.

Therefore, in those cases where the company is not a party to the agreement – which form most cases – it is usually affirmed that it is impossible to derive corporate consequences from a breach of obligations set out in shareholders' agreements. The resulting rule would be that the binding effect of shareholders' agreements is exclusively contractual and thus cannot have legal effects vis-à-vis the company.[7]

Based on this this principle, some secondary rules are derived by scholars and applied by the courts, among which: (a) there should be no legal consequences for the corporation of a breach of a shareholders' agreement, even if all shareholders are bound also by the agreement;[8] (b) there can be no sanctions set out in the articles of

[6] *Mock* (fn. 3), 216.

[7] *Bachmann,* in Gummert/Schäfer (eds.), Münchener Handbuch des Gesellschaftsrechts, 2023, n. 46.

[8] *Pentz,* in Goette/Habersack/Kalss (eds.), Münchener Kommentar zum Aktiengesetz, Vol. I, 6th ed., 2024, § 23, n. 200.

association as a reaction to a breach of a shareholders' agreement;[9] (c) the vote of the non-performing shareholder will be deemed to be valid, for Company Law purposes; (d) the shareholder's fiduciary duty is not affected by shareholders' agreements[10] under the Law of Obligations.

In what specifically concerns enforcement of the obligations set out in a shareholders' agreements, doubts have been casted on the possibility of specific enforcement of obligations (especially voting obligations) emerging from a shareholders' agreement or on the validity of certain contractual penalties for a breach of shareholders duties.

However, the content and limit of some of these rules has been recently disputed.[11]/[12] In certain cases, involving omnilateral shareholders' agreements (i. e., agreements involving all shareholders) it has even been argued that the separation principle should not apply, as a rule, if third party interests are not at stake.[13]

One of the most important limitations to the extension of the principle of separation is given by its very foundations. In fact, the principle of separation can only have the power to limit the primary and secondary forms of protection of obligations if it is based on valid principles of Contract law or other cogent principles of Company law.

2. Foundations of the principle of separation

The principle of separation can be based on several and concurring legitimate grounds. A shareholders' agreement is a *res inter alios acta*, in relation to the Company, its articles of association and to the shareholders that are not a party to the agreement. Additionally, there are some mandatory rules of Company Law that cannot be set aside in the articles of association and, therefore, neither can they be opted out through a shareholders' agreements. Finally, because the articles of association are public and give rise to a new legal person, third party protection must be granted to good-faith third parties that interact with the Company, relying on those articles and on the reality as depicted in the commercial registry.

However, if these are the foundations of the principle of separation, they also help us define its limits and test the soundness of some legal rules that are argued to derive from it.

The identification of imperative rules of company law and the legitimate interests of third parties is comparatively less complex when compared to the matter of the general limits that contract law imposes on the production of effects in the sphere of

---

9 *Koch,* in Koch (ed.), Aktiengesetz, 18th ed., 2024, § 23, n. 47.

10 *Pentz* (fn. 8), § 23, n. 202.

11 *Bachmann* (fn. 7), n. 47, on the question of the extent to which a challenge to shareholders' resolutions can be based on the breach of a shareholders' agreement and the extent to which a shareholders' agreement can (or should) be used when interpreting the articles of association. Against this possibility: *Koch* (fn. 9), § 23, n. 47.

12 *Bachmann* (fn. 7), n. 54, on whether a shareholders' agreement can influence the content of the shareholders' duty of loyalty towards the company. Against this possibility: *Koch* (fn. 9), § 23, n. 47.

13 *Carneiro da Frada*, Forjar o Direito, 2015, 459 ff.

third parties. I will therefore focus the rest of my analysis on this basis and its application to the protection of obligations arising from shareholders' agreements.

III. Shareholders' agreements as *res inter alios acta* and privity of contract

As mentioned, the main foundation of the principle of separation is that the shareholders' agreement is a *res inter alios acta* in relation to the Company, its articles of association and to the shareholders that are not a party to the agreement. This foundation rests on the principle of *privity of contract,* the core of which is generally acknowledged in modern legal systems (albeit with relevant differences, regarding its scope and exceptions).

According to the general rules derived from the principle, rights created through contract can only be acquired by the contracting parties (and not by third parties) and liabilities can only be imposed upon contracting parties (and not to third parties).[14] The scope of the rules is sometimes expanded, so as to include all legal interests and consequences emerging from a contract: whether favorable or adverse, they can be acquired by/imposed upon no one but the parties to the contract.

A principle with the widest scope possible would be the following: a contract cannot have legal consequences for third parties.

This ample formulation, which is sometimes invoked in the context of shareholders' agreements and the principle of separation, can only be accepted with several exceptions, and to the extent that *legal* and *contractual consequences* of a contract are distinguished. By *contractual effects* I mean those legal consequences that are derived directly from a contract based on the will of the parties, because and to the extent that the parties have agreed upon them. And by *legal effects of a contract,* I mean those indirect consequences that a contract will have, that can affect third parties and whose content and extent are determined by law.

In summary terms, it can be said that, with a few well-defined exceptions, the contractual effects of contracts only occur in the sphere of the parties. The legal effects of contracts are realized in the sphere of the parties and third parties, depending on the law itself.

1. Indirect legal effects of a contract vis-à-vis third parties

A first level of *indirect legal consequences* refers to those changes in the legal positions of the parties to the agreement, that indirectly affect third parties, to the extent that those third parties' legal positions are somewhat dependent on the legal position of the parties to the contract.

[14] *Beatson/Burrows/Cartwright,* Anson's Law of Contract, 2016, 613 ff.

Take C, for example, who is a creditor of A, party to a contract recently concluded with B. C's position as A's creditor is indirectly altered because, on the one hand, B now competes with C for A's assets, as a general guarantee of their credits. On the other hand, C may be entitled – in certain conditions are met – to exercise A's credit against B when this proves essential for the satisfaction of the guarantee of his own claim.[15]

The performance of a contract can also have indirect consequences on the legal positions of third parties. In principle, if A undertook to transfer the asset X to B and performs its contractual obligations, asset X will be transferred to B and will no longer be available for C (a creditor of A), for the satisfaction of its claim.

The indirect consequences can consist of a combination of juridical and factual effects: if A agrees with B to fill with diesel a central-heating tank that can be used by all owners of an apartment building, the performance by A of her contractual obligations will *factually* and *juridically* benefit C, D and E, who are also owners of apartments in that building.

The enforcement of a contract can also have indirect consequences on the legal positions of third parties. The judicial enforcement of the contractual obligations undertaken by A vis-à-vis B will be made at the expense of the assets of A, and that will affect all creditors of A, even if they are third parties in relation to the contract between A and B.

It is also discussed, in limited cases, whether a contract that has been entered between A and B can create a legal advantage for C, being qualified as contract with protective effect for third parties (or contract protecting third parties).[16] A contract protecting third parties (*Vertrag mit Schutzwirkungen zugunsten Dritter*) will not create a right of the third party to demand performance of the obligations emerging from the contract but extends secondary duties of care and protection to third parties. In these cases, the contract concluded between A and B has indirect legal effects, based on the law, on the legal position of C, who will benefit from the protective effectiveness of the duties of conduct arising from the contract, and will be entitled to compensation if these duties are violated.

Case law has also developed certain conditions that, when met, can create in third parties the secondary duty not to knowingly interfere with the performance of a contract.[17]

---

[15] Articles 606ff., Portuguese Civil Code ("CC").

[16] This concept has been developed by case law, which has based the protective effectiveness of the contract for third parties on four conditions: (a) the proximity of the third party to the obligational programme; (b) a legitimate protection interest on the part of the creditor; (c) the debtor's awareness of this protection interest; (d) the need for protection. In German law: *Klump*, in J. von Staudingers Kommentar zum Bürgerlichen Gesetzbuch mit Einführungsgesetz und Nebengesetzen – Buch 2, Recht der Schuldverhältnisse- §§ 328–345, 2020, § 328, n. 92ff. For Portuguese law *Costa Gonçalves/Mendes Correia*, Cadernos de Direito Privado, 74 (2021) 47ff. English law also acknowledges cases where a contract can give rise to tortious duties of care to third parties: *Beatson/Burrows/Cartwright* (fn. 14), 644ff.

[17] *Beatson/Burrows/Cartwright* (fn. 14), 653ff.

2. Direct contractual effects of a contract vis-à-vis third parties

As mentioned above, while the principle of privity of contract expresses a well-founded general rule – no rights or obligations will be acquired by/imposed upon third parties through a contract – important exceptions must also be considered.

The most important exception refers to the possible acquisition of credit rights by third parties, where that intention is shared by the contractual parties. In these cases, through a contract for the benefit of a third party, direct positive contractual consequences can emerge vis-à-vis a third party: the obligor will promise to the obligee to render his performance not to the obligee, but to a third party and therefore the latter will acquire a right to demand performance from the obligor.[18]

3. Indirect and direct effects and shareholders' agreements

Having briefly considered the extent and limits of the general principle of privity of contract it is now useful to return to the principle of separation.

In Portuguese law, article 17/1 of the Portuguese Commercial Companies Code ("PCCC") is sometimes invoked as the normative basis for the principle of separation. However, this provision only excludes the contestability of acts carried out by the company or acts carried out by the shareholders on the basis of shareholders' agreements. This is consistent with the limits and distinctions made above: the obligations created through the shareholders' agreement are not binding upon the company, as a third party, namely in what concerns the validity of the company's acts.

However, no special rule can be drawn from this regarding the indirect, legally-based effects of a contract on the company. If shareholder A has not yet fully performed his obligation to contribute to the capital of company X, the latter is his creditor. If this same shareholder A assumes an obligation to sell shares to shareholder B, through a shareholders' agreement, company X will have another potential competitor, regarding shareholder A's assets, for the satisfaction of their credits.

It should also be noted that the direct object of shareholders' agreements are shareholders' legal positions, in the form of rights or duties: voting rights, rights to a dividend, shares in a company, duties to finance the company, etc. Shareholders will agree with each other certain obligations regarding the exercise of those rights and the performance of those obligations.

Therefore, a strict separation principle in terms of legal effects/consequences is not only lacking any normative basis but would be contradictory. A shareholder cannot perform its obligations emerging from a shareholders' agreement without exercis-

---

[18] Articles 443 ff. CC; § 328 BGB. A genuine contract for the benefit of third parties must be distinguished from contracts where the parties agree that the obligor will render performance to a third party, but without giving the latter the right to demand performance. In German law, this distinction is made between *echter Vertrag zugunsten Dritter* and *unechter Vertrag zugunsten Dritter*.

ing – directly or indirectly – its shareholder's legal positions, and that will have at least some indirect effects on the company. If shareholder A of company X undertook to vote in a certain way pursuant to a shareholders' agreement and performs accordingly, the vote will be effective and bind company X (in the absence of *other* grounds for invalidity). And this will also be the case, even if shareholder A has appointed a mandatary with authority to vote in his name and on his behalf: the vote casted by A's representative will be binding upon the company, even if it is made in performance of an obligation created through a shareholders' agreement.[19]

On the other hand, there are some legal effects that have the shareholding position as an object, and whose occurrence does not depend on the will of the company. These legal effects (e.g., effects of transfer or of creation of encumbrances) can also result from agreements other than shareholders' agreements: if the applicable conditions are met, the company will have to comply with a pledge created over shares of shareholder A, irrespectively of the fact that this encumbrance was created pursuant to a shareholders' agreement or to an autonomous pledge agreement.

The indirect legal consequences can also be beneficial for the company. There is no principled reason to exclude the possibility of qualifying a shareholders' agreement as a contract with protective effect for third parties (the company), if the above-mentioned conditions are met. In this scenario, the company would not be able to demand performance of the obligations emerging from the agreement but would be entitled to secondary protection, through damages, in case the parties breach duties of care and protection.

Finally, the Company and shareholders that are not party to the agreement can acquire rights and demand its performance if the shareholders' agreement can be interpreted as a contract for the benefit of a third party.

All these rules are consistent with the principle of privity of contract. In principle, shareholders' agreements do not create *new* obligations or duties for the company, or *new* rights or entitlements (with the exception of the shareholders' agreement as a contract for the benefit of a third party). Therefore, and also as a rule, they will have no legal consequences for the company. The company is not bound by the agreement and the breach of the emerging obligations does not integrate the universe of facts that trigger typical Company law remedies.

However, this principle has two important limitations. On the one hand, there are certain indirect consequences that *any* contract can have on third parties, that occur by virtue of the law, and shareholders' agreement are no exception.

---

[19] This will also be the case when the shareholders' agreement provides for the transfer of shareholder A's corporate rights, which are enforceable in general (corporate and obligational) terms against third parties. An example would be the transfer of shareholder A's shares resulting from the (voluntary or coercive) performance of a shareholders' agreement, or the transfer of his dividend claim against the company to a third parties (which can be seen as a full or partial credit assignment, pursuant to the general rules). The company will have to acknowledge the third party as shareholder or creditor, even if the legal effect of transfer has occurred pursuant to the shareholders' agreement.

The second limitation is that, while shareholders' agreements do not create, in principle, *new* obligations or rights for the company, they will create *new* obligations and rights for the parties to the agreement, the object of which are shareholders' positions. The voluntary or coercive exercise of these rights and obligations will also have indirect effects for the company. The company will not have *new* obligations regarding those positions, but neither can it invoke *exceptions* or *defences,* relieving it from obligations that were already in its sphere. If shareholder A promises to vote in a certain fashion, company X will not be relieved from its duty to accept the vote casted, only because the voting right is being exercised pursuant to a shareholders' agreement.

IV. Enforcement of shareholders' agreements

1. Introduction

The previous analysis can shed some light to disputed issues regarding the enforcement of shareholders' agreements.

The general rule according to which no Company law remedies will be available for the breach of shareholders' agreements is consistent with general contract law: the company is not a party to the shareholders' agreement, and for that reason the agreement does not create new rights or duties in its legal sphere. Additionally, and also as a rule, no reference to the shareholders' agreement will be found in the articles of association and in the supplementary and mandatory rules of company law: therefore, the breach of a shareholders' agreement will not be qualified as a fact that triggers Company law remedies, such as the exclusion of shareholders or the invalidity of shareholders' resolutions.

However, apart from Company law remedies, when discussing the enforcement of obligations emerging from a shareholders' agreement, a mystical force should be rejected to the separation of principle. The limits to the enforcement of a shareholders' agreement should be based on the general Contractual principles (as the privity of contract) mentioned above, on mandatory Company law rules, or on the need to protect third-party discernible interests. In the absence of these forceful reasons, general enforcement mechanisms should be available in relation to the obligations emerging from shareholders' agreements.

2. Ancillary contractual mechanisms

Certain contractual mechanisms are usually employed to prevent breaches to the obligations assumed in a shareholders' agreement. Among others, call options are used, providing the abiding shareholders (or designated third parties) with an option to acquire the shares of the non-compliant party, as well as put options, providing the abiding shareholders (or designated third parties) with an option to sell the shares to the non-compliant party.

In other cases, a representative is appointed, with a non-revocable power of attorney, to carry out the necessary acts for compliance with the shareholders' agreement, or an escrow agreement is set in place, providing the escrow agent with powers to comply with the agreement.

For the same reasons, contractual arrangements to reduce the practical risk of a breach of contract should be admitted, especially in agreements regarding certain limitations or prohibitions of transfers of shares. Shares can be assigned to a trustee for safekeeping, with the agreement that the trustee may only dispose of them in accordance with the agreed restrictions on disposal.[20] A third party will be involved, and will interfere with the company, indirectly, but the sound grounds underlying the principle of separation will not be affected.

3. *Primary protection*

a) Interim measures

In Portuguese Civil Procedural Law, interim measures are generally available to a party desiring to assure the provisional protection of a claimed right, whose effectiveness would be threatened with the delay of the main proceedings. Interim measures can be aimed at preventing a violation of the claimed right (safeguarding its future exercise), at provisionally regulating the exercise of rights, or at anticipating the effects that have been petitioned in the main proceedings.

However, and because interim measures are based on a *summario cognitio* and not in a full-fledged assessment and, in certain conditions, will be decided *ex parte*, without the involvement of the respondent, it is widely accepted that they cannot anticipate in an irreversible fashion the final form of relief that is being petitioned in the main proceedings.[21]

In this context, it is discussed in Portuguese law whether an interim measure can be obtained by a party to the shareholders' agreement, preventing another party from breaching the obligations emerging therein. In what concerns voting agreements, it has been argued that an interim measure ordering the shareholder to vote in a certain fashion would anticipate the final relief petitioned in the main proceedings and therefore should be considered inadmissible.[22] However, this argument does not seem to apply to an interim measure *prohibiting* the shareholder to vote in a certain resolution. In this case, the vote of the relevant shareholder will not be casted in a way that alleg-

---

[20] *Lutter/Schneider*, ZGR 1975, 187.

[21] *Castro Mendes/Teixeira de Sousa*, Manual de Processo Civil, Vol. I 2022, 593; *Lynce de Faria*, A Tutela Cautelar Antecipatória no Processo Civil Português, 2016, 253 ff.

[22] *Trigo*, Os Acordos Parassociais sobre o Exercício do Direito de Voto, 1998, 227; *Perestrelo de Oliveira*, Acordos Parassociais, 2025, 175. Holding the opposite view, *Ferreira Gomes*, M&A – Aquisição de Empresas e de Participações Sociais, 2022, 362.

edly complies with a shareholders' agreement, thus creating an irreversible situation: the relevant shareholder will have to accept a partial and temporary limitation of his voting rights, based on the summary cognition of interim measures, but in a manner that does not anticipate the final protection sought in the main proceedings.[23]

The level of irreversibility that cannot be anticipated through interim measures is a matter to be discussed on Procedural law grounds. However, the principle of separation does not seem to provide an additional ground to exclude the possibility of recourse to interim measures regarding the obligations emerging from a shareholders' agreement.

b) Enforcement action

In Portuguese law, it is generally accepted that a creditor can resort to a declaratory claim and petition the court to order the debtor to perform the obligations assumed in shareholders' agreements.[24]

However, most authors conclude that this mechanism will have little practical impact in case of voting agreements, since, as a rule, a judgement ordering the debtor to comply will not be issued in good time (i. e. before the relevant general meeting takes place).[25]/[26] This may be the case in most cases concerning voting agreements, but it

---

[23] An example can be helpful: (i) shareholder B claims that the shareholders' agreement requires shareholder A to vote X and not Z; (ii) if the votes of shareholder A are not needed to pass resolution X or Z, the interim measure does not create an irreversible situation: A will not vote X or Z, pursuant to the interim measure, but his votes will be indifferent for the outcome; (iii) if the votes of shareholder A are needed to pass resolution X, and the shareholders' agreement effectively requires him to vote in X, the interim measure does not create an irreversible situation; resolution X will not pass, but can be resubmitted later, after shareholder A is judicially ordered to vote X in the main proceedings; (iv) if the votes of shareholder A are needed to pass resolution X, and the shareholders' agreement does not require him to vote in X, the interim measure does not create an irreversible situation: resolution X will not pass, and if resubmitted later, he can freely vote against it.

[24] *Trigo* (fn. 22), 215–216; *Leal,* Revista de Direito das Sociedades, 1 (2009), 179; *Ferreira Gomes* (fn. 22), 362. Also, *Mock* (fn. 3), 220–221, noting that sometimes the other parties to a shareholders' agreement will only discover a breach at the moment of the vote, which will render interim measures or enforcement actions untimely.

[25] *Cordeiro/Reis,* in Cordeiro (ed.), Código das Sociedades Comerciais Anotado, 5th ed., 2022, Art. 17. n. 32.

[26] It could be argued that the breach of an obligation emerging from a shareholders' agreement can in certain circumstances create a justified concern with future breaches of obligations emerging from the same agreement, and that in such case an enforcement claim should be available to the creditor, allowing him to petition an order for the debtor to comply with voting obligations in future resolutions. This route can be grounded on articles 557.º and 610.º of the Portuguese Civil Procedure Code. An enforcement claim could also be useful, if the resolution taken in breach of a shareholders' agreement has not created an irreversible situation (e. g., the resolution taken with the non-compliant vote has rejected a certain operation [a merger], that can still take place in the future). In those cases, the shareholder can be ordered to request a new shareholders meeting, to submit the relevant operation to a shareholders' resolution and to vote favourably. In relation to this last possibility, it has been argued that the resubmission of the same resolution would be contrary to the principle of separation (*Ferreira Gomes* [fn. 22], 364–365), but it does not seem to be the case: shareholders are free to resubmit issues to a shareholders' resolution, and to change their vote. The resubmission re-

should be noted, on the one hand, that the obstacle does not stem from the principle of separation (but from practical reasons), and on the other hand, that enforcement action should be considered as admissible, in general, for other types of shareholders' agreements.

c) Specific performance

In Portuguese law, in certain instances, the obligee will be entitled to judicially demand the specific performance of the obligation undertook by the obligor. One of the mentioned instances concerns the obligations assumed through a promissory agreement (*contrato promessa*), i.e., a contract through which the parties undertake to enter a future contract.

The juridical nature of the obligation assumed by the debtor (the obligation to issue a declaration of intent, as a means to produce certain juridical effects) is considered sufficient grounds to allow the court to substitute itself for the debtor in the correspondent specific performance and to overcome the obstacles to this form of relief, which would emerge from the personal nature of the obligation.

Under Portuguese law, the possibility of specific performance is expressly provided for only in relation to the obligation to contract, assumed through a promissory contract. However, most of the doctrine admits that specific performance can be generically extended to cases in which the debtor has assumed an obligation to make a declaration of intent.[27]

This is relevant for those shareholders' agreements that concern the exercise of voting rights. In these cases, the contracting parties undertake to exercise or not to exercise its voting rights according to certain rules. Therefore, as a matter of principle, specific performance of these obligations should be accepted.

In Portugal, however, some doctrine contests the possibility of specific performance of voting obligations assumed in shareholders' agreements, on several grounds:[28] (a) the vote thus cast would have corporate effects, and not merely obligational ones, which would be inconsistent with article 17.º/1 of the Portuguese Commercia Companies Code and the principle of separation;[29] (b) specific performance to overcome a breach of obligations would only be available in those cases where such

---

quest and the vote are acts of the shareholder. The Company's acts are not being subject to judicial enforcement. However, these routes would not substantially change the situation of the obligee, because in future resolutions, he could vote against the judicial order and, in principle, be subject to damages only.

[27] *Cordeiro,* in Cordeiro (ed.), Código Civil Anotado – Vol. II – Das Obrigações em Geral, 2021, Art. 830, n. 48 ff.; Trigo (fn. 22), 217; *Torres Ereio/Aragão Homem,* Revista de Direito Civil, 3 (2016), 651–662.

[28] I will only analyse obstacles to specific performance of corporate nature. Some authors contest this possibility on general grounds, arguing that specific performance is only available in those instances specifically stipulated in the law, i.e., in those cases where the obligee has promised to enter a future contract (*Ventura,* O Direito, 124 (1992), 83–84).

[29] *Cordeiro/Reis* (fn. 25), n. 32. However, in exceptional cases, the Authors accept that the auton-

performance has been rendered impossible, because a general meeting had taken place and a corporate resolution had been made (in which the obligee has casted a vote contrary to the undertakings of the shareholders' agreement);[30] (c) The personal dimension of the exercise of the voting right would render impossible a substitution of the shareholder.

These arguments do not seem to provide sufficient grounds for refusing specific performance of voting obligations emerging from shareholders' agreements.[31]

In what concerns the principle of separation, it does not provide any grounds against specific performance, in those cases where specific performance is still possible. It is true that the specific performance of voting obligations will have consequences vis-à-vis the company, but those consequences are of a legal and indirect nature: they result indirectly from the forced performance of a valid obligation taken over by the shareholder.

In specific enforcement, the court only issues the declaration owed by the shareholder (i.e. the vote),[32] it does not issue the corporate resolution, nor does it fix or determine its effects.[33] The court's decision does not produce effects different from those that would be generated by the shareholder's vote, and it does not substitute itself for the company in determining these effects. If the shareholder's vote is abusive, the resolution can be cancelled; if the shareholder could not be admitted to vote, the company can disregard the vote; if the vote is in the minority, the resolution will not pass. None of these consequences will be decided by the court, but by the company.

The Company must of course accept the vote of a certain shareholder: but this is a duty that it already had. The specific performance of the agreement does not create any new duties for the Company. The only difference is the way in which the vote is casted, which is a matter of the shareholder, not of the Company: the vote will be issued *judicially* and not *autonomously*.

Additionally, it would be surprising – to say the least – that the legislator recognized the validity of contractual obligations having as object the exercise of voting rights and at the same time would empty such obligations, by hindering the creditor to obtain its enforced performance, in general terms.[34]

In what concerns the (im)possibility to perform, it is true that the availability of specific performance only arises in those cases where the obligations are not already extinguished due to impossibility. But this is not a consequence of the principle of separation, it is a consequence of the Law of Obligations and is extendible to all other obligations (in which impossibility can be instantiated). Thus, this discussion only

omy between a shareholders' agreement and the corporate sphere can be surpassed, if the principle of good faith so requires.

[30] *Ventura* (fn. 28), 84.

[31] For German law, where specific performance of voting agreements is generally admitted, *Röhricht/Schall*, in Hirte/Mülbert/Roth (eds.), *Aktiengesetz*, Vol. II, 5th ed., 2016, § 23, n. 335.

[32] *Ferreira Gomes* (fn. 22), 366.

[33] *Noack*, Gesellschaftervereinbarungen bei Kapitalgesellschaften, 1994, 73

[34] *Torres Ereio/Aragão Homem* (fn. 27), 694.

covers the obligation to vote on future resolutions (i. e. those that have not yet been passed), on matters not yet submitted to resolution, or in the context of the company resolutions aimed at revoking or substituting former ones (i. e., when the resolutions previously passed are susceptible to change).

However, even in those cases, it could be argued that specific performance is only available as a reaction to a breach of a duty, and when such breach occurs, in the form of non-performance or non-conforming performance, it will no longer be possible to perform, because a resolution has been taken and cannot be challenged on grounds of a shareholders' agreement.[35] To contest such a position, it can be argued that there are certain forms of breach that have not rendered performance impossible, and that provide sufficient justification for the court's intervention, through specific performance: (a) cases where the shareholder was not present in the meeting and the vote had to be postponed; (b) cases where the shareholder has indicated beforehand that he will not comply with the voting commitments;[36] (c) cases where the resolution taken with the non-compliant vote of the obligee of a shareholders' agreement is invalid (by reasons other than the breach of the shareholders' agreement) and the subject will be resubmitted;[37] (d) cases where the submission of a later resolution with the same object is possible and useful, among other reasons, because the former one has not been executed or registered, or a substitution of a registered/executed resolution is still useful.[38]/[39]

Finally, in what concerns the personal character of the exercise of voting rights, it could be argued that the court cannot replace the company nor to appoint a representative of the shareholder, for the exercise of the voting right in compliance with the shareholders' agreement.[40] This line of reasoning, however, does not seem com-

---

[35] *Leal* (fn. 24), 183. To a certain extent, this line of reason is intertwined with a different and more general discussion, of whether specific performance is available for all forms of breach of a duty to make a declaration of intent (delay in performing, anticipatory declaration of non-compliance, etc.) or only in case of definitive non-performance. For those who consider that specific performance should be available as a reaction to all forms of breach (with the limit of the impossibility of performance), there will be instances where specific performance can be of use to the creditor.

[36] *Leal* (fn. 24), 183. A special case of this sort consists of resolutions of a recurring nature (i. e., where the same object is submitted to the shareholders at a later date): *Ferreira Gomes* (fn. 22), 367.

[37] In these cases, the compliant shareholders can simultaneously request the court to declare the invalidity of the resolution and to substitute the non-compliant shareholder in the exercise of its vote, in a way that corresponds to the performance of the shareholders' agreement, through specific performance, approving an alternative proposal, which was defeated in the past. *Torres Ereio/Aragão Homem* (fn. 27), 682 ff.

[38] Shareholder A undertook to vote in favor of a capital increase (article 85.º/1 PCCC) or a pluriannual investment plan submitted by the board of directors to the shareholders (pursuant to article 373.º/2 PCCC), if previously approved by a meeting of the parties to a shareholders' agreement. The parties approve of the operation. However, shareholder A votes against it in the shareholders meeting and the resolution does not pass. Shareholders B and C, also parties to the shareholders' agreement can resort to specific performance of the obligations, petitioning that the court casts a favorable vote instead of shareholder A in a future resolution with the same object.

[39] *Torres Ereio/Aragão Homem* (fn. 27), 693 ff.

[40] *Almeida,* Sociedades Comerciais, Valores Mobiliários, Instrumentos Financeiros e Mercados, Vol. I, 2022, 120.

patible with the express normative stipulation of specific performance in cases where the obligee has committed to enter a future contract with the obligor: in these cases, the obligation has also a personal dimension, but the legislator has considered that primacy should be granted to the right of the creditor to obtain performance as agreed.

Also, as a rule, in Portuguese law, shareholders can be represented at company resolutions, which can be invoked as an argument for a certain fungibility in the exercise of voting rights. On the other hand, the personal character of a certain obligation, as an obstacle to specific performance, is usually invoked in those cases where the personal freedom of the obligee must be assured contemporary to performance (donations, labor agreements, etc.). When compared with those cases, the personal character of the exercise of voting rights does not seem to trigger the same concerns.[41]

Specific performance of other types of shareholders' agreement should be even less problematic and is generally admitted by Portuguese scholars.[42] The specific performance of obligations regarding the transfer of shares is widely accepted in Portuguese doctrine.[43]

4. *Secondary protection and damages/penalties for nonperformance*

In general terms, the debtor must compensate the creditor for the losses resulting from the breach of an obligation.[44]

The parties to the shareholders' agreement can promise to pay a penalty for nonperformance.[45] However, at least in Portuguese and German law, the penalty will be subject to judicial equitable reduction, if it is disproportionately high.[46]

In this context, it could be suggested that the use of contractual penalties would be an indirect way to grant *erga omnes* efficacy to shareholders' agreements. Again, a distinction must be drawn: the principle of separation does not cater for a (non-existent) right of the shareholder to breach the shareholders' agreement without meaningful consequences. Therefore, contractual penalties may be scrutinized, but pursuant to the general limits set by the Law of obligations: they can be reduced because they are disproportionate to the potential damages, but not because they effectively dissuade the parties to a shareholders' agreement of a breach.

---

[41] *Trigo* (fn. 22), 217–218; *Ferreira Gomes* (fn. 22), 367.

[42] *Leal* (fn. 24), 179: *Almeida* (fn. 38), 298; *Pais de Vasconcelos,* A Participação Social nas Sociedades Comerciais, 2006, 64.

[43] *Almeida* (fn. 38), 120; *Leal* (fn. 24), 179; *Torres Ereio/Aragão Homem* (fn. 27), 663–665.

[44] §§ 280(1) BGB; Article 798.º CC.

[45] *Cordeiro/Reis* (fn. 25), n. 36.

[46] § 343(1) BGB; Article 812.º CC

V. Conclusion

Shareholders' agreements are autonomous and differentiated in relation to the articles of association, in that they create rights and obligations concerning the exercise of shareholders' positions that are subject to different rules and must respect imperative Company law provisions and third-party interests protected by the publicity granted to the articles of association.

However, in terms of the legal effects of shareholders' agreements, the same principles and exceptions governing all contracts should apply. Therefore, among other consequences, shareholders' agreements can have indirect legal consequences vis-à-vis the company. This is especially manifest in case of enforcement of the obligations created by shareholders' agreements, the object of which is the exercise of shareholders' positions. To the extent that the enforcement does not imply the creation of *new* duties to the company and is consistent with procedural law, the principle of separation does not create new obstacles.

Determining the adequate foundation of the principle of separation, in line with the principle of privity of contract, will be fruitful to identity its limits. In terms of enforcement, obstacles based on the principle of separation should only be accepted, in principle, if based on cogent principles of Contract law or other cogent principles of Company law.

V. Conclusion

Unanimous Shareholders' Agreements: A comparative overview

José Ferreira Gomes

Abstract: This article examines the legal nature and effectiveness of unanimous shareholders' agreements across jurisdictions. It contrasts their contractual character with the binding force of articles of association, analysing leading cases from England, the United States, and Germany. The discussion highlights how courts and legislatures have, in close corporations, increasingly allowed unanimous agreements to prevail over mandatory rules, reflecting shareholders' autonomy when third-party interests are not at stake. Building on comparative insights, the article argues that the principle of separation between company and shareholders is not an absolute barrier but a functional safeguard. Where shareholders can self-protect and no external interests are harmed, unanimous agreements should be effective toward the company, forming part of a broader "associative ordering" of corporate relations.

I. Introduction

Shareholders agreements are typically construed as an ordinary contract between all or a subset of shareholders, aimed at supplementing the general rules of company law and the provisions of the articles of association the company has adopted.

As in any other contract, a shareholder agreement binds only the parties to the agreement. They have no effect on the company or any third party. This means that no acts of the company or its shareholders can be challenged on the basis of these agreements.

According to the "principle of separation" between the company and its members, the company, as a juridical person, is governed only by the applicable legal provisions, its articles of association and the acts of its governing bodies. It cannot be governed by agreements entered into between its shareholders other than the articles of association.

They differ from the articles of association that create the company as an autonomous juridical person and govern its life over time, projecting its effects towards the company (and, therefore its corporate bodies), its current and future members, and any third parties with whom it interacts in the market.

For this reason, in many legal systems it is said, generally speaking, that the articles of association must be interpreted in an *objective* manner, much like the interpretation of a law, and not as an ordinary contract, considering the will of the parties. It is said that only this makes it possible to safeguard the company's position (as an autonomous legal entity) and all its stakeholders, towards its founding shareholders.

Shareholders' agreements, on the other hand, because they bind only the parties to it, are subject to the general rules of interpretation of contracts, under which the actual or presumed will of the parties takes on greater or lesser importance.

Frequently, shareholders include the company as a party to the agreement in an effort to bind it to its provisions. This is solution is subject to debate in different legal systems. It seems clear, however, that the company is not at freedom to contract out of mandatory legal rules.

For example, in England, in the case *Russel v Northern Bank Development Corp.* (1992),[1] the House of Lords held that while the agreement could bind the shareholders, it could not bind the company itself. The shareholders cannot use an agreement to circumvent mandatory company law regarding the exercise of "statutory powers".[2] "Statutory powers" are presumed to include any matter the 2006 Companies Act requires to be resolved upon by a general meeting. The board of directors cannot restrict shareholders' decision powers by entering into contracts in respect of these matters.[3]

In the US, in the recent case Moelis (2024),[4] the Delaware Court of Chancery held that the company cannot restrict the board's discretion to manage the business and affairs of the corporation by entering into an agreement with stockholders, even if it is the controlling shareholder.[5]

> "[i]nternal corporate governance arrangements that do not appear in the charter and deprive boards of a significant portion of their authority contravene Section 141(a)".[6]

The court points out that such an internal governance arrangement is clearly distinct from external commercial contracts (such as a credit agreement) that constrain specific acts otherwise entrusted to the board.

[1] [1992] BCLC1016 (HL).

[2] *Ferran*, Cambridge Law Journal, 53:2 (1994), 343 ff.

[3] *Zakrzewski*, in Mock/Csach/Havel (ed.), International Handbook on Shareholders' Agreements: "England and Wales"; Csach, 2018, 247, 258 ff.

[4] West Palm Beach Firefighters' Pension Fund v. Moelis & Company, C.A. No. 2023-0309-JTL (Del. Ch. Feb. 23, 2024) (Laster, V.C.).

[5] In this case, the Court held that a shareholder agreement entered into by the controlling shareholder, three of his affiliates, and the Company could not constrain the board's powers under the law. Directors cannot contract away their fiduciary duties.

[6] According to this famous legal provision: "the business and affairs of every corporation organized under this chapter shall be managed by or under the direction of a board of directors, except as may be otherwise provided in this chapter or in its certificate of incorporation.".

II. Questioning the separation between the company and its members: The US and the German legal systems

However, in many legal systems, regardless of whether mandatory rules or enabling rules prevail, the separation between the company and its members has been called into question when *all* shareholders are parties to the agreement. This is especially true in face of close corporations. Faced with unanimous shareholder agreements,[7] courts have often allowed substance to prevail over form.

For example, *in the US*, since the 1960s, it was accepted that *omnilateral* or *unanimous* stockholders' agreements can shape the governance of close corporations to the specific interests and needs of their business plan. In particular, they have accepted that these contracts can circumvent the long-established case law that considered shareholders' agreements that directly interfered in management decisions to be invalid.[8]

It became clear to both courts and legislatures that the existing statutory model of a corporation bore no relationship to the needs and operations of the close corporation.[9] The typical mandatory rules are often aimed at protecting shareholders and other investors whenever there is a separation of ownership and control of the company. If no such separation exists, why should shareholders' freedom of contract be restricted? Whenever the shareholders are in a position to selfprotect their own interests by contract, they do not require the protection of certain company law rules.[10]

Currently, the law of most States recognises that unanimous shareholders' agreements can prevail over certain legal rules,[11] in many cases based on § 7.32 *Model Business Corporation Act* (MBCA).

---

[7] That was the case in Russel v Northern Bank Development Corp.

[8] They have thus departed from the 1948 landmark decision of the New York Court of Appeals in the case Long Park v. Trenton-New Brunswick Theatres Co., 297 N.Y. 174, 77 N.E.2d 633 (1948), which held invalid an unanimous shareholders' agreement in a *close corporation* that gave management powers to specific shareholders, because it *would "sterilise"* the board of directors and thus contravened mandatory law. More than a decade before, in *Fells v. Katz*, 256 N.Y. 67, 175 N.E. 516 (1931), the same court held ineffective a shareholders' agreement under which a certain person would be president of the company for a period of ten years, during which the board of directors could not remove him. See *O'Neal/Thompson*, Close Corporations and LLCs Law and Practice, 3rd ed., 2004, §§ 4:3 ff.

[9] *Siegel*, Columbia Law Review, 72 (1972), 604, 606 ff.

[10] As highlighted in the 1933 decision of the Supreme Judicial Court of Massachusetts, in the case Continental Corp. v. Gowdy: "Generally speaking, public policy requires compliance with statutes regulating the management of corporations. But whether the effect of a particular law can be avoided by contract depends upon the purpose for which the law was enacted."

[11] In some States, their effects vary depending on whether they are included in the corporation's charter or in the bylaws. However, in some of these states, despite this requirement, case law has come to accept the prevalence of shareholders' agreements not included in the company's constitutive documents, insofar as they were entered into between all the shareholders. *O'Neal/Thompson* (fn. 8), § 4:3 ff.

§ 7.32 of the MBCA, which dates back to 1991, recognises the validity of unanimous shareholders' agreements that bind the close corporation (and its directors), being inconsistent with certain legal provisions otherwise mandatory. It gives greater contractual freedom to the shareholders of close corporations, who can thus adapt them to the specificities of their business project.[12]

"§ 7.32 Shareholder Agreements

(a) An agreement among the shareholders of a corporation that complies with this section is effective among the shareholders and the corporation even though it is inconsistent with one or more other provisions of this Act in that it:

(1) eliminates the board of directors or restricts the discretion or powers of the board of directors;

(2) governs the authorization or making of distributions whether or not in proportion to ownership of shares, subject to the limitations in section 6.40;

(3) establishes who shall be directors or officers of the corporation, or their terms of office or manner of selection or removal;

(4) governs, in general or in regard to specific matters, the exercise or division of voting power by or between the shareholders and directors or by or among any of them, including use of weighted voting rights or director proxies;

(5) establishes the terms and conditions of any agreement for the transfer or use of property or the provision of services between the corporation and any shareholder, director, officer or employee of the corporation or among any of them;

(6) transfers to one or more shareholders or other persons all or part of the authority to exercise the corporate powers or to manage the business and affairs of the corporation, including the resolution of any issue about which there exists a deadlock among directors or shareholders;

(7) requires dissolution of the corporation at the request of one or more of the shareholders or upon the occurrence of a specified event or contingency; or

(8) otherwise governs the exercise of the corporate powers or the management of the business and affairs of the corporation or the relationship among the shareholders, the directors and the corporation, or among any of them, and is not contrary to public policy.

(b) An agreement authorized by this section shall be:

(1) set forth (A) in the articles of incorporation or bylaws and approved by all persons who are shareholders at the time of the agreement or (B) in a written agreement that is signed by all persons who are shareholders at the time of the agreement and is made known to the corporation;

(2) subject to amendment only by all persons who are shareholders at the time of the amendment, unless the agreement provides otherwise; and

(3) valid for 10 years, unless the agreement provides otherwise.

(c) The existence of an agreement authorized by this section shall be noted conspicuously on the front or back of each certificate for outstanding shares or on the information statement required by section 6.26(b). [...]

(d) An agreement authorized by this section shall cease to be effective when the corporation becomes a public corporation. [...]

---

[12] As pointed out in its official comment.

(e) An agreement authorized by this section that limits the discretion or powers of the board of directors shall relieve the directors of, and impose upon the person or persons in whom such discretion or powers are vested, liability for acts or omissions imposed by law on directors to the extent that the discretion or powers of the directors are limited by the agreement. [...]"

On a different tone, *in Germany* – very influential at least in Continental Europe, as you all know – the topic has long been subject to an intense debate. The strict separation between articles of association and shareholders' agreements has been questioned by at least three decisions of the BGH, in 1959, 1983 and 1986.

In the *case decided by the BGH on 12 March 1959*,[13] all the shareholders of an AG (public limited company) entered into a contract with a former director, under which they undertook to vote to exclude his liability. In breach of this agreement, the company filed a civil liability claim against him.

In view of unanimous shareholders' agreement, the BGH took the view that everything should proceed as if the resolution to exclude liability had actually been passed. According to the BGH, a contract concluded between all its members can be enforced against the company and its corporate bodies when the use of its different legal personality constitutes an abuse of rights.[14]

The *decision of the BGH of 20 January 1983* ruled a case in which the members of a GmbH (private limited company), who were also members of an OHG (partnership), disputed whether the private limited company could take a stake in an English company competing with a partnership.

The plaintiff argued, on the one hand, that the private limited company could not acquire a shareholding in the English company also because there was an unanimous shareholders' agreement prohibiting the participation in company competing with the partnership.

The BGH agreed with this argument. It allowed the shareholders' agreement to penetrate the corporate sphere, holding that a resolution approved by a majority of the shareholders to participate in another company, although in accordance with the articles of association, could be challenged if all the shareholders had previously entered into an agreement to the contrary. Unlike in its 1959 decision, in its 1983 ruling the BGH did not refer to its case law on the piercing of the corporate veil.[15]

In its *decision of 27 October 1986*, the BGH confirmed the position expressed in 1983. At issue was the dismissal of a director that was also a shareholder of a GmbH. Under its articles of association, dismissal could be decided by a simple majority and without just cause. However, since all the shareholders had agreed that the director's dismissal depended on the his consent, in the absence of such consent, the resolution could be challenged.

---

[13] BGHZ 29, 385, NJW 1959, 1082.

[14] *Hoffmann-Becking*, ZGR 1994, 447 ff.

[15] This was criticised by *Happ*, WM 1983, 168 ff. Also *Ulmer* and *Winter*, *e.g.*, argue that challenging corporate decisions based on the breach of shareholder agreements is a matter of corporate veil lifting and, as such, is only admissible in exceptional cases. See *Ulmer*, NJW 1987, 1853 ff.; *Winter*, ZHR, 154 (1990) 259, 277 ff. *Hoffmann-Becking* critically analyses the path of the corporate veil lifting, arguing that it should only be pursued after all possibilities conferred by the duty of loyalty to the company have been exhausted (despite the BGH rejecting this understanding in its 1983 decision). See *Hoffmann-Becking* (fn. 14), 457 ff.

Unlike the 1959 decision, which was not given much importance, the 1983 and 1986 judgments of the BGH were heavily criticised, particularly for their lack of dogmatic reasoning.

In fact, their reasoning is based not on dogmatic considerations, but on reasons of procedural economy. In the words of the BGH, "there is no reason to refer the shareholders who have been defeated by the breach of contract to a complicated action against the shareholders in order to resolve the issue by ordering them to vote in the opposite direction".

Several commentators argued that this case law is inconsistent with the "principle of separation" between the company and shareholders' spheres, "apparently without great dogmatic scruples".[16] This principle, they said, should only be set aside in situations of clear abuse of rights.[17]

It was also argued that this decision violated the fundamental principle that basic organisational rules should be able to be determined beyond doubt by anyone outside the company and should therefore be included in the articles of association.

In the opposite direction, three authors from Tübingen stood out in 1990s. First Noack, and then Zollner and Westermann, advocated overcoming the strict construction of the "principle of separation" of the articles of association towards the shareholders' agreements in favour of a unitary perspective, expressed in what Noack called an "associative ordering in a broader sense" ("Verbandsordnung im weiteren Sinne").[18]

This unitary ordering would comprise mandatory and dispositive legal rules, articles of association, resolutions of the corporate bodies, and shareholders' agreements. Together these rules would shape the legal relationships established within the private limited company, insofar as this did not conflict with the rights of third parties.[19]

In one sentence, very similar to consolidated case law in the US: "the idea of separation, as long as third-party interests are not involved, is nothing more than a petitio principii".

Despite the weight of these authors' positions, the majority of legal scholarship remained unchanged, arguing the importance of the principle of separation, which may be set aside in exceptional cases of abuse of juridical personality, by lifting the corporate veil.

---

[16] *Hoffmann-Becking*, fn. 14, 446.

[17] Cfr., *v. g.*, *Happ* (fn. 15), 172; *Hoffmann-Becking* (fn. 14), 450 ff. In view of the 1983 decision, the latter also points out that the decision of the shareholders at stake could not even be challenged on the grounds of abusive voting or breach of the duty of loyalty, since it did not run counter to the interests of the GmbH, but only to those of the OHG (448).

[18] *Noack*, Gesellschaftervereinbarungen, 1994, 101, 107 ff.

[19] *Noack* (fn. 18), 107 ff. See also the critical analysis of *Ulmer*, "'Satzungsgleiche' Gesellschaftervereinbarungen bei der GmbH? Zum Für und Wider der Trennung zwischen Satzung und schuldrechtlichen Gesellschafterabreden", in FS Volker Röhricht zum 65 Geburtstag, 2005, 633, 634 ff.

Even the BGH ended up tacitly distancing itself from its prior decisions without any explanations in a judgment of 7 June 1993,[20] and, years later, in another one of 24 November 2008:[21] shareholders' agreements – even if unanimous – do not determine the content of the duty of loyalty, cannot be used to interpret the articles of association and do not serve as grounds for challenging company resolutions.[22]

However, this was not the end of the story, as the BGH apparently gave a step back in a decision of 15 March 2010.[23]

III. The shockwaves in different European countries: The "principle of separation" as starting point, but not the finish line in the decision of specific cases

The debate in Germany had shockwaves in many other European countries, including Portugal, Spain.

Personally, I have argued that the "principle of separation" is the starting point of any discussion, but not necessarily the finish line in the decision of specific cases.

The company is a "creature of the law" or a "*Lebensgesetz*" that, as Ronald Close famously explained, replaces the coordination of economic activity through market exchanges, thereby reducing transaction costs.[24]

It encompasses the regulation of *(i)* the organisation and functioning of the company (enabling its self-determination in legal transactions), *(ii)* its relations with its shareholders and *(iii)* the relations of its shareholders with each other.[25]

In this context, the company can be seen as an institutionalised mechanism for managing conflicts of interest in promoting the shareholders' common project.

It is akin to a political system that ensures the representation and discussion of different understandings of what the business project is and should be, and how the potentially conflicting interests of the shareholders are and should be accommodated. In this way, it aims to eliminate, or at least minimise, pathological situations.

The way in which these interests and perspectives are articulated within the institutional framework varies according to the type of company in question. Each type

---

[20] GmbHR 1993, 497, DNotZ 1994, 313.

[21] ZIP 2009, 216.

[22] See *Dörrscheidt*, Grenzen der Gestaltungsfreiheit bei omnilateralen außerstatutarischen Gesellschafterabreden, 2009, 47 ff., which presents a detailed analysis of developments up to 2009. See also, *v.g.*, *Koch*, in Koch/Hüffer, AktG, 12th edition, § 23, n. 47; *Sailer-Coceani*, in Münchener Handbuch des Gesellschaftsrechts, 4, 4th ed., 2015, n. 14; *Pentz*, in Münchener Kommentar zum Aktiengesetz, 1, 4th ed., 2016, § 23, n. 200–202.

[23] NZG 2010, 988. About this ruling, see, v. g., *Noack*, NZG 2010, 1017 ff.

[24] *Coase*, Economica, 4:16 (1937), 386 ff.

[25] This threefold dimension of regulation is inherent to corporate regulation as a whole and typically is primarily based on legislation. It is therefore incorrect to associate this threefold dimension (solely) with the articles of association. See *Noack* (fn. 18), 102 ff.

of company is a microsystem that regulates an institution designed to collectively manage potentially conflicting interests and perspectives on a business project.

In this sense, company law is aimed above all at protecting the interests of the shareholders (present and future) who, through the company, develop their business project.

As a rule, without prejudice to the rules specifically aimed at protecting third parties who interact with the company – including those relating to directors' authority to bind the company or to the realisation and conservation of share capital – company law *only indirectly* benefits those who contract with the company.

Thus, for example, the rules on the structure, composition and operation of company bodies, being a condition of the juridical person's self-determination in legal transactions and aimed at promoting and safeguarding the company's interests (and therefore the common interests of the shareholders as shareholders), indirectly benefit all those who contract with the company.

Whether you agree with this solution or not, the idea behind it is that everyone benefits from the stability of the company thus promoted.[26]

That being said, the principle of separation is not an end in itself. Understood in *strict and absolute terms*, it is tributary to a dogmatic construction of legal personality that is today highly debatable.

The affirmation of the company's autonomy (as a juridical person) vis-à-vis its shareholders cannot be a conceptualist exercise in which the underlying substance is forgotten: the company is a legal instrument for the realisation of a business project by the shareholders. For this reason, the company cannot be seen merely as a third party in the relationship between all the partners.

Despite the criticism it was subject to, I agree with Noack's assertion that this conceptual rigour is not compatible with the recognition, by case law and legal scholarship, that there are direct legal relationships between the shareholders of the company.[27]

Shareholders' contractual freedom cannot be restricted simply by invocating the separation principle. The assertion that this principle is of fundamental importance in company law is not enough.[28]

It is not enough to say that (omnilateral) shareholder rules cannot shape company life because they do not fulfil the *publicity requirements* of the articles of association.

Those who invoke this principal, have the onus of explaining what this principle aims at safeguarding in each specific case.[29]

Allow me to repeat: *the separation between the company and the shareholders spheres is not an end in itself; it aims at preventing certain corporate legal rules from being circumvented by the shareholders.*

---

26 *Ferreira Gomes*, Da administração à fiscalização das sociedades, 2015, 69 ff.

27 *Noack* (fn. 18) , 164.

28 *Schön*, Schuldrechtliche Gesellschaftervereinbarungen, 2018, 151 ff.

29 *Noack* (fn. 18), 164.

If there are no adequate grounds to restrict contractual freedom, unanimous shareholders' agreement should be deemed effective towards the company.[30]

The rules regarding the organisation and operation of the company that have an impact on third parties must necessarily be included in the articles of association. The legal requirements on form, formalities and publicity must be complied with.

Whenever third parties are not affected, a restriction on the shareholders' contractual freedom is hard to justify. If they can self-protect their own interests *ex contractu*, they do not require the protection of certain legal rules.

Future shareholders are also safeguarded. If they adhere to the shareholders' agreement, they accept its impact on the company. If they don't, the agreement is no longer unanimous and the general rules apply.

I therefore agree with Noack's perspective on an "associative ordering in a broader sense" ("Verbandsordnung im weiteren Sinne").

According to this perspective, the effectiveness of the unanimous shareholders' agreement towards the company is not limited to cases of abuse of the company's legal personality that allow for the lifting of the corporate veil.

This has an impact on the effectiveness of shareholders agreements that regulate the management and supervision of the company, on one hand, and shareholders' resolutions, on the other hand.

[30] *Noack* (fn. 18), 164.

Russian roulette clauses, fair price and business ethics

Some remarks from the Italian Fintecna case

Nicola de Luca

Abstract: The article tackles the issue of the legitimacy of clauses located in contracts between private individuals and designed to break up joint ownership. The affirmative solution allows to state that even in company statutes or shareholders' agreements, an anti-deadlock clause is permissible: upon the occurrence of a specific trigger event, it allows each party to buy the other's shareholding at a certain named price or to sell its own at the same price. Referring to the terms of an important case solved by the Italian Court of Cassation (Fintecna), the author takes the position that the validity of the anti-deadlock clause does not depend on its requesting that the price named by one party, to make either a purchase or a sale, corresponds to at least a certain fair price. Nor can it be argued that taking advantage of the other party's difficult situation, in contrast to good faith, would allow a judge to redetermine the purchase price, imposing a fair price. The parties must therefore necessarily identify solutions ex ante to possible abuses, in order to prevent the other party from taking unfair advantage at a later date.

I. Paintings, statues, and diamonds are no cakes to cut

The Italian Civil Code[1], as many other European Civil Codes, deals with the division of property that is indivisible or not comfortably divisible: a painting, a statue, a piece of jewellery. These are not cakes to cut. The law provides for that they are sold at auction, so that the cash paid can be divided. However, in case one co-owner seeks for the allotment in kind of the property, this is not sold by auction to third parties, provided that the other co-owners may obtain an equitable compensation in cash. Thus, this rule makes it clear that the law does not protect the interest of co-owners to maximizing the value of the property through the sale to the bidder offering the highest price. Rather, the referred rule grants that the interest of some co-owners seeking to share money out of the sale of the common property does not jeopardize also non-economic interests of other co-owners, such as those arising from affection to the piece of property: these are commonly referred to as idiosyncratic interests in a law and economic approach.

[1] *E.g.*, Articles 560, 720, 846 (repealed), 1111, 1112, 1114 of the Italian Civil Code.

The interest to be allotted the property in kind cannot be fulfilled but to one co-owner or group of co-owners acting jointly. In case of multiple requests, one must prevail. Courts have wide discretion in the criteria of choice. Usually, they will select the single co-owner or the joint co-owners having the largest share of interest. On the contrary, and for the reasons stated above, the Italian Supreme Court[2] confirmed that courts may not award the piece of property to the co-owner who offers more cash to the others. Indeed, the law does not protect an interest to the maximization of the value from the sale. For instance, in case co-owners have an equal share – i. e. 50 % – 50 % – courts may do nothing but proceed to a sale by auction.

The same ruling of the Italian Supreme Court, however, usefully pointed out that the fact that preference cannot be assigned to the highest bidder depends on the interests that the law intends to protect in the absence of an agreement. The law, however, does not prevent the co-owners from entering into an agreement among themselves to assign preference to the highest bidder, i. e., setting up an auction amongst themselves. Considering this statement, an important question arises as to whether, instead of an auction to the highest bidder, co-owners may also enter into a so-called Russian roulette[3] agreement, providing for a shotgun mechanism. Such an agreement grants one or all the co-owners with the right to set an equitable price for the shares of the property, while remitting to the other co-owner the right to choose whether to buy (the other's share of the undivided property) or to sell (her own).[4]

A positive solution to this question requires analytic demonstration.

---

[2] Italian Court of Cassation, VI Section, 20 March 2019, n. 7869, in Foro italiano, Rep. 2019, ad vocem *Successione ereditaria*, n. 264, and (*in extenso*) in Vita notarile, 2019, 828.

[3] Such expression first appeared in the tale 'Russian roulette' by the American writer, *George Surdez*, published in the Collier's Magazine on 30 January 1937, regarding "the strange case of Sergeant Burkowski, who died many deaths, and his friend Feldheim, who had to explain one of them to their superior officers". The tale describes the dangerous games played by soldiers of the French foreign legion in North Africa. Reference to the 'roulette' is easy to understand, given that a revolver's cylinder rolls as the wheel of a casino roulette. The adjective Russian refers to the nationality of Burkowski. However, that is probably an homage to *Mikhail Lermontov*, and his novel 'A hero of our times' of 1840, containing the tale 'A fatalist'. There Lermontov tells the story of lieutenant Vulich, an officer of the Tsar's army of Serbian origins who strongly believed in predestination. To show that destiny is unmodifiable, he takes a pistol and asks the major whether it was loaded. The major did not remember. Then he says: "'Gentlemen, I ask you not to move from your places!' said Vulich, putting the muzzle of the pistol to his forehead. Everyone seemed petrified. 'Mister Pechorin,' he added, 'take a card and throw it up.' I took from the table, as I remember it now, the ace of hearts, and threw it upwards. Everybody stopped breathing; all eyes, full of fear and some undefined curiosity, ran from the pistol to the fatal ace, which was slowly falling, tumbling in the air. At the moment it touched the table, Vulich pulled the trigger … a misfire!".

[4] American and Canadian Courts often solve deadlock situations also in the absence of an agreement, by ordering that one party names a price and the other chooses whether to buy or sell. In the US, see e. g. Fulk v. Washington Service Associated, Inc., No. 17747-NC, 2002 WL 1402273 (Del. Ch. June 21, 2002); in Canada, see e. g.: Kinzie v. Dells, 2010 BCSC 1360 (Can. B.C.); Whistler Service Park Ltd. v. Ocean Glacier Creek Dev., 2005 BCSC 1942 (Can. B.C.); Lee v. Lee, 2002 BCSC 1077 (Can. B.C.); Safarik v. Ocean Fisheries Ltd. (1996), 17 B.C.L.R. 3rd 354 (Can. B.C.C.A.).

II. "I cut… or better, I name price, you choose:" the shotgun mechanism

All agree that, in case a division in kind is possible, it is fair that one party cuts the cake, and the other chooses the slice. In case the division in kind is not possible, one must question whether "I name the price, you choose" is an equivalent solution. Some may doubt that it is possible to grant one party of the agreement (or even all parties) with the right to name the price, as this forces the other party to buy or sell (and in case she does not choose, to understand silence as a consent at selling or buying). The doubt arises because, in general terms, the law does not permit to have agreements whose effectiveness or performance depend on condition precedents based on one party's mere will.[5]

As regards Russian roulette clauses, however, such a doubt is ungrounded, as the shotgun mechanism does not create condition precedents based on one party's mere will, rather it grants to the other party the right to a choice. Indeed, the law[6] confirms the validity of agreements granting to one party the right to choose the other party's performance among some, or the right to terminate the contract at will, or the right not to proceed to the closing after testing of the product; in addition, it is commonly acknowledged that call and put options may be agreed upon, early termination clauses are valid (and consumers always benefit from such clauses), prices for services may be unilaterally modified (whilst the other party may only withdraw), and so on. In other words, the law generally allows that freely negotiated contracts create situations in which one party makes a decision binding on the other party.

Within the range of decisions which a contract may grant to one party (the party "shooting first"), it is possible to also include the right to decide the price of a sale, in order to terminate the situation of co-ownership in the piece of indivisible property (and, as we will see, in the share capital of a company).

Moreover, some may doubt that it is possible to grant to one party to the contract the right to price the piece of property, so that the other chooses. Indeed, arbitration clauses – also aiming at making prices[7] – generally refer to a third independent party the power to decide. This doubt too is, however, ungrounded.

Indeed, freedom of contract is not prevented from awarding to one of the parties the right to name prices, as far as determination is linked to objective criteria or in case the contract places the choosing party on neutral stance. This situation occurs in circumstances governed by Russian roulette clauses, as the shotgun mechanism entrusts the recipient with the right to buy or sale, not the party naming the price.

A famous quote from Judge Easterbrook[8] is most appropriate in this regard: concerning shotgun mechanisms, "the possibility that the person naming the price can be forced either to buy or to sell keeps the first mover honest."

---

[5] *See*, e.g., Article 1355 Italian Civil Code.

[6] *See*, e.g., Articles 1286, 1520, 1556 Italian Civil Code.

[7] Articles 1349 and 1473 Italian Civil Code.

[8] In *Valinote v. Ballis*, 295 F.3d 666, 667, 7th Cir. (2000).

III. An uncertain outcome keeps the first mover honest

The forgoing leads to the conclusion that if the co-owners of an indivisible piece of property wish to regulate *ex ante* how to terminate in the future the situation of co-ownership, by avoiding that the common asset is sold at auction, they can agree on a Russian roulette clause.

The right to terminate co-ownership may be activated upon the occurrence of certain events, including a disagreement over the shifting use of the property, or even at will and at any time.

Given the existence of non-economic interests of the co-owners, the named price need not be related to objective value of the property, rather may take into account any value of affection being relevant for them: in plain words, the named price may be completely arbitrary, as long as it makes sense for the co-owner who pulls the trigger. Moreover, as long as the first mover does not have a choice whether to buy or sell, it is perfectly reasonable that the named price encourages the other party to buy (through the determination of a low price) or sell (through the determination of a high price), depending on the intention of the naming party.

IV. Business deadlocks and shotguns

Let's now complicate our case and consider properties that are not unique and indivisible, rather that acquire greater value when combined. Consider the floors of a building belonging to two separate owners but intended by mutual agreement to be organised for leasing as a hotel to a third party, under separate though converging contracts. When the leases expire, should one of the owners feel that she no longer wishes to lease her property to the third hotelier, she would implement a choice that would also reverberate on the other owner. It is far from fanciful, then, to imagine an agreement between the two separate owners aimed at ensuring that – in a situation of disagreement over the destination of the properties – any of them could offer to buy the other's or sell her own property. Here, too, the determination of the purchase or sale price may be freely left to the offeror. The price, here, is not likely to be influenced by elements of affection, rather predominantly by economic reasons. Also these reasons, however, are subjective, as not all have similar chances to exploit commercial opportunities, not all have similar economic means, and so on. In a classic economic perspective, while the first mover must name a price at which she is indifferent as to buy or sell – the property and the money have same marginal utility – the recipient may have a preference based on a business rationale: indeed, the decision to buy or sell should exclusively depend on her economic perspectives.

The discussion has now straightforward reached the focus point, that of corporate shareholdings. It is sufficient to imagine that the building intended for a hotel is altogether contributed to a company equally owned by the two partners, who can then enter into the Russian roulette agreement so that, in the event of a deadlock or at will, all shares giving access to the real estate company management concentrate on a single hand.[9] It is now necessary to understand whether or not the discussion on co-ownership and combined ownership, and the conclusions reached there, are also valid for agreements regarding shareholdings: mainly, doubts have been raised whether or not for shotgun mechanisms included in the corporate statutes, instead of shareholders' agreements, the named price must at least equal fair price.

V. Named price, fair price: remarks from the Italian Fintecna case

Italian law requires that, as the shareholder is forced to dispose her shares, redeemed shares must be paid at fair price.[10] Fair is a price which is determined taking into account the asset value of the shares (i. e., the value of the company's net assets), the investment value (i. e., the expected earnings) and the market value, if any.[11]

Some professional associations and commentators[12] are of the opinion that such a rule is also applicable to Russian roulette clauses included in the corporate statutes, while for those agreed to in shareholders' agreements fair pricing would not be necessary. Other professional associations and commentators[13] maintain that fair pricing is not at all mandatory, as in all shotgun mechanisms the choice as to buy or sell lies with the recipient,[14] who is therefore not forced to sell at the named price.

---

[9] The academic debate is wide. In English, see *Brooks/Landeo/Spier*, (2010) 41 Rand Journal of Economics 649–673; *Landeo/Spier*, (2013) 121 Economic Letters, 390–394; *id.*, (2014a) 81 University of Chicago Law Review 203–227; id., (2014b) 31 Yale Journal on Regulation 143–187. In German, see *Agstner/Fleischer*, ZGR 2024, 933–958. In Italian, see next footnotes.

[10] Article 2437-sexies Italian Civil Code.

[11] Article 2437-ter Italian Civil Code.

[12] Consiglio Notarile di Milano, Massima n. 181/2019, Clausola "anti-stallo" di riscatto o di acquisto forzato di partecipazioni sociali (c.d. clausola della "roulette russa" o clausola del "cowboy") (artt. 2437-sexies, 2473-bis c.c.) (9 July 2019). See also, *Rescio*, in Rescio/Speranzin (ed.), Patrimonio sociale e governo dell'impresa. Dialogo tra giurisprudenza, dottrina e prassi in ricordo di G.E. Colombo, 2020, 355, at 377 ff. and *Notari*, in Analisi Giuridica dell'Economia, 2021, 383, at 401 ff.; *Limatola*, Lo "stallo decisionale" nelle s.p.a. Disciplina legale ed autonomia statutaria, 2024, 227 ff.

[13] Consiglio Notarile dei Distretti Riuniti di Firenze, Pistoia e Prato, Massima n. 73/2020, La clausola "russian roulette": rilevanza organizzativa e autonomia statutaria. See also, *Rosapepe*, www.ilsocietario.it, 2017; *Divizia*, in Società, 2018, 434; *Mazzoletti*, in Notariato, 2018, 301; *Bernardi*, in Rivista di Diritto Societario, 2018, 617; *Leto*, in Rivista del notariato, 2018, 86; *Sciannaca*, in Giurisprudenza commerciale, 2019, II, 861; *C. Pasquariello*, in Società, 2021, 154; *Perreca*, in Banca, borsa, e titoli di credito, 2020, II, 939. Also add, *de Luca*, in Rivista di diritto civile, 2022, 863.

[14] *See*, e.g., *Landeo/Spier*, (2014b) (fn. 7), at 143, 148 s., maintaining that "shotgun mechanisms, where the court mandates one owner to name a single buy-sell price and compels the other owner to either buy or sell shares at the named price, should play a larger role in the judicial management of business divorce. Since the party proposing the offer may end up either buying or selling shares, the party has an incentive to identify and name a fair price"; […] "since the party making the offer may end up on either side of the transaction, the incentive to make a "law-ball offer" is eliminated".

In a landmark case, the Italian Supreme Court (upholding the Cour of Appeals and the District Court's decisions) has confirmed that the named price needs not equal fair price, at least in cases where the Russian roulette clause is included in a shareholders' agreement.[15] In my view, also clauses included in the corporate statutes do not require that the named price at least equals fair price.[16]

Indeed, the choice as to whether placing the shotgun mechanism in the corporate statutes, or in the shareholders' agreements, only affects the interests of shareholders: indeed, while Russian roulette clauses included in shareholders' agreements only bind the founders (or those being parties to the side agreement), clauses included in the corporate statutes also bind future shareholders, without any need for their specific consent or approval. This choice – as similarly does the choice to introduce any other limit to the circulation of shares: pre-emption rights, approval clauses and so on – does not entail consequences on the governance of the company, nor affects third parties as such and, in particular, does not require any specific protection for shareholders who will be recipient of a buy/sell notice in the future, regardless of whether those shareholders were originally part of the decision to include the deadlock-breaking provision in the corporate statutes. Thus, there is no reason to treat differently clauses included in the statutes and in shareholders' agreements.

It should be added that introducing limitations on the circulation of shares of already incorporated companies generally requires a majority vote: thus, dissenting shareholders are permitted to dispose their shares, not to veto the decision. In contrast, all agree that introducing a Russian roulette clause in the corporate statute of an already incorporated company requires unanimous consent of all shareholders:[17] indeed, European company law[18] requires that all clauses permitting compulsory redemption of shares, as e.g. the drag-along clause, must be provided for before the shares are issued; hence, they may affect existing shares only in case all shareholders agree. This confirms that all shareholders receiving a buy/sell notice based on a Russian roulette clause have specifically consented to the clause, or at least were aware of the existence of such a clause before becoming shareholders.

---

[15] Italian Court of Cassation, I Section, 25 July 2023, n. 22375, in Foro italiano, 2023, I, 3515; Court of Appeals Rome, 3 February 2020, in Foro italiano, 2020, I, 1383; District Court Rome, 19 October 2017, in Giurisprudenza italiana, 2018, 1136 (it is fair to disclose that I have acted as attorney-at-law for Fintecna, the winning party).

[16] See, *de Luca* (fn. 13), at 881 ff.

[17] *See*, by analogy, Trib. Milano, 24 March 2011, in Banca, borsa, e titoli di credito, 2013, II, 59, discussing the validity/effectiveness of a shareholders' resolution by majority vote aiming at introducing a drag-along clause.

[18] Article 82(1)(a), Directive 2017/1132/EU. *See*, among others, *de Luca*, European Company Law, 2nd ed., 2021, at 205 ff.

VI. Fair price and business ethics. Shooting a man in the back is not honest, but it gives no right to claim damages

Russian roulette clauses may encourage opportunism of shareholders, in case of asymmetry. Asymmetry may regard information, operational capacity, or financial resources. Many commentators have investigated what remedies shall or may be put in place in cases where the right to pull the trigger of a shotgun mechanism is done to the exclusive advantage of the naming party, who may also act in bad faith.[19] This situation brings us immediately to the issue of business ethics which is the Leitmotiv of this conference.

What happens if the first mover names a very low price only because she is perfectly aware that the recipient cannot choose to buy instead of selling? Is it honest to shoot a man in the back?

Let's assume that the recipient has suffered a fire at her own home, which is uninsured, and having no available financial resources, has taken out a mortgage, to repay which she must devote a substantial part of her income, the rest of which is necessary to support the family. The naming party is thus sure that, even by offering a low price, the recipient is burdened by the mortgage and, having no possibility to expand credit, will not be able to buy, instead of selling.

As much as the example may suggest feelings of sympathy, this is no valid reason for doubting of the validity of the Russian roulette clause.[20] Rather, as the buy/sell notice leads to sign a separate sale and purchase agreement, one must understand whether or not the malicious exercise of the Russian roulette clause permits to question the validity of such a contract (the Sale and Purchase Agreement).[21] The answer is negative, but in circumstances in which the price is so trivial that the shares are worth at least a double: in these cases, indeed, taking advantage of a situation of need allows the recipient to bring an action for annulment.[22] The contract is annulled unless the acquiring party offers to economically rebalance its conditions.

As only the acquiring party may offer to increase the price at a fair level to avoid annulment, also the foregoing confirms that the law never grants the recipient of the notice a right to a fair price. Therefore, in cases the seller may not seek for the annulment of the sale and purchase agreement, it would be nonsense to allow her to claim for damages, which would be easily identified in the difference between the paid price and the (alleged) fair price. Such a difference is not, under a thorough private law perspective, a damage to be restored.

Shooting a man in the back is not honest, but it gives no right to claim damages.

---

[19] *See* references in footnote 9.

[20] *Contra*, unconvincingly, *Cotillo*, in Contratto e impresa, 2023, 309, at 312 ss.

[21] It is generally agreed that, before the signing of the SPA, it is possible to freeze the exercise of the call option right, through the *exceptio doli generalis*. In those circumstances, however, the party feeling abused has the burden to prove that the other party has acted in bad faith, i. e. it exercised its rights aiming at causing damage.

[22] 'Rescission', under Article 1448 Italian Civil Code.

V. Conclusions

Entering into a Russian roulette agreement is a useful tool in case co-owners of an indivisible property foresee the need to terminate co-ownership avoiding a sale at auction. A similar clause may serve as deadlock-breaking-provision in cases a business divorce is necessary. The shotgun mechanism, generally, keeps the first mover honest. Thus, the named price must not equal at least fair price (neither in cases where the clause is included in the corporate statutes). However, shareholders' opportunism may lead to name unfair prices, in situations where the recipient has not a real choice to buy instead of selling. Given that the law grants protection only in extreme cases, the parties to the Russian roulette agreement must consider this possible scenario and protect their future interests at the time when they have bargaining power to do so. Predetermined conditions to the exercise of the buy/sell provisions, price floors, and earn-out clauses are only some examples of the variety of useful tools avoiding opportunism and granting at the same time that freedom of contracts is not compromised.

Between Contractual Freedom and Ethical Limits: The Admissibility of Russian Roulette Clauses in Shareholders' Agreements under Portuguese law

Catarina Coelho

Abstract: this paper explores the legal admissibility, ethical implications, and practical consequences of including a Russian roulette clause in shareholders' agreements of closed limited liability companies under the legal framework of Portuguese law. It argues that Russian roulette clauses are not necessarily invalid.

I. Introduction

A shareholder agreement[1] may contain a diverse set of clauses. In this paper, we focus on the admissibility of Russian Roulette clauses under Portuguese Law.

This topic touches upon the broader issue of introducing ethics into shareholder agreements, particularly in relation to imposing limits on contractualism beyond the financial strength of one party over a weaker one.

In this paper, we will outline key issues associated with the inclusion of Russian Roulette clauses. Our primary objective is to assess whether there are potential validity issues associated with parties stipulating such clauses within the legal framework of Portuguese Law. We acknowledge that these issues can be explored in greater detail in future works; the present analysis is limited in scope, as dictated by the constraints of this publication.

This paper will specifically focus on *sociedade por quotas* (closed limited liability companies) under Portuguese Law, due to their practical importance in this context. Not only there are multiple companies, in Portugal, that opt for the company type *sociedades por quotas,* but also, as we will explain, Russian Roulette clauses are especially relevant where there is an agreement between two shareholders, which is only possible in certain kinds of companies – such as *sociedades por quotas.* Hence, they will be the focus of our paper.

[1] Under Portuguese Law a shareholder agreement may be defined as "an agreement between two or more shareholders (in that capacity), beyond the bylaws, which regulates corporate relations, with merely binding effects amongst the parties that signed them (inter partes)." *Perestrelo de Oliveira*, Acordos Parassociais, 2025, 7.

It is assumed that these clauses are contracted within the shareholder agreement, not company bylaws. The analysis of joint ventures,[2] listed companies, and venture capital[3] is beyond the scope of this paper. Similarly, we will not address other types of shoot-out clauses, such as the Texas shoot-out,[4] sale shoot-out,[5] or fairest sealed bid.[6]

We will not delve into the juridical nature of these clauses, as an in-depth analysis would extend beyond the scope of this paper and the broader context of this publication. Additionally, we will not explore whether these clauses compromise the interest of the company as a limit on shareholder agreements.[7]

Finally, we will not examine specific procedures for determining the price or the consequences of choosing a particular method. Nor will we analyze whether a fair price needs to be stipulated within the Russian Roulette clause.[8] Remedies related to the breach of these clauses will also not be discussed.

In light of the subject matters analysed in the present paper, we will begin by examining the structure and characteristics of a Russian Roulette clause (*II.*). Next, we will explore its admissibility under Portuguese Law, considering the space provided for private autonomy in shareholder agreements (*III.*). Following this, we will assess situations in which a contract concluded after the triggering of this clause may be considered unconscionable (*IV.*) and cases where it might involve an abusive exercise of rights (*V.*). Additionally, we will discuss the issues raised under Portuguese Law by the creation of an artificial deadlock (*VI.*). We will then analyze the legal consequences of triggering a Russian Roulette clause from a company law perspective (*VII.*). Finally, we will draw our conclusions in light of analysis of the previous points (*VIII.*).

---

[2] We should nontheless hightlight the importance of this kind of clauses in joint ventures. For an analysis of it see *Nadorff/McNeal*, Oil and Gas, Natural Resources, and Energy Journal 3 (2020), 411, 411–19; *Schulte/Sieger*, NZG 2005, 24, 24–31.

[3] As Schroeder and Welpot state, this kind of clause is also typical in venture capital contracts. *Schroeder/Welpot*, NZG 2014, 609, 611.

[4] In this type of clause, the offers of the party's must be superior in each round. In that scenario a third party is involved, and the parties should send him its offers to acquire the shares of each party. The party that presents the highest offer prevails and acquires the shares of the other party. *Schroeder/Welpot* (fn. 4) 611. Stating that Texas shoot out is a variant of the Russian roulette clause, *Schmolke*, Grenzen der Selbstbindung im Privatrecht, 2014, 556.

[5] A sale shoot-out occurs when the parties initiate the negotiations with an offer to sell by one of the parties. If the other refuses to buy, it is obliged to sell its shares by a lower value. In this variant a third party is not involved and it continues until one of the parties accepts the offer to sell of the other. *Schroeder/Welpot* (fn. 4) 611.

[6] In this case, a third party is involved since the beginning. The parties will send to the third party in a sealed envelop an offer to buy the shares of the other party in a fixed price. This third party will decide which of the two offers it considers adequate. The clause can contain an evaluation method of the price that the third party may use to determine which of the offers contains an adequate price. *Schroeder/Welpot* (fn. 4) 611.

[7] Analysing this issue, see *Cunha*, Direito das Sociedades Comerciais, 7th ed., 2019, 246 ff.; *Trigo*, Os Acordos Parassociais sobre o Exercício do Direito de Voto, 2nd ed., 2011, 180–181; *Cunha*, in Abreu (ed.), Comentário do Código das Sociedades Comerciais, 2nd ed., 330–331.

[8] As it is analysed, for instance by Nicola de Luca in the present book, in "Russian roulette clauses, fair price and business ethics. Some remarks from the Italian Fintecna case".

II. What is a Russian Roulette clause?

A Russian roulette clause[9] (or buy-sell[10]) is a possible form of shoot-out clauses[11] and it is identified as a "business divorce clause"[12] or as a "deadlock resolution clauses", given that it is a clause that operates when, in cases of an internal dispute, provides a way out of a deadlock.[13]-[14] Deadlocks can create significant challenges for a company, including economic difficulties and damage to shareholder relationships.[15]A divergence of opinions or standpoints among shareholders may obstruct the approval of decisions in the general assembly, potentially leading to a halt in the company's activities due to the lack of decisions.[16] It occurs when 2 shareholders or 2 groups of shareholders, with equal percentage of voting rights, arrive at a deadlock.[17] This situation may arise in joint ventures (though their analysis is beyond the scope of this paper) as well as in small and medium-sized companies. [18]This type of clause can also be included to force a buy-out.[19]

Russian Roulette clauses "allows the shareholder initiating the resolution process, to offer to the other shareholder(s), its entire share at a specified price, whereby the other shareholder(s) can either accept this offer within specified time and acquire the

---

9 This denomination stems from the uncertain outcome of the triggering of the clause. *Valdini/Koch*, Gesellschafts- und Wirtschaftsrecht 2016, 179, 179–182.

10 *Fleischer/Schneider*, European Company and Financial Law Review 2012, 35, 38.

11 A shoot-out clause carries the following structure: "the first part defining a trigger or deadlock event", and the second detailing the process to be followed once the procedure is triggered." *Fleischer/Schneider* (fn. 11) 38. For a similar use of the concept, *Bock*, Gesellschaftsvertragliche Gestaltungen zur Auflösung von Pattsituationen in der Gesellschafterversammlung, 2020, 138. For other kinds of shoot-out clauses see *Fleischer/Schneider* (fn. 11) 39 ff.

12 *Perreca*, Banca, borsa, titoli di credito 2020, 939, 940.

13 *Stojanovic*, South East European Law Journal 2023, 5, 14; *Schmolke* (fn. 5) 556.

14 Bock distinguishes between deadlock situations and less serious divergences, that the author qualifies as *Pattsituationen*. *Bock* (fn. 12) 28. Höck submits, in light of German Law, a definition for a „deadlock". *Höck*, Russian-Roulette-Klauseln und Shoot-Out-Klauseln, 2021, 54 ff. According to this author, a deadlock amounts to: " a permanent decision-making blockade of one or more company bodies, which is based on a deadlock or a different distribution of votes and results in their inability to act. This decision-making blockade can lead to significant negative effects on the economic situation of the company and even threaten its existence.". Ibid 68. It is important that the shareholders arrive at a permanent deadlock, in the sense that the parties cannot reach an agreement in relation to none of the available options. Ibid 64–65. Deadlocks may occur due to general assembly resolutions that affect the shareholders' special rights or when a shareholder is excluded, a director is let go or dividend distribution, or due to an investment by the shareholders. Ibid 69–70.

15 *Bock* (fn. 12) 23.

16 *Bock* (fn. 12) 25; *Schroeder/Welpot* (fn. 4) 610. Under Italian Law, the lack of activity of the general assembly of the company may lead to its dissolution, as per article 2484, no. 3 of the Italian Civil Code. *Perreca*, (fn. 13) 940.

17 *Bock* (fn. 12) 24. Rarely, a deadlock clause is established on companies where there is a great share dispersion, or where there isn't two clear groups or interests. *Facci*, Le nuove leggi civili commentate 2020, 765, 770.

18 *Bock* (fn. 12) 28.

19 *Thomas/Ryan*, The Law and Practice of Shareholders' Agreements, 4th ed., 2014, 137.

share of the initiating shareholder or sell all of its/their own shares to the initiating shareholder at the initiating offer's price.".[20]

As Fleischer and Schneider illustrate:

> "Party A (the party wishing *to* leave or take over *the* company) initiates the procedure by making an offer, either (1) to sell all their shares to Party B, or (2) to purchase all of Party B's shares for a specific price. Party B can then freely decide whether to buy or sell".[21]

This example depicts the classical variant. In a modification of this clause, called the "one way sell Russian roulette", Party A makes only one offer to sell or transfer its shares to Party B. If Party B refuses, it is obliged to sell its shares to Party A by the price established by Party A.[22]

It has been stated that a Russian Roulette clause consists of two steps: (i) the trigger event or deadlock, which identifies the situation that activates the clause (commonly associated with a deadlock), and (ii) the execution procedure, which outlines the steps to be followed in the event of a deadlock.[23]

This clause should regulate the consequences of the parties failing to reach a decision within a specified period of time, such as by providing that the offer is deemed accepted, or that the purchase price is adjusted – either increased or decreased.[24] Under Portuguese Law, it is permissible for the silence of one of the parties to produce such legal effects, provided this consequence is expressly stipulated, in accordance with Article 218 of the Portuguese Civil Code.[25] This is considered a more efficient approach, since it ends only after two offers.[26]

Additionally, it is recommended that a cooling-off period be contractually established, providing the parties with an opportunity to reflect on the consequences of triggering a Russian Roulette clause and to consider reaching an amicable agreement before resorting to its activation.[27]

This type of clause has the advantage of reducing the likelihood of litigation concerning the price offered for the acquisition of shares. It aligns the interests of the parties, as the selling shareholder will seek the highest possible price, while the remaining shareholder aims to pay the lowest.[28] Additionally, it helps ensure that the price ultimately offered is adequate and acceptable for both parties and facilitates an orderly exit from the company.[29] It will also motivate the parties to reach an agreement, even before initiating this procedure, thus avoiding the costs of a possible liti-

---

[20] *Stojanovic* (fn. 14) 15.

[21] *Fleischer/Schneider* (fn. 11) 38.

[22] *Schroeder/Welpot* (fn. 4) 611.

[23] *Fleischer/Agstner*, Zeitschrift für Unternehmens- und Gesellschaftsrecht 2024, 933, 937. Also mentioned by *Hornung*, Leaver-, Vesting- und Shoot-Out-Klauseln, 2018, 215.

[24] *Fleischer and Agstner* (fn. 24) 937.

[25] *Oliveira* (fn. 2) 218.

[26] *Fleischer and Schneider* (fn. 11) 38–39.

[27] *Schulte/Sieger* (fn. 3) 26.

[28] *Schroeder/Welpot* (fn. 4) 610.

[29] *Schroeder/Welpot* (fn. 4) 611; *Valdini/Koch* (fn. 10) 181.

gation.[30]The uncertainty surrounding which party will be required to exit the company creates an incentive for the parties to seek an amicable resolution.[31]

However, there are some risks associated with a possible unjust outcome when triggering this kind of clause.

If there is a financial imbalance between the parties one can question whether this is a just method of dispute resolution, where the financially stronger party can pressure the other into acquiring or selling his/her shares for a lower price (taking advantage of its precarious financial position).[32] In addition, if one of the parties is prevented from acquiring the shares (due to Tax or strategic reasons) there is also risk of abuse.[33]Additionally, this clause is adequate when both parties wish to remain in the company. When one party doesn't, one of the parties may leverage this information in order to acquire the others shares at a lower price.[34]

Ultimately, there is a risk that one party may abuse the mechanism to pressure the other into transferring their shares.[35] However, the key question is whether such risks justify the argument that these types of clauses should be deemed invalid under Portuguese Law. This issue will be examined in the following section.

III. Russian Roulette clauses under Portuguese Law: a validity issue?

This analysis should begin by considering the extent of private autonomy granted to shareholders in shareholder agreements under Portuguese Law (*III.1.*), and, in light of that, proceed to analyze the admissibility of such clauses (*III.2.*).

1. The room for private autonomy in shareholder's agreements

Shareholders' agreements are admissible under Portuguese Law, as confirmed by Article 17, no. 1 of the Portuguese Companies Code.

However, shareholders' agreements are not subject to extensive regulation, nor is there a legal framework that prescribes which types of clauses should be considered admissible or inadmissible. This absence of regulation entails that there is significant scope for private autonomy in the drafting of shareholders' agreements.[36]

Considering that Company's Law is still a branch of civil law, the principle that everything which is not expressly prohibited is permitted remains applicable here.[37]

---

[30] *Schroeder/Welpot* (fn. 4) 611.

[31] Ibid 612.

[32] Ibid 612.

[33] Ibid 613.

[34] Ibid 613.

[35] *Valdini/Koch* (fn. 10) 179.

[36] Also highlight the applicability of freedom of contract to shareholder agreements in its content and on the liberty to agree upon them, *Antunes*, Direito das Sociedades em Revista 2021, 13, 17.

[37] *Martins*, Parassocialidade e transmissão de valores mobiliários, 1996, 224.

Nevertheless, this autonomy is not without limits. Shareholders' agreements, like any other contract, are subject to normative constraints.[38] They must comply with mandatory normative provisions[39] and cannot involve obligations that are physically or legally impossible, indeterminable, or contrary to public policy (*ordem pública*) and common decency (*bons costumes*)[40]. In addition, shareholders' agreements must respect the restrictions set out in Article 17, no. 2[41] and no. 3[42] of the Portuguese Companies Code.

It is against this legal background that the admissibility of *Russian Roulette* clauses should be assessed.

2. Are Russian Roulette clauses admissible under Portuguese Law?

As for the limitations arising from Article 17, no. 2 and no. 3 of the Portuguese Companies Code, none will, in principle, be relevant in relation to a Russian Roulette clause, as this type of clause does not pertain to the conduct of directors, members of the supervisory bodies, or to voting agreements.

One provision that might raise questions regarding the validity of a *Russian Roulette* clause is Article 280, no. 2 of the Portuguese Civil Code, which establishes that any contract contrary to public policy or common decency shall be deemed null and void.

These are inherently broad concepts, open to multiple interpretations. Among the possible meanings attributed to these terms, we consider that *public policy* refers to the fundamental principles of a given legal system – those values and norms that the State and society deem should prevail over the will of private parties expressed through contractual agreements.[43] In turn, we adopt the interpretation of *common decency* as referring to the "prevailing standards of sexual, familial, and social morality, or to the ethical and deontological rules applicable within a specific field".[44] In

---

[38] *Antunes* (fn. 37) 26.

[39] *Oliveira* (fn. 2) 48.

[40] *Antunes* (fn. 37) 26. Also stating that shareholder agreements can be considered null and void due to being legally impossible, *Gomes*, in Castro (ed.), Estudos em Honra de João Soares da Silva, 2021, 341, 346; M&A – Aquisições de Empresas e de Participações Sociais, 2022, 356.

[41] Under said article of the Portuguese Companies Code: "2 – The agreements referred to in the preceding paragraph may relate to the exercise of voting rights, but not to the conduct of stakeholders or other persons in the exercise of management or supervisory functions."

[42] Under this article of the Portuguese Companies Code: "Agreements by which a shareholder undertakes to vote are null and void: a) Always following the instructions of the company or one of its bodies; b) Always approving proposals made by the latter; c) Exercising the right to vote or abstaining from exercising it in return for special advantages".

[43] *Mota Pinto*, Teoria Geral do Direito Civil, 3rd ed., 552.

[44] *Cordeiro*, Tratado de Direito Civil, Vol. II, 5th ed., 600. Also adopting this concept of common decency, *Fernandes*, Teoria Geral do Direito Civil II – fontes, conteúdo e garantia da relação jurídica, 5th ed., 2017, 626.

this sense, *common decency* reflects impositions of the legal system that are exterior to the to the contract itself.[45]

With regard to public policy, we do not consider that any fundamental principle is called into question when parties mutually agree to include such clauses.

However, in what concerns common decency, one might question whether this type of clause should be considered invalid, given that it might be considered unethical in accordance with the prevailing social morality to exploit one party's financial position in relation to the other.[46] Namely, consider a hypothesis where one party is perfectly aware of the other's financial problems and strives to take advantage of said fact to acquire the others shares initiating the procedure set out in a Russian roulette clause.

While this conduct may certainly be objectionable, we consider that it does not reach the threshold required for invalidity, given the typical characteristics of a Russian Roulette clause as previously described.

They establish an equal procedure applicable to both parties, ensuring that neither shareholder can unilaterally decide to exclude the other. Moreover, neither party knows in advance which of them will ultimately acquire the other's shares, preserving a balance of power and fairness in the process.[47]

In light of that, it would highly constrain the party's autonomy to dictate that said clauses would be immediately invalid, especially if a financial equilibrium existed when the shareholder agreement was concluded.[48] In addition, the invalidity of an agreement exists from the moment of its conclusion, not merely in a posterior moment.[49] Therefore, it is not persuasive to argue that this kind of invalidity can arise only when triggering said clause.

---

[45] *Cordeiro*, Tratado de Direito Civil, Vol. II, 5th ed., 499.

[46] In German doctrine, there are some that argue that this kind of clauses are contrary to article 138, 1 of the BGB, since they are contrary to "common decency". Mentioning it, *Höck* (fn. 15) 135. Highlighting the risks of stipulating these kind of clauses, *Wedemann*, Gesellschafterkonflikte in geschlossenen Kapitalgesellschaften, 2013, 498–500. Also alerting that in cases where shareholders establish a shoot clause that admit its triggering in a free manner they should be considered invalid under article under article 138 of the BGB, due to their proximity to "Hinauskündigungsklauseln" (in practice, altough formally shareholders will have equal rights, in practice will refrain from something to the fear of other shareholder initiating a proceeding against him or leaving the company in financially unviable terms), *Baumann*, Ausstieg aus einem paritätischen Equity-Joint-Venture, 2023, 247. A decision of the German Supreme Court held that the stipulation of a *Russian Roulette* clause serves a legitimate purpose: it provides a mechanism to resolve deadlocks and a means for the exclusion of a shareholder when justified circumstances exist. As such, it can be considered admissible. *Mayer*, Shoot-Out-Klauseln im deutschen GmbH-Recht, 2019, 92–93.

[47] In German doctrine this point is raised by *Höck* (fn. 15) 129; *Schaper*, DB 2014, 821, 823. In similar terms, *Baumann* (fn. 47) 249.

[48] *Höck* (fn. 15) 138. Admitting russian roulette clauses under the principle of private autonomy, *Mayer* (fn. 4) 120.

[49] *Fernandes* (fn. 45) 493. In german doctrine, this argument is presented by *Baumann* (fn. 47) 250.

This evaluation might be different if the right to trigger the Russian roulette clause would only be attributed exclusively to the will of one of the party's.[50] However, that does not constitute the typical configuration of a Russian Roulette Clause.

Hence, it would be a stretch to consider that in most situations the Russian Roulette Clause would fulfill the requirements to be considered null,[51] without a case-by-case assessment of the specific terms and context in which it appears within a shareholders' agreement.

Naturally, in all scenarios, the drafting of said clause can shed light on its admissibility in the particular case.[52]

However, the limits imposed to private autonomy are not limited to its most extreme consequence, its nullity. It is still worth questioning the possibility of this contract being considered an unconscionable contract (*i. e.,* the contract when someone, exploiting the situation of need, inexperience, lightness, dependence, mental state or weakness of character of another, obtains from him, for himself or for a third party, the promise or granting of excessive or unjustified benefits).

IV. Can the contract that executes the transfer of shares as set out in a Russian Roulette clause be considered an unconscionable contract?

Given the risks associated with agreeing to this type of clause as outlined above, it is worth questioning whether, when enforced in certain scenarios, it could give rise to an unconscionable contract (*contrato usurário*) – particularly with respect to the terms governing the transfer of shares from one party to the other.[53]

Under Portuguese Law, an unconscionable contract exists only in very exceptional circumstances, due to the stringent requirements established by Article 282 of the Portuguese Civil Code. The legal consequence may be the annulment of the contract – such as the contract arising from the purchase of shares – or its modification in accordance with principles of equity.

Unconscionability considers both the one who exploits and the one that is exploited in a given transaction, as well as considering the characteristics of the contract that was concluded.[54]

It would require that a situation of inferiority exists (be it, due to necessity, inexperience, or weakness) and this inferior situation was essential to the issuance of the

[50] *Höck* (fn. 15) 141.

[51] Also considering that Russian Roulette clauses should not be considered invalid under Portuguese Law, *Oliveira* (fn. 2) 223; *Oliveira*, Corporate Finance, 3rd ed., 2024, 114.

[52] *Mayer* (fn. 47) 90.

[53] If, there is an effective coercion and not merely an exploration of a difficult situation, the contract may be said to have been only agreed upon due to duress, and it could be also annulled under article 255 of the Portuguese Civil Code. However, that will not amount to a typical situation in the contracting of or in the triggering of a Russian Roulette Clause.

[54] *Cordeiro* (fn. 45), 499.

legal declaration (meaning that, if it weren't for that situation, the legal declaration would not have been issued, or it would have been issued with a different content). This "necessity" can be of an economic, moral, or physical nature. It is not required that the necessity situation be real; it can be putative. The situation of necessity can even apply to legal entities. In this case, one could argue that the existence of the necessity situation is evident, being an economic necessity, in the sense that, if it weren't for financial problems, the business would not have been concluded.[55]

Furthermore, on the part of the usurer, it must exploit the inferior situation of the injured party.[56] The "exploitation" refers to the advantage the usurer consciously takes of the inferior situation in which the injured party finds itself. It is required that the usurer is aware of this situation and is conscious of the exploitation, regardless of their intention to abuse the inferiority of the declarant.[57]

Finally, there must exist a substantial non-equivalence between performances or a non-justification for said benefit.[58]

It is, in abstract, given the requirements above set out, possible to ponder how the execution of the Russian Roulette clause that results in the purchase and sell of ones shares to the other, could be considered an unconscionable contract and it shows that the Portuguese legal system sets out further boundaries to the concluding of unethical contracts.

Furthermore, this analysis would be incomplete without considering one of the primary safeguards against unethical conduct under Portuguese Law – the institute of abuse of rights.

V. Abuse of rights and the Russian Roulette Clause

Abuses and the existence of unbalanced situations that are triggered due to the observance of a Russian Roulette Clause is often highlighted as an issue in other jurisdictions.[59]

To analyze whether the triggering of a Russian Roulette Clause can amount to an abusive conduct under Portuguese Law, a brief description of the institute of abuse of rights in Portuguese Law is required (*1.*). Against this background, we will examine potential abusive conduct in the triggering of a *Russian Roulette* clause (*2.*) and its regulation under Portuguese Law (*3.*).

---

[55] *Sequeira*, in Proença (ed.) Comentário ao Código Civil, 2. ed., 699–701.

[56] *Cordeiro* (fn. 45) 497. This author stresses that the exploitation may be merely objective, and it may not imply the knowledge of the weakness of the exploited party. Ibid 498. Also demanding the existence of an exploitation by one of the parties, but also considering that it should be conscious, *Vasconcelos/Vasconcelos*, Teoria Geral do Direito Civil, 2024, 676.

[57] *Sequeira* (fn. 56) 699–701.

[58] *Cordeiro* (fn. 45) 499.

[59] For instance, in german law, *Schmolke* (fn. 5), 557.; *Schroeder/Welpot* (fn. 4) 614; Under Italian law see *De Luca*, Orizzonti del Diritto Commerciale 1 (2024), 257, 264.

1. Very brief description of the institute of abuse of rights under Portuguese Law

Under Portuguese Law, the institute of abuse of rights addresses the legitimacy of exercising a right,[60] *i. e.*, whether a person who holds a given right may exercise it freely, or whether its exercise is subject to limitations imposed by the legal system.[61]

An abuse of rights exists not only where the actions of the holder of a certain right exceed the purpose (from an economic and social perspective) of its creation by the legal system but also when not strictly legal values are breached (those related with common decency). This is grounded by the idea that rights are recognized by the legal system since they pursue certain values and purposes.[62]

Among the various situations that could potentially meet the criteria for abuse of rights arising from the exercise of the right to buy or sell shares under a *Russian Roulette* clause, it is worth considering whether Article 334 of the Portuguese Civil Code may be invoked, and in which categories of cases this would be applicable.[63]

2. Which exercise of rights, arising out of a Russian Roulette Clause, may be considered abusive?

To date, Portuguese case law has not examined or clarified the situations in which the exercise of rights under a Russian Roulette clause might amount to an abuse of rights. However, some have been suggested under another legal system: *(i)* financial disparity, *(ii)* fiscal disadvantages and other legal obstacles, *(iii)* interest divergence, information asymmetry or strategic disadvantages.[64]

On financial disparity cases, the financially stronger shareholder would trigger the clauses' procedure, and make a strategic offer to acquire the others shares, knowing that the counterparty would not be able to match it. The counterparty would be forced out of the company and to sell its share at an unreasonably low price.[65]

---

[60] It is understood that the exercise of subjective rights is not without limits. *Fernandes* (fn. 45) 612.

[61] *Fernandes* (fn. 45) 613.

[62] *Fernandes* (fn. 45) 624. Much more could be said about the doctrine of abuse of rights under Portuguese Law. However, given the scope of this paper, it is not the appropriate place to provide a detailed account of the circumstances in which the exercise of a right may be deemed abusive. For a more comprehensive analysis of this institute, see, namely, *Cordeiro*, Da Boa Fé no Direito Civil – Vol. II, 1984; *Cordeiro*, Tratado de Direito Civil, Vol. V – Parte Geral – Exercício Jurídico, 3rd ed., 2018; Sá, Abuso do Direito, 2005.

[63] In accordance with the prevailing position from Portuguese legal scholars and case law, there certain groups of conducts that are considered to be, in abstract, potentially abusive. *Fernandes* (fn. 45) 626–627. We will not describe them in depth, but we will highlight possible issues concerning the triggering of a Russian Roulette clause and their connection to abuse of rights.

[64] *Höck* (fn. 15) 160–164. Also highlighted by the OLG Nürnberg, Urteil vom 20.12.2013, 12 U 49/1.

[65] *Höck* (fn. 15) 160–161.

Regarding the second group of cases, it concerns situations where there is fiscal or other regulatory or legal disadvantages that present obstacles to selling or buying one of the shareholders' shares.[66]

The last group of cases relates to situations where one of the parties no longer has an interest in remaining a shareholder in the company, which impairs the value offered by the other shareholder to acquire its shares. In addition, where a shareholder has more knowledge of the area in which the company is inserted and the possible projection of the value of its shares, it may use that to his advantage in determining the price offered.[67]

In light of the above, and drawing from the group of cases mentioned above within the institute of abuse of rights,[68] we will now consider where the situations described might be qualified as an abusive exercise of rights.

3. Disproportion between the benefit resulting from the exercise of rights arising out of a Russian Roulette Clause and the resulting sacrifice for the other shareholder

Without discarding all hypothetical abusive conducts related with our hypothesis,[69] we will focus, in particular, on cases involving an imbalance of rights or dispropor-

---

[66] *Höck* (fn. 15) 161–163.

[67] *Höck* (fn. 15) 163–164.

[68] It is accepted, by several authors, the following conducts as an illicit exercise of one's rights, as delimitated by several group of cases. The *exceptio doli generalis* amounts to a "reaction, by paralysing or preventing the malicious and therefore abusive exercise of the right, through the attribution of a potestative right to the person against whom the right is exercised", *Fernandes* (fn. 45) 627. It is debated, under Portuguese Law, the relevance to be attributed to this group of cases. Ibid. *Venire contra factum proprium* connects to the "the prohibition of contradictory behaviour which, in terms of the exercise of the which, in terms of exercising the right, considers it inadmissible to act contrary to another action previously taken by its holder", *Fernandes* (fn. 45) 628. Formal inalegalibilities translate "the nullity derived from the lack of legal form of a particular business cannot be claimed, otherwise there will be an 'abuse of law' contrary to good faith", *Cordeiro*, (fn. 63) 333. *Suppressio* connects to the delayed exercise of a right, such much so, that the counterparty legitimately ceases to believe that such right will be exercised, due to this circumstance, its exercise is prevented. *Fernandes* (fn. 45) 628. *Tu quoque* entails that "a party who has breached obligations imposed should not be allowed to exercise a right recognised in it by invoking a fact on the part of the opposing party to which that behaviour was not unrelated". *Fernandes* (fn. 45) 628. Disequilibrium in the exercise of rights connects to conducts contrary to the good faith due to the consequences of their exercise and are categorized as follows: "the useless harmful exercise; the demand for what must be returned immediately – dolo agit qui petit quod statim redditurus est; and the disproportion between the advantage of the exercise for the holder and the resulting sacrifice for others". *Fernandes* (fn. 45) 629.

[69] For instance, in accordance with legal scholars of Italian Law, some conducts may be considered abusive as cases of *exceptio doli*. Namely, in a situation where one of the parties, aware that the other is not in a stable or solid financial position offers to acquire its share for a low price (since it is aware that the other will likely accept it in its conditions) this can amount to a illicit act where the sole motive to offer such a price is to harm the other party. In that case, the exercise of that right may be paralyzed. *De Luca*, Orizzonti del Diritto Commerciale 1 (2024), 257, 266. Also raising this issue, *Perreca*, Banca, borsa, titoli di credito 6 (2020), 939, 950.

tionality – specifically, situations where there is a disproportion between the benefits obtained through the exercise of the right to purchase a shareholder's shares as a result of triggering a Russian Roulette clause and the corresponding sacrifice imposed on the other shareholder.

It is understood as a situation in which there is a disproportion between the benefits gained by the party exercising a right and the burdens imposed on others by the exercise of that same right, resulting in harm to others in a manner that becomes intolerable.[70]

The imbalance in the exercise of a certain right (due to its effects or consequences) is considered abusive since it is contrary to the good faith.[71]-[72] The way in which the right is exercised should substantially exceed its limits.[73]

In such cases, although there is a legitimate formal ground to exercise rights, it should be considered whether the consequences of said act and control the compatibility with the legal system, when considered as a whole, render it an illicit exercise.[74]

Where one of the parties is placed is an insufferable position, not having the economic means to present a viable offer to acquire the other shareholder's shares and having to accept any offer that the other presents, one might be before a case of abuse of rights. This may happen in financial disparity cases, where the price offered is substantially lower than the shares market price, can an abusive exercise of rights be pondered, in a given case.

In the second group of cases, identifying an abuse of rights will typically remain difficult where fiscal or legal disadvantages are present in acquiring the shares, for not achieving the threshold necessary to argue that an illicit exercise exists. If, however, as in the first group of cases, those disadvantages are accompanied by financial disparities, there may be a basis to contend that disproportionality exists.

In the third group of cases, a shareholder's mere lack of interest in the company will rarely be sufficient to constitute an abuse of rights, even if it results in a depreciation of the offer to purchase the others shares. Where a shareholder's interest lies in exiting the company – and the value of the shares reflects that intention – this would generally not be regarded as abusive. However, the same cannot be said in situations where there is a significant imbalance in knowledge or expertise between the parties. In such cases, where one shareholder is unable even to perceive the harm being inflicted upon them, the exercise of rights may be deemed illicit, if that has an impact on the value offered for the shares.

This analysis is naturally subject to the circumstances of the given case.

---

[70] *Cordeiro* (fn. 63) 385. Also adopting this notion, *Fernandes* (fn. 45) 630; *Candeias*, Revista da Faculdade de Direito da Universidade de Lisboa 64(1) 2023, 885, 917.

[71] "Good faith" in interpreted as, in accordance with article 334 of the Portuguese Civil Code, as the "fundamental values of the system itself, which assigns the rights in question", *Cordeiro* (fn. 63) 410–411.

[72] *Cordeiro* (fn. 63) 379.

[73] *Fernandes* (fn. 45) 632.

[74] *Cordeiro* (fn. 63) 389.

Considering the existence of a disequilibrium of rights, its consequences of are multiple, going from the suppression of the abusive exercise, the cessation of it or to indemnify the other party.[75]

The most appropriate remedy should be determined in a case-by-case analysis.

Having analysed the above mentioned cases, it is relevant to access a specific situation, since it can have not only an impact on the shareholder agreement itself but also in the company itself – the creation of "artificial deadlocks".

VI. Artificial deadlocks: its effect on the shareholder agreement and the company

One specific scenario that can lead to abuses is the deliberate triggering of a deadlock event, whereby a shareholder intentionally obstructs several decisions at the general assembly, creating an "artificial deadlock."[76]. One shareholder could deliberately block the approval of a certain resolution or consciously create obstacles to reach a certain milestone.[77]

In these cases, the shareholder could be blocked from exercising its right to trigger a deadlock, since it would be considered abusive, where it is created with the purpose of harming the other shareholder as per article 334 of the Portuguese Civil Code.[78]

It should nonetheless be pondered, from a companies' law perspective, whether there can be consequences from creating artificial deadlocks or whether this amounts to a situation only relevant under the shareholders' agreement.

One can ponder whether the votes emitted by the shareholder can render the deliberation invalid, but only where the requirements set out on article 58 (1), (b) of the Portuguese Companies Code[79].

In German law it is suggested that influencing the weaker shareholder, to vote in a way that damages the company, may be considered abusive.[80] Even only damaging other shareholders, for selfish ends, causing a deadlock, even if in line with the company's interests, can be considered abusive for breaching the duty of loyalty that binds shareholders.[81]

In both cases, it can be pondered, as per article 58, 1, b) of the Portuguese Companies Code, it is possible to request the annulment of a deliberation where a voting

[75] *Cordeiro* (fn. 63) 413; *Fernandes* (fn. 45) 633–634.

[76] *Höck* (fn. 15) 170.

[77] *Höck* (fn. 15) 170.

[78] Considering it as a situation of abuse under German Law, see *Höck* (fn. 15) 170–171.

[79] For a detailed approach concerning what kinds of cases constitute an abusive deliberation, *Abreu*, Do Abuso de Direito, 1983, 167–195. Studying, more generaly, the subject matter of deliberations under Portuguese Law see *Furtado*, Deliberações dos Sócios – Comentário ao Código das Sociedades Comerciais 1993.

[80] *Höck* (fn. 15) 166.

[81] *Höck* (fn. 15) 167.

right is exercised with the purpose of damaging the company or its shareholders, or, whenever, to obtain unfair benefits for itself or a third party, a certain deliberation is approved.[82] This depends on whether the resolution would have passed even without the exercise of the voting right by said shareholder. In such cases, annulment is no longer possible, as the resolution would have been approved regardless of the abusive votes.[83] This assessment is referred to by legal scholars as the "resistance test".[84]

It must be demonstrated that there is an intention to obtain special advantages, and that the deliberation serves as an appropriate means to achieve that purpose.[85] It is not consensual amongst legal whether this kind of deliberation must necessarily be enacted with the purpose of harming the company and other shareholders.[86]

Special advantages are understood as patrimonial gains attributable by deliberation, admitted to shareholders or non-shareholders, but not to all that are present in the company in a similar situation than the ones beneficiated, as well as the gains that would not be granted, to people that are not before a similar situation that the others, to who doesn't occupy a similar hypothetical position in the company.[87]

It should be demonstrated that there is an intention to harm either the company or the other shareholder and the deliberation is an adequate mean to fulfill said purpose.[88]

The harm caused by the deliberation (as a consequence either from the special advantage assured by the deliberation or of the measure established by the deliberation that intends to harm the company or the other shareholders) is suffered by the company or other shareholders.[89]

In addition, the intention to cause harm (*dolo*) may be either direct or merely eventual: it is sufficient that the shareholder foresees, as a possible consequence of exercising their voting right, the obtaining of a special advantage or the infliction of harm upon another shareholder or the company.[90]

The term *harm* (*prejuízo*) may be interpreted broadly and does not necessarily require an economic disadvantage. Accordingly, it can be argued that the repeated obstruction of decisions essential to the fulfillment of the company's purpose – such

[82] It is considered that abusive deliberations amount to deliberations where a shareholder pursues a certain interest, harming the shareholders' interest and without it amounting to the company's interest. *Olavo Cunha* (fn. 8) 731.

[83] Ibid 732.

[84] *Abreu*, in Abreu (ed.) Código das Sociedades Comerciais em Comentário – Artigos 1.º a 84.º, 2nd ed., 2017, vol. I, 715.

[85] Ibid 713.

[86] Considering that it does not and mentioning the debate, *Abreu* (fn. 85) 713. Menezes Cordeiro appears to argue that it suffices the purpose to harm the company or the shareholders, *Cordeiro*, Direito das Sociedades, 4th ed., Vol. I, 2020, 712.

[87] *Abreu* (fn. 85) 713–714.

[88] *Abreu* (fn. 85) 713.

[89] *Abreu* (fn. 85) 714.

[90] *Abreu* (fn. 85) 715.

as refusing to approve matters that would benefit the company – may satisfy this requirement. In cases of artificial deadlocks, the intent to cause harm must be established. Additionally, it must be demonstrated that the resolution would not have been approved by the other shareholder.

If such requirements are satisfied, it becomes possible to petition a judge for the annulment of the deliberation in judicial proceedings, provided the petition is filed within 30 days from the closing date of the general assembly. This remedy is available only if the shareholder did not cast a decisive vote that resulted in the approval or rejection of the deliberation. In scenarios where there are only two shareholders, it is logical to allow annulment where the deliberation failed to obtain approval.

Still from a strictly companies law perspective, one could even ponder whether this conduct could even result in the exclusion of a shareholder as per article 242, (1) of the Portuguese Companies Code[91], considering a case where the parties have not agreed, in the company bylaws, causes for exclusion, as admitted in article 242 of the Portuguese Companies Code.[92]

The requirements are (i) in the case of the shareholder, that a disloyal or severely disrupting of the functioning of the company exists and (ii) in what regards the company, that said conduct causes relevant, actual or potential damages to the company.[93]

There may be grounds to exclude the shareholder under the referenced article, considering that creating an artificial deadlock can severely disrupt the company's operations and cause significant damage.[94] Consider a scenario where all major corporate decisions are prevented by the shareholder, due to its negative vote, and no majority is possible in matters that are essential for the prosecution of the companies activities. This situation is specially severe in limited liability companies (*sociedades por quotas*) since several major decisions encompass the competence of the General Assembly[95] (in case there isn't a derogation by the shareholders in the company's by-

[91] This amounts to a judicial action that shareholders may proceed in the event that a shareholder with his unloyal or severely upsetting conduct to the company's function, may exclude him or where it may cause serous damages.

[92] *Cordeiro/Espírito Santo*, in Código das Sociedades Comerciais Anotado, 5th ed., 2022, 846.

[93] Ibid 849. See also, *Ferreira*, O direito de exclusão de sócio na sociedade anónima, 2009, 86–87.

[94] *Cunha*, in Abreu (ed.) Código das Sociedades Comerciais em Comentário, 3rd ed., Vol. III, 2023, 635.

[95] As demonstrated by article 246 of the Portuguese Companies Code, as follows: "1 – The following acts, in addition to others indicated by law or the articles of association, shall be subject to a shareholders' resolution:

a) The call for and return of supplementary contributions; b) The amortisation of shares, the acquisition, disposal and encumbrance of own shares and consent to the division or transfer of shares; c) The exclusion of members; d) The dismissal of managers and members of the supervisory body; e) The approval of the management report and accounts for the financial year, the allocation of profits and the treatment of losses, f) Exonerating managers or members of the supervisory body from liability; g) The bringing of actions by the company against managers, partners or members of the supervisory body, as well as the withdrawal and settlement of such actions; h) Amending the articles of association; i) The merger, demerger, transformation and dissolution of the company and the re-

laws) and it is possible to equate that in situations where an omission can represent a financial missed opportunity for the company (*v.* g., an immovable good at a below market price apt to pursue the company's activities) the company's lack of decision-making due to the conduct of one of its shareholder should be grounds to cause potential damages.

Another possible disturbance is the frequent use of the right to veto from one of the shareholders or the use of the special right of "double vote" (*voto duplo*).[96]

Hence, where a shareholder creates an artificial deadlock that is apt to fulfil said criteria, the procedure of excluding a shareholder under article 242 of the Portuguese Companies Code entails that: (i) there is a deliberation, (ii) a judicial proceeding is initiated, with the company's directors or designated representatives responsible for filing the legal action, (iii) and the share is acquired or there is a share amortization.[97]

Considering that in one of our possible hypotheses the company only has 2 shareholders, it should be pondered whether article 242 (2) of the Portuguese Companies Code, that imposes the need to conduct a deliberation prior to filing a judicial proceeding, still applies.

According to a first position, the necessity to deliberate would amount to an unnecessary formalism considering that the shareholder is prevented to vote, the will of the other would be sufficiently complied with by filing an action, and this is the only will that requires protection to the formation of the deliberation. Others consider that the deliberation should, nonetheless, be held, in light of the difference that exists between the deliberation and the filing of the action and considering that it should not be equated the will of the shareholder and the will of the company.[98]-[99]

---

turn to business of a dissolved company; 2 – If the articles of association do not provide otherwise, it is also up to the shareholders to decide on: a) The appointment of managers; b) The appointment of members of the supervisory body; c) The sale or encumbrance of immovable property, the sale, encumbrance and lease of premises; d) The subscription or acquisition of shares in other companies and their sale or encumbrance."

[96] As highlighted under German Law by *Höck* (fn. 15) 64–65. This is also a relevant statement under Portuguese Law given that it is possible to atribute special rights to shareholders in the company's bylwas under article 24 of the Portuguese Companies Code and it is accepted that one is the right to veto in the modification of the company's bylaws or the right to double vote. *Dias*, Os Direitos Especiais dos Sócios, 2015, 249–250.

[97] *Almeida*, Sociedades Comerciais, Valores Mobiliários, Instrumentos Financeiros e Mercados, Vol. I – As sociedades comerciais, 2022, 392–393.

[98] *Cunha*, in Problemas do Direito das Sociedades, 2002, 201, 204–205; Cunha, (fn. 95) 638–641. Following this reasoning, *Cordeiro/Espírito Santo* (fn. 99) 850.

[99] To add on the above, it should be mentioned that considering article 246, no. 1 (c) of the Portuguese Companies Code, it is mandatory to hold a deliberation in the general assembly on the exclusion of shareholders. In addition, under article 251, no. 1, (d) of the Portuguese Companies Code, the excluded shareholder is prevented from exercising its right to vote in this situation, because it is presumed by the law that a conflict of interests exists where a shareholder votes in a deliberation of its own exclusion. *Abreu*, in Abreu (ed.) Código das Sociedades Comerciais em Comentário, 3rd ed., Vol. IV, 2025, 74–75. Given that in a company with only 2 shareholders the exclusion of one of them, without judicial control, would depend on the others will, it is argued by some authors that a gap exists that should be filled with recourse with article 2 of the Portuguese Companies Code (that al-

We align with the second position, namely, since the legal personalities of the company and the shareholder are distinct. Thus, it is required that the General Assembly convene first, as mandated in such cases by Article 246, No. 1(c) of the Portuguese Companies Code. Only after this can the shareholder submit the matter to the court.

It should be highlighted that only where the multiple situations that give rise to a deadlock are created, an exclusion may be pondered, due to the stringent requirements imposed by the law to exclude a shareholder.

VII. Immediate consequences of validly triggering a Russian roulette clause under Portuguese Companies Law

Considering the applicability of Portuguese Law to a shareholder agreement, and in the event of its validity/lack of an abusive exercise of rights arising out of a Russian Roulette Clause, we will analyse the immediate consequences of triggering a Russian roulette clause.

We are of the view that the effects of shareholder agreements are merely *inter partes,* even where the ones that concluded the shareholder agreement are the total number of shareholders in the company, that is, when we are before an omnilateral agreement (which will be likely to occur, as above explained, to assure the efficiency of the Russian Roulette clause).[100] However, they have, if complied with, consequences that affect the company.

In what concerns article 229, no. 2 of the Portuguese Companies Code, the transfer of *quotas* doesn't need to be consented where it is transferred to another shareholder, and it should be communicated in writing to the company (228, no. 3 of the Portuguese Companies Code). Caution must nonetheless be had in relation to a scenario where one shareholder acquires the other's share and, due to that fact, only one remains a shareholder.

In that case, said shareholder has one year to find another party to acquire said share, or else the company can suffer an administrative dissolution as per article 142, no. 1, p. (a) of the Portuguese Companies Code.

Another possibility, under Article 270-A, no. 2 of the Portuguese Companies Code, is the creation of a one-person shareholder company. This option is voluntary, not mandatory. It may occur following the procedure outlined in Article 270-A, no. 3 of the Portuguese Companies Code.

---

lows recourse to the Portuguese Civil Code), dictating the application by analogy of article 1005, no. 3 of the Portuguese Civil Code that states that the exclusion may only occur with recourse to the court. *Cordeiro/Espírito Santo* (fn. 99) 849.

100 The issue is namely debated by *Frada*, in Estudos em homenagem ao Professor Doutor Carlos Ferreira de Almeida, 2011, 121; *Gomes* (fn. 41) 341–394. We adopt the arguments adopted by Perestrelo de Oliveira, that stands that only in very limited cases can good faith impose that the shareholder agreement has efficacy beyond the signing parties, *Oliveira* (fn. 2) 71–73.

When there is only one shareholder, they may alternatively choose to enter into contracts with multiple partners, pursuant to Article 270-D, No. 4 of the Portuguese Companies Code, instead of forming a one-person shareholder company.

VIII. Conclusions

In light of the above, we hereby present our conclusions concerning the stipulation of a Russian Roulette clause in a shareholder agreement under Portugues Law:

1. The triggering of a Russian Roulette clause (in one of its variants) results in the acquisition of all shares of one of the shareholders to the other or him selling them in the event of a deadlock.
2. A Russian roulette clause can raise ethical issues, however, under Portuguese Law, they cannot be deemed automatically invalid.
3. There are multiple ways to respond to an illicit act committed by a shareholder who has agreed to sign a Russian Roulette clause.
4. Beyond contract annulment, deliberation annulment, and exclusion of the wrongful shareholder, there are additional means to restore boundaries and impose consequences that go beyond addressing unethical behavior.
5. Ethics play a strong role in Portuguese civil law and even Companies Law, when the conduct of a shareholder is sufficiently harming to other shareholders but mostly to the company itself. The recourse to civil law in companies' law in what concerns shareholder agreements helps solve possible ethical issues in companies' law.

Voice, exit and sustainability: an EU perspective

Paulo Câmara

Abstract: This article discusses legislative responses to shareholder intervention in sustainability matters. We argue that while EU law framework on shareholder voice in sustainability is balanced and sufficient, EU takeover law responses are, in this respect, prone to criticism. The reasons for this criticism relate, on the one hand, on the disclosure needs from ESG-minded investors to ensure properly informed takeover-related divestment decisions. On the other hand, the need for TOD reform is also anchored on the possibility of takeovers leading to shifts in sustainability policies and corporate purpose statements of the target company. Furthermore, competing bids may lead to opposing sustainability plans from the competing bidders. Finally, as takeovers trigger a material impact on share prices, additional disclosures are required to ensure the efficiency and integrity of the markets. The proposed changes to the TOD would be minimal to favour better competition and therefore would not go against the objectives embodied in the current EU Competitiveness Compass approach.

Keywords: AGM, EU Shareholders Rights Directive, EU Takeover Directive, EU law, takeovers, ESG, sustainability preferences, disclosure duties, competing bids, market for corporate control, shareholder activism, shareholder proposals, shareholder voting rights.

I. Introduction

The current juncture marks a critical inflection point in the evolution of the European Union's regulatory framework for sustainability, leading to the need to analyse *legislative responses to shareholder intervention in sustainability matters*. The impetus for this reassessment stems from the Omnibus package,[1] which proposes targeted adjustments to the Taxonomy Regulation (2020),[2] the Corporate Sustainability Reporting Directive (CSRD: 2022),[3] and the Corporate Sustainability Due Diligence Directive (CSDDD: 2024).[4]

---

[1] *European Commission*, Proposal for a Directive amending Directives 2006/43/EC, 2013/34/EU, (EU) 2022/2464 and (EU) 2024/1760 as regards certain corporate sustainability reporting and due diligence requirements (2025).

[2] Regulation (EU) 2020/852 of the European Parliament and the Council of 18 June 2020.

[3] Directive (EU) 2022/2464 of the European Parliament and of the Council of 14 December 2022.

[4] Directive (EU) 2024/1760 of the European Parliament and of the Council of 13 June 2024.

This analysis differentiates between two principal modalities of shareholder response to corporate ESG conduct: the exercise of voting rights ("voice") and the divestment or transfer of shareholdings, particularly within the context of public takeovers ("exit"). These mechanisms encapsulate the foundational avenues through which shareholders express alignment or dissent with a company's sustainability trajectory, thereby functioning as critical levers in the broader architecture of ESG shareholder accountability.[5]

Regarding the exercise of voting rights, we will deal with the intersection between the EU Shareholder Rights Directive and the legislative interventions on ESG reporting (CSRD/ESRS) and sustainability due diligence (CSDDD). In terms of voting practices, both in the US and the EU, shareholder votes in ESG matters are becoming more frequent.

Takeovers are public offers targeted at shareholders whose degree of acceptance determines the success or unsuccess of the bid. Therefore, takeover regulation is intrinsically focused on ensuring informed decision-making by shareholders.

However, there are several motives that imply an adaptation to this paradigm and that brig relevance to ESG factors in the context of takeovers. On the one hand, the increasing number of ESG-driven investors[6] determines the importance, at least for those investors, of ESG commitments taken by the offeree and by the offeror.

Furthermore, M&A activity increasingly considers ESG risks in due diligence processes.[7] Moreover, takeovers have an impact on shares prices[8] which explains the relevance of material information for an efficient functioning of the market.

Finally, takeovers can lead to changes in the sustainability policies of the target companies, with (positive or negative) externalities caused for workers, the value chain, and the environment.[9] It is important to note that the current concept of stakeholder that stems from EU Law includes namely all the individuals or groups whose interests are affected or could be affected – positively or negatively – by the undertaking's activities and its direct and indirect business relationships across its value chain.[10]

These factors, taken together with the growing attention paid to corporate practices and investment and divestment[11] decisions as ways to contribute to the alignment

---

[5] See *Broccardo/Hart/Zingales*, Journal of Political Economy, volume 130, number 12, December 2022.

[6] *Barzuza/Curtis/Webber*, 93 Southern California Law Review 1243, 2020; *Hart/Zingales*, University of Chicago Business Law Review, Summer 2022, Vol.1, Issue 1 (2022) 197, 204–207; *Hirst/Kastiel/Kricheli-Katz*, 2023 Wisconsin Law Review 977, 2023.

[7] *Afsharipour*, University of Pennsylvania Journal of Business Law, Volume 26, Issue 4, 2024, available at SSRN 5017362.

[8] See namely *Pound/Zeckhauser*, The Journal of Business, Vol. 63, No. 3, 1990, 291–308; *Ordóñez-Calafí/Thanassoulis*, Journal of Corporate Finance, Volume 60, 2020.

[9] *Levitt/Bond*, European Corporate Governance Institute Working Paper 1011/2024.

[10] ESRS 1 § 22.

[11] *Becht/Pajust/Toniolo*, European Corporate Governance Institute – Finance Working Paper No. 900, 2023.

with Paris Agreement goals and other sustainability objectives forces us to rethink the legal framework of takeover bids and their articulation with the universe of investors with preferences for sustainable investments.

This article proceeds as follows. To adequately address the problem, we begin by examining EU law and voice practices in ESG topics (II.). We then turn to analyse the market for corporate control (III.), in articulation with new takeover dynamics that derive from the ESG context and with the growing relevance of shareholder sustainability preferences. This paves the way to discussing the need for reform (IV.). Finally, some concise proposals are presented regarding the revision of the TOD (V).

II. Voice

1. EU Law

Directive (EU) 2017/828 of the European Parliament and of the Council of 17 May 2017 – commonly referred to as the Shareholder Rights Directive II (SRD II) – amended Directive 2007/36/EC with the objective of enhancing long-term shareholder engagement and improving corporate governance in EU-listed companies. The Directive was adopted in response to concerns that shareholders, particularly institutional investors, were insufficiently involved in AGM voting decisions.[12]

SRD II introduced several key reforms aimed at strengthening shareholder rights and facilitating active participation at shareholder meetings. Intermediaries must ensure timely and accurate transmission of information between companies and shareholders, including voting forms and meeting notices.[13] Shareholders must receive confirmation that their votes have been validly recorded and counted.[14] Intermediaries are also obliged to facilitate the exercise of shareholder rights, whether directly or through authorized representatives.[15] This includes enabling electronic voting and ensuring cross-border shareholders can participate effectively. Finally, institutional investors and asset managers must publicly disclose their shareholder engagement policies and report annually on their implementation.[16] This includes how they monitor investee companies, exercise voting rights, and manage conflicts of interest.[17]

---

[12] *Böckli et al.*, SSRN 2568741, 2015; *Zetzsche*, Journal of Corporate Law Studies, 17(2), 2017, 379–414.

[13] Article 3b of Directive (EU) 2017/828 of the European Parliament and of the Council of 17 May 2017.

[14] Article 3c/2 of Directive (EU) 2017/828 of the European Parliament and of the Council of 17 May 2017.

[15] Article 3c of Directive (EU) 2017/828 of the European Parliament and of the Council of 17 May 2017.

[16] Article 3g of Directive (EU) 2017/828 of the European Parliament and of the Council of 17 May 2017.

[17] *Ringe*, ECGI WP 501/2020; *Siems*, European Business Organization Law Review (EBOR), Vol. 6, pp. 539–552, 2005.

The Directive has had a positive impact on facilitating the active exercise of voting rights in the EU. On the one hand, by mandating shareholder identification and the transmission of voting materials, SRD II has reduced barriers to participation, particularly for cross-border and minority shareholders. On the other hand, SRD II has institutionalized shareholder engagement, encouraging long-term investment strategies and more informed voting behavior.[18]

As we have seen, SRD II was adopted with the explicit aim of strengthening shareholder engagement in EU-listed companies. By contrast, the Corporate Sustainability Reporting Directive (CSRD) – supplemented through the European Sustainability Reporting Standards (ESRS) – does not contain provisions that directly refer to shareholder intervention or engagement. Its primary objective is to improve the quality and comparability of sustainability-related disclosures by companies.

Along other stakeholders, shareholders are recipients of sustainability information. Moreover, annual sustainability report implies that shareholders and stakeholders will access much more granular information on sustainability matters.

The CSRD adopts a double materiality framework, requiring companies to report both on how sustainability matters affect their financial performance and how their activities impact society and the environment.[19] However, it does not assign a role to shareholders in shaping or reviewing these disclosures. Namely, the double materiality assessment required under the European sustainability reporting framework constitutes a board-led evaluative function, with no formal mechanism for shareholder involvement. Given the extensive array of sustainability-related data points mandated by the European Sustainability Reporting Standards (ESRS) – including metrics spanning environmental, social, and governance domains – the process of determining material impacts and risks is inherently managerial in nature. As a result, the authority to define, assess, and disclose such data points resides squarely within the powers of the company's board.

The European Union's Corporate Sustainability Due Diligence Directive (CSDDD), adopted in 2024, introduces a new framework of corporate responsibility for sustainability matters, including explicit obligations in relation to climate governance. A central provision is the requirement that companies within scope must adopt and implement a climate transition plan that aligns with the temperature objectives of the Paris Agreement, notably the 1.5°C target.[20] The plan must identify concrete emission reduction targets for 2030 and beyond, disclose Scope 1, 2, and (where relevant) Scope 3 greenhouse gas emissions, and articulate key operational and financial measures to achieve decarbonisation objectives over time.

Unlike shareholder-driven initiatives such as "Say on Climate" votes – where investors request advisory votes on climate strategies – the CSDDD does not mandate

[18] *Câmara*, Governação Societária e Propósito, 2025, 480–481; *Ferran*, European Business Organization Law Review (EBOR), Volume 23, 507–539, 2022.

[19] *Câmara*, Governação Societária e Propósito, 2025, 405, 428, 470, 530.

[20] Article 15 CSDDD.

that companies submit their transition plans to shareholders for approval at the AGM.

2. The divergence in 'say on sustainability' practices

At global level, there has been a widespread development of voting proposals within the framework of ESG matters. The picture, however, is different if we compare Europe and the US.

In the US, shareholder proposals in sustainability matters are mostly advisory, contrary to the EU, where they are commonly binding.[21]

Until 2024, there has been a clear trend of increase of AGM decisions in ESG matters.[22] In the U.S., shareholder proposals are a combination of pro-ESG filings and anti-ESG proposals. Asset managers once heralded for championing ESG principles – BlackRock, Vanguard, State Street – have pulled back, with alleged concerns over politicization of ESG activism. Moreover, pro-ESG proposals usually receive a low level of support: in the US, the median support level of all shareholder proposal was at 20.6 % for 2024.[23] Social proposals on DEI remains contentious in the U.S., and following the election of Donald Trump, proposals to push-back diversity policies are on the rise. Lastly, shareholder proposals in ESG generally do not involve changes in by-laws.[24]

On the contrary, in Europe, climate shareholder proposals remain at stable moderate levels and are better received by institutional investors.[25]

3. The Case Against Further Regulatory Intervention

As shareholder activism relating to ESG concerns becomes increasingly visible across global capital markets, there is an inevitable debate over whether regulatory mechanisms should be introduced to mandate or incentivize investor engagement. While such proposals may stem from legitimate concerns regarding corporate sustainability, a prescriptive legal framework mandating specific forms or degrees of shareholder activism warrants cautious scrutiny.

---

[21] *Cools*, Climate Proposals: ESG Shareholder Activism Sidestepping Board Authority, in Kuntz ed., Research Handbook on Environmental, Social, and Corporate Governance (2023); *Square Well Partners*, Global Review of Shareholder ESG Proposals: 2022–2023.

[22] *Broccardo/Hart/Zingales*, Journal of Political Economy, volume 130, number 12, December 2022; *Runyon*, New ESG developments in 2024 proxy season suggest changes in shareholder engagement, Thomson Reuters Institute, (20 Aug 2024); *Square Well Partners* (fn. 21).

[23] *Mishra*, Harvard Law School Forum on Corporate Governance (June 3, 2024).

[24] *Fisch/Robertson*, Shareholder Proposals and the Debate over Sustainability Disclosure, in Enriques/ Strampelli (eds.), Board-Shareholder Dialogue: Policy Debate, Legal Constraints and Best Practices, 2023.

[25] *FTI*, Shareholder activism on ESG matters: the 2023 proxy season experience, (June 26, 2023); *Johnson*, ESG Dive (Feb. 5, 2025).

The diversity of corporate governance cultures, ownership structures, and investment behaviors – particularly between the US and the EU – renders uniform regulatory intervention both impractical and potentially counterproductive. The EU's regulatory framework already facilitates stewardship through mechanisms such as the Shareholder Rights Directive II (Directive (EU) 2017/828), which promotes long-term shareholder engagement without prescribing activist behavior.[26]

Mandating shareholder activism across these divergent contexts may trigger several unintended consequences. First, such intervention could erode the authenticity of investor engagement by reducing it to a box-ticking exercise, devoid of strategic intent. Second, smaller shareholders may face disproportionate compliance burdens, particularly in jurisdictions where market access and corporate disclosure are already constrained.[27] Third, compulsory activism risks politicizing ESG discourse within corporate governance, shifting the focus from nuanced fiduciary deliberation to ideologically driven mandates.[28]

Rather than prescribing shareholder participation, regulators should focus on strengthening the procedural and structural conditions that enable meaningful engagement. This includes promoting transparency in voting behavior, facilitating access to proposal mechanisms, and improving ESG-related disclosure standards. Such measures are more likely to preserve the autonomy of investors and the contextual responsiveness of activism.

In conclusion, the strategic value of ESG-related shareholder activism resides in its voluntary, investor-led nature. It should be regarded as a dynamic governance practice – one that evolves through market dialogue, stakeholder pressure, and fiduciary discretion. Accordingly, EU legal intervention ought to aim at enabling such practices, as it presently does, not legislating their content or frequency.

III. Exit: The market for corporate control revisited

From the standpoint of the economic rationale of takeovers, the starting point for analysing the articulation between sustainability and the market for corporate control lies in pointing out the initial treatment of the disciplinary function of the corporate control market as set out by Henry Manne. In his seminal article on the subject, dated 1965, the author pointed out that the role of this market would depend, in the first place, on the positive correlation between management efficiency and the evolution of market prices – if management proves to be less efficient, the market will be tempted to penalise the value of the shares, causing their price to fall.[29] The win-

---

[26] See II 2 above.

[27] *Square Well Partners* (fn. 21).

[28] *Morningstar Sustainalytics*, Investor Voting Behavior on ESG Resolutions, ESG Dive, 2024.

[29] *Manne*, Mergers and the Market for Corporate Control, (1965) 112; Id., La posizione dell'azionista nel diritto delle società americano, (1965), 491.

dow of opportunity opened by such a price drop would be decisive, as it would make it more attractive for those hoping to run the company more efficiently to launch a takeover bid.[30] In addition, the market for corporate control would overcome the difficulty of court evaluation of the performance of company management, as well as the application of the *business judgement rule*, thereby increasing investor protection.

Manne recognised five fundamental benefits derived from market for corporate control: the reduction of heavy bankruptcy proceedings; the improvement of management efficiency; the intensification of protection for non-controlling investors; the increase in capital mobility; and the increase in efficiency in the distribution of resources.[31] The protection of workers and other *stakeholders* in the context of the bidding market is left out of this catalogue.[32]

It is worth examining this classical presentation of the market for corporate control[33] under three angles related to sustainability, that we will address below: a) relevance of price share movements; b) shareholder protection attached to the market for corporate control; and c) takeovers' relevance for stakeholders.

1. *Relevance of price share movements*

According to Henry Manne's approach to the subject, the disciplinary function of takeover bids is inextricably linked to share prices' movements. The better the company's performance, the higher the share price tends to be and, consequently, the more remote the possibility of a hostile takeover. This idea does not lead necessary to a strictly financial perspective on the mechanics of takeovers. The external pressure on the performance of listed companies can also be determined by environmental, social or governance factors. In these companies, as we know, unsatisfactory business results tend to lead investors to sell their holdings, which in turn leads to a fall in share prices on the market, due to the decrease in demand for securities (*Wall Street rule).* The devaluation of shares can namely be caused by events relating to environmental and social sustainability, which have a growing influence on share prices. This erodes stock prices and favours the emergence of hostile takeovers. This is why *takeover bids* can also play a *disciplinary role in* these matters.[34]

---

[30] *Manne* (fn. 29), 112–113.

[31] *Manne* (fn. 29), 119. In other works, the author would reveal himself to be ostentatiously critical of corporate social responsibility. See. namely *Manne*, Review of Richard Eeells, Corporation giving in a free society, (1956), 195–203; Id., Corporate responsibility, motivation, and reality, in Collected Works of Henry Manne (2009; original article is from 1962), 125–138.

[32] *Weiss*, Der angemessene Handlungsrahmen der Zielverwaltung in der Übernahmesituation (2009), 26–27.

[33] For other aspects of evolution of the market for corporate control, see *Roth/Hopt/Opalski*, Basic Issues Surrounding the TOD's Transposition, ECGI WP n. 794/2024

[34] See namely *Coffee* Jr, 84 Colum. L. Rev. 1145, 1984; *Dyck/Zingales*, Journal of Finance, Volume 59, Issue2, April 2004, 537–600 ; *Zingales*, Costs and Benefits of Financial Market Regulation, 2004, 14–16, 38–39.; *Baghat/Romano*, Empirical Studies of Corporate Law, 2005, 18–89; *Burkart*, Economics of Takeover Regulation, Stockholm, 1996; *Easterbrook/Fischel*, 36 Business Lawyer, 1981, 1733–

More importantly, with the generalised disclosure of information on sustainability commitments from large companies, under the CSRD/ESRS, this will influence the market for corporate control and the dynamics of M&A in general and takeover bids.[35] When calculating the value of the offer price, the offeror will usually consider social and environmental risks that could affect the value of the offeree company. In addition, the market price is also affected by the labour environment and environmental constraints: the permeability to hostile bids may therefore be related to options or omissions on issues relating to the offeree company's commitments (or lack thereof) regarding ESG.

2. Shareholder protection attached to the market for corporate control

In respect to shareholder protection, Henry Manne famously asserted that "the market for corporate control gives power and protection to shareholder commensurate with their interest in corporate affairs".[36] Our viewpoint is that in the current market landscape claims an adaptation in takeover laws to ensure shareholder power and protection.

It should be noted that shareholders with sustainability preferences may show different behaviours, preferring to hold their shares (i. e. to reject the offer) if they are satisfied with the social or environmental performance of the offeree company or the positive evolution it has registered. They may also decide to reject the offer because the offeror has in mind sustainability commitments which are contrasting with those in force at the target company.

On the side of the shareholders as recipients of the offer, the decision to sell in a takeover bid can also be motivated as an instrument to remove assets at risk of devaluation for environmental or social reasons (*brown assets*) from their *portfolio.* Such a transfer, however, does not reduce the overall environmental impact of the assets transferred to third parties.[37]

1750; Id, 91 Yale Law Journal, 1981, 698–737; *Jensen/Meckling*, Journal of Financial Economics, October, 1976, V. 3, No. 4, 305–360; *Rubak/ Jensen*, Journal of Financial Economics, Vol. 11, Issues 1–4, 1983, 5–50. Critical views of the disciplining effect centre on the less positive long-term evaluation of integration, can be found in *Franks/Mayer*, Hostile takeovers and the correction of managerial failure, 1996, 163–181; *Sjåfjell*, Yearbook of European Law, Volume 27, Issue 1, 2008, 387–398.

[35] *Fernandes*, Climate Finance, 2023, 199–205; *Gartenberg/ Yiu*, Corporate Purpose and Acquisitions, 2021; *Afsharipour*, ESG and Board-Shareholder Engagement in M&A, 2023, 5–21; on the US experience, *Petrucci/Subramanian*, Pills in a World of Activism and ESG, 2022, 5–8.

[36] *Manne* (fn. 29), 112.

[37] *Dirty assets are just shifted from one firm to another*, as *Armour/Enriques/ Wetzer* point out in Dark and Dirty Assets. It is also worth mentioning studies which show that the sale of polluting assets to companies with a closed shareholder structure or in low-regulation environments leads to an *increase* in GHG emissions. See also *Zhou*, The Curse of Green Shareholder Oversight: Evidence from Emission Spillover of Divested Plants, 2022.

Conversely, if the execution of sustainability policies generates disappointing financial results that may open the door to a decrease in the share price and the vulnerability of a hostile takeover bid.[38]

Finally, competing bids may confront different sustainability policies and corporate purpose plans that offerors have in mind for the target company. In these cases, shareholders will be having the opportunity to choose between several bidders and their choice may be motivated by the sustainability of their respective projects.

3. Takeovers' relevance for stakeholders

Finally, it is important to retain that, structurally, takeover bids are presented as offers aimed at holders of shares or other securities issued by the offeree company: they are presented by a potential or actual shareholder (the offeror) to the offeree company's shareholder universe (the addressees of the offer).[39] This has traditionally led to takeover bids being seen as operations in which only the interests of the shareholders are relevant, who are ultimately responsible for the success or failure of the bid.[40]

This traditional position regarding the exclusive implications of the bid for shareholders should be re-examined, at least in partial terms. On the one hand, it is known that takeover bids can have significant effects on employment, and there is a high percentage of bids which, to take advantage of synergies between the offeror and the offeree, culminate in the sale of significant parts of the offeree and the elimination of jobs.[41]

On the other hand, remuneration policies in listed companies increasingly include forms of share allotment, which is why we can typically find a portion of shares held by employees. The fact is that a high concentration of shareholdings in the hands of employees could reduce the chances of success of unsolicited offers.[42]

Similarly, takeovers can lead to changes in climate and corporate governance policies of the target company. There has been an influx of takeover bids on the market with important social or environmental objectives, motivated by the offerors seeking

---

[38] *Gilson*, Corporate Governance versus Real Governance, 2022, 10.

[39] *Câmara*, Manual de Direito dos Valores Mobiliários⁴, 2018, 671; *Ventura*, Estudos Vários sobre Sociedades Anónimas, 1992, 118–122.

[40] In this regard, *Easterbrook / Fischel*, The Economic Structure of Corporate Law, 208; *John Teall*, Governance and the market for corporate control, 2007, 8–11.

[41] It should be noted that the empirical balance depends on the market considered. On the one hand, *Kershaw*, Principles of Takeover Regulation, 2016, 12–14, refers to a mixed empirical assessment in the British context, which prevents generalised statements about the negative labour effects of *takeover* bids (much more sceptical in this respect: *Mayer*, Firm Commitment, 2013, 98–99. In the US, the picture is usually more penalising for workers. Among many: *Bebchuk et al*, Stakeholder Capitalism in the Time of COVID: Appendix, 2022; Id., How Twitter Pushed its Stakeholders under the (Musk) Bus, 2023; *Schleifer/Summers*, Breach of Trust in Hostile Takeovers, 1988, 41–53; Lipton/Rosenblum, A New System of Corporate Governance, 1991, 214.

[42] For example, when BNP Paribas launched its bid for Société Génerale in 1999, the participation of the company's employees was decisive in the failure of the takeover bid.

to bring about changes in the social and environmental policies of the offeree companies. One example is the bid presented in 2022 by Brookfield and Atlassian (led by activist Mike Cannon-Brookes) for the Australian company AGL, whose business is based on coal-fired power stations, which Atlassian wanted to close.[43]

In this context, the decision to sell in a takeover bid may seek to express a reaction of dissatisfaction with the offeror's ESG options. This last case can be illustrated with Heinz's failed bid for Unilever's share capital in 2017: the offeree company's strong ties to its employees and the community, its culture focused on the long term and its environmental commitments were decisive reasons for the failure of Heinz's bid.[44]

In sum, takeovers may impact severely the target's sustainability commitments and they may also lead to shifts in sustainability policies and corporate purpose statements of the target company.

IV. The need for a sustainability-driven EU takeover law

The influential Pennington Report (1974) – which laid out the foundations for the TOD – included a chapter on protection of employees of the offeree company but no significant reference was made to other stakeholders.[45] Therefore, unsurprisingly, the Takeover Bids Directive also adopted the sole-stakeholder paradigm as it only refers to workers of the target company as relevant stakeholders.

The concerns expressed about the protection of *workers* was one of the reasons for the delay in approving the text of the European Takeover Bids Directive.[46] The final text, approved after fifteen years of debate,[47] would namely force the offeror to provide information to the employees of the offeree company and to disclose its intentions regarding the impact of the bid on employment conditions, as discussed below.[48] In addition, the Directive clearly states that member states must ensure that the board of the offeree company acts, pending the takeover bid, *in the interests of the company as a whole.*[49] The TOD, however, does not prevent more demanding rules on stakeholder protection from being adopted by Member States.[50]

---

[43] *Morton el al*, AGL rejects takeover bid by Mike Cannon-Brookes, Guardian, 20-Feb.-2022; Fernyhough, Mike Cannon-Brookes: Australia's first green corporate raider, FT, 14-May-2022.

[44] *Polman/Winston*, Net Positive, 2021, 1–6.

[45] *Pennington*, Report on Takeover and Other Bids, 1974, 84–86.

[46] Directive 2004/25/EC of the European Parliament and of the Council of 21 April 2004 on takeover bids.

[47] On this development, see *Ari Savela*, Hostile takeovers and directors, 2000, 315–345.

[48] Art. 3(1)(b) and 6(1–3), 8(2) and 9(5) Directive 2004/25/EC of the European Parliament and of the Council of 21 April 2004.

[49] Article 3(1)(c) Directive 2004/25/EC. The other language versions are convergent ("dans l'intérêt de la société dans son ensemble"; "im Interesse der gesamten Gesellschaft "; "nell'interesse della società nel suo insieme"). On this provision, see *Clarke*, The role of employees in the Takeover Bids Directive, 2016, 41–45.

[50] *Grundmann*, Europäisches Gesellschaftsrecht, 2004, 447.

It is important to understand how EU takeover law falls short of responding to these new concerns regarding stakeholder interests[51] in the context of takeover bids.

The TOD rules governing the offeree's report do not attach any implication to the corporate purpose or to the sustainability policies of the target company. Through this report, the board of directors of the offeree company must comment on the repercussions of the bid on the interests of the offeree company in general and, in particular, on the interests of its employees and their working conditions and on the places where the company carries out its activity.[52]

In this context, it should be recognised that the target's purpose statements, and sustainability policies presents itself as a necessary basis for discussion in the board report – particularly when the offeror company has an adverse position in relation to nature or ambition of the offeree company's environmental or social commitments.[53]

The essence of the current rules is anchored in the disclosure duties in the takeover documents.[54] It should be noted that the TOD includes various features that emphasise the position of employees. In fact, the offeror's document must include information on the offeror's intentions regarding the continuity or modification of the business activity of the offeree company, of the offeror, insofar as it is affected by the bid, and, in the same terms, by companies with which they are in a controlling or group relationship, regarding the maintenance and conditions of employment of the employees and managers of the aforementioned entities, namely any repercussions on the locations where the activities are carried out and regarding the maintenance of trading on a regulated market in the securities that are the subject of the bid.[55]

The offeror must also inform its employees' representatives or, failing that, the employees of the content of the offer documents as soon as they are made public.[56] This duty of information does not involve discussion or consultation with the workers or their representatives but does not exclude the labour duties that apply in this area.[57] No involvement with other stakeholders is mandated, namely in relation to climate-related organisations.

Finally, the Directive entails a procedural possibility of obtaining a reaction from employees to the offer.[58] If, before the start of the offer, the management body receives

---

[51] See also *Sjåfjell/Anker-Sørensen*, The Duties of the Board and Corporate Social Responsibility (CSR), 2017, 39–40.

[52] Art. 9/5 TOD.

[53] *Conac*, Rivista Orizzonti del Diritto Commerciale, n.º 3, 2019, 507 (considering that the PACTE law extends the defensive space of the target); *Forrest Alogna*, Les Echos, August 2018, 5 (dismissing the idea that the purpose functions, in itself, as a defensive measure); *Colin Mayer*, What is Wrong with Corporate Law?, 2022, 9.

[54] *Giesberts*, Anot. § 4, Kölner Kommentar zum WpÜG, (2003), 223.

[55] Art. 6/3 i) TOD.

[56] Art. 8/2 TOD.

[57] Similarly, in the German legal system: *Hirte*, annot. § 10 WpÜG, Kölner Kommentar zum WpÜG, 303.

[58] The law does not establish a right for employees to have their say in the event of a revised offer, which conveys the idea that the right to have their say only applies to the initial project. In any case,

an opinion from the workers, directly or through their representatives, on the repercussions of the offer on employment, it must disclose it as an annex to the report it has drawn up.[59] It should be noted that this is not a duty to issue a comment. There is not even a minimum content to be observed regarding the workers' comments.[60] However, the law does not provide the same possibility for other interested parties to react, such as suppliers, or representatives of the community in which the offeree company operates.

As mentioned above, even if the employees abstain to comment on the bid, the management report of the offeree company must refer to the repercussions of the bid on the interests of its employees and their working conditions and on the places where the company carries out its activity.[61] In fact, the Directive requires the report to comment on the repercussions of the bid on the interests of the offeree company[62] (*on all the company's interests,* in the terminology of the Directive)[63], which provides a basis for understanding that the report should include an analysis of the implications of the bid on other *stakeholders, in* addition to employees, if this proves relevant. However, this should be expressly clarified in the text of the Directive.

V. Proposed changes to the TOD

Based on the precedent analysis, we specifically identify points of the Directive that should be reviewed and changed. The TOD's response to these issues is incomplete in three critical topics, as explained below.

---

a distinction must be made. If substantial aspects of the offeror's project are revised, the right to a new hearing should be recognised. On the other hand, simple revisions of the consideration are only relevant to the shareholders and not to the *stakeholders, and* therefore do not provide the possibility of a new statement by the labour group. *Hirte*, Kölner Kommentar zum WpÜG, 749, in an apparently more open direction, without making the distinction advocated in the light of § 27 *WpÜG*; and *Roh*, annot. § 27, Frankfurter Kommentar zum WpÜG³, 2008, 527.

59 Art. 9/5 TOD. The Directive does not set out the effects of late submission. Under German law, it is considered that the duty to publish remains, in honour of the interests of transparency at stake, even if it refers to a document submitted after the deadline (thus *Hirte*, annot. § 27 WpÜG, Kölner Kommentar zum WpÜG, 747; supporting autonomous disclosure on the internet: *Roh*, anot. § 27, Frankfurter Kommentar zum WpÜG³, 2008, 527; apparently against, *Kubalek,* Die Stellungnahme der Zielgesellschaft Zu öffentlichen Angeboten Nach Dem WpÜG, 2011, 102.

60 On the compensation of damages that the employees' report can cause, under German law: *Weishaupt*, Schadensersatzansprüche der Wertpapierinhaber der Zielgesellschaft im Falle einer fehlerhaften Stellungnahme nach § 27 WpÜG, 2007, 220–224.

61 Kubalek's view is different, as under German law he sees the defendant's report as a document devoid of any concern for the protection of *stakeholders* (fn. 59) 100–103.

62 Art. 9/5 TOD.

63 Recital 17 and Article 9/5 of Directive 2004/25/EC.

1. *Extending the content of takeover offeror's disclosures*

The current EU takeover regime reveals an exclusive focus on workers as the sole type of relevant *stakeholders*. The Takeover Directive refers 26 times to employees, and makes no mention of supply chain companies, the environment, or the target company's relevant community.[64] Any indication of the effects of the takeover on the environmental and social sustainability (in the extra-labour field) of the offer is omitted. The most significant omission from the information regime in force concerns the offeror's plans in terms of environmental policy and sustainability in broader terms.

As we have pointed out, the market for corporate control is increasingly integrated by operations to transfer assets for social environmental reasons (*brown spinning* or *green spinning*). This has two alternative effects: in ESG-minded offeree companies with a high sense of corporate purpose, takeovers makes it possible for shareholders to share the sustainability premium (aka *greenium*); alternatively, takeovers may operate as offers to the acquisition, promoted by activists, of companies with no or little ambition in terms of sustainable action, in order to reinforce the degree of their commitments in terms of sustainability.

It is worth noting that the duty to collect and take into account the sustainability preferences of investors – which is dealt with in the European portfolio management and investor advice MiFID II regime in the context of the duties of suitability[65] – is not applicable in the context of the takeover bid regime. On receiving an order to accept a takeover bid, the financial intermediary is limited, in the most common cases,[66] to execute the order, and is not responsible for assessing whether the order meets the sustainability preferences of the client. From a regulatory point of view, it would be far more complex and disruptive to change the current MiFID II system of financial intermediation duties than to simply expand the information to be included in the content of takeover bid documents.

For this reason, the information in the offeror's project should be extended to clarify whether the offeror intends to maintain or change the sustainability policies and the corporate purpose statements, and in which direction.[67] Currently, the information only covers "the offeror's intentions with regard to the continuity or modifica-

[64] It should be noted that the offeror's strategic plans must describe the possible repercussions on the places where the companies operate, which ultimately relates to the implications of the bid for the community (art. 6/3 i) TOD). see *Sjåfjell*, in European Company Law In Accelerated Progress, (Steef M. Bartman, ed.), Alphen aan den Rijn, Kluwer Law International, 2006.

[65] Commission Delegated Regulation (EU) 2021/1253 amending Delegated Regulation (EU) 2017/565.

[66] The service of executing and transmitting orders requires an analysis of the client's knowledge and experience, as the most basic component of the duty of suitability. However, the order to accept a takeover bid is in principle subject to the derogation from this duty (*execution-only*) set out in art. 25/4 MiFID II, as the requirements set out in this rule are usually met (client initiative; shares listed on a regulated market; absence of a conflict of interest on the part of the intermediary; prior warning issued by the intermediary). See in general *Câmara* (fn. 39), 447–448.

[67] In the same vein, albeit on a generic level: *Sjåfjell* (fn. 64) 37–38.

tion of the business activity of the offeree company, of the offeror, to the extent that it is affected by the bid, and, under the same terms, by companies with which they are in a controlling or group relationship, with regard to the maintenance and conditions of employment of the workers and managers of the entities referred to, in particular any repercussions on the locations where the activities are carried out and with regard to the maintenance of trading on a regulated market in the securities that are the subject of the bid". Aspects to be included in the offeror's documents should include information on policies, objectives, and targets to manage material sustainability matters, confirmation or revision of climate transition plans and other significant aspects relating to the execution of the corporate purpose and sustainability objectives.

2. Extending the content of the target's board report

In a future legislative amendment, the report of the company in question should be extended in the same way.[68] Regarding ESG issues, it would be important for this report to go beyond the interests of its employees in their working conditions and in the places where the company operates. It would be relevant that this board report would also analyse the offeror's project in terms of the corporate purpose and environmental sustainability of the target company, in similar terms to what is proposed for the offeror's documents.

3. Enabling other stakeholders' reactions to the bid

Finally, it would be justified to improve the regime of *stakeholder* reaction during the pendency of the bid, which is currently limited to the labour component. Regarding the repercussions of the bid, a possibility (rather than a duty) could be established for bondholders, consumer associations and environmental organisations with specific (e.g. geographical) links to the offeree company to issue comments within the same time frame as comments from employee representatives.

Our proposal is to maintain the approach of the Directive regarding timing in the sense that other stakeholders' reaction would only be appended to the report where the board of the offeree company receives in good time such separate opinion. Therefore, this proposal would not slow down the bid process but would allow relevant comments to be submitted for an overall consideration of the implications of the bid, while also providing reports from the offeree with a more integrated and complete perspective. A future broadening of the *stakeholders* eligible for consideration of the offer would prove useful for a more informed decision on the part of the shareholders as recipients of the offer.

[68] On the content and function of this report, see *Câmara* (fn. 39), 683–687.

VI. Conclusion

Following our analysis to EU legislative responses to shareholder intervention in sustainability matters, we conclude that while EU law framework on shareholder voice in sustainability is balanced and sufficient, EU takeover law responses are, in this respect, prone to criticism. The reasons for this criticism relate, on the one hand, on the disclosure needs from ESG-minded investors to ensure properly informed takeover-related divestment decisions. On the other hand, the need for TOD reform is also anchored on the possibility of takeovers leading to shifts in sustainability policies and corporate purpose statements of the target company. Furthermore, competing bids may lead to opposing sustainability plans from the competing bidders. Finally, as takeovers trigger a material impact on share prices,[69] additional disclosures are required to ensure the efficiency and integrity of the markets.

We are conscious that, at this juncture, regulatory burden in the EU has reached a peak of complexity we concur with the views namely expressed in the Draghi Report (2024) and the EU Competitiveness Compass (2025) (which are underlying the Omnibus package proposals) according to which a simplification of the EU regulatory framework is much needed as a condition for competitiveness of the EU economy.[70]

The proposed changes to the TOD would be minimal to favour better competition and therefore would not go against the objectives embodied in the current EU Competitiveness Compass and Omnibus approach.

[69] *Pound/Zeckhauser*, The Journal of Business, Vol. 63, No. 3, 1990, 291–308; *Ordóñez-Calafí/Thanassoulis*, Journal of Corporate Finance, Volume 60, 2020.

[70] *Draghi*, The future of European competitiveness Part B | In-depth analysis and recommendations, 2024, 317–322; *European Commission*, A Competitiveness Compass for the EU, 2025; Id. Proposal for a Directive amending Directives 2006/43/EC, 2013/34/EU, (EU) 2022/2464 and (EU) 2024/1760 as regards certain corporate sustainability reporting and due diligence requirements, 2025.

Breach of Shareholders Agreements

Catarina Monteiro Pires

Abstract: This paper examines the breach and termination of shareholders' agreements under Portuguese law, with particular attention to the legal remedies available. It further explores the implications of termination in multilateral agreements, the boundaries of contractual autonomy as defined by Article 809 of the Portuguese Civil Code, and the function of call options within the framework of shareholder agreements.

I. Introduction

This paper ponders a particularly nuanced issue: the application of the law of obligations to commercial contracts. Although it is widely recognized that commercial contracts are distinct from civil contracts, this distinction warrants a more in-depth analysis as to its consequences.

Since the Commercial Companies Code (CSC) came into effect on November 1, 1986, Portuguese law has expressly acknowledged the validity of shareholders' agreements.[1] Under Portuguese law, shareholders' agreements are recognized as typical legal transactions, with a legal basis in Article 17 of the Portuguese Companies Code (CSC).[2] Article 17(1) of the Portuguese CSC provides that shareholders' agreements are those entered into between several shareholders or all shareholders, provided they act in that capacity.[3] The term "shareholders' agreement" refers to a legal transaction entered into between shareholders of a company, which may or may not in-

[1] *Ventura*, in Estudos Vários sobre Sociedades Anónimas, Almedina, 1992, 123ff., *Trigo*, Os Acordos Parassociais sobre o Exercício do Direito de Voto, 1998 and also *Trigo*, in Problemas do Direito das Sociedades, Almedina, 2002, 169–184, *Leal*, RDS 2009, 135ff., *Câmara*, in Saldanha Sanches (ed.), Estudos em memória do Prof. Doutor J. L. Saldanha Sanches, vol. II, 2011, 813 Coutinho de Abreu, Curso de Direito Comercial, vol. II, 8th ed., 2024, 159f., et seq, *Engrácia Antunes*, RDS 25 (2021), 13; *Perestrelo de Oliveira*, Acordos parassociais, 2025.

[2] In accordance with Article 17, paragraph 1, of the CSC: "[s]hareholder agreements made between all or some shareholders, in which they, as shareholders, commit to conduct not prohibited by law, are effective among the participants, but based on them, actions of the company or shareholders towards the company cannot be contested.".

[3] Other significant provisions include (1) Article 19 of the Securities Code for publicly traded companies.

volve all shareholders.[4] Mere concerted action is not sufficient to establish a shareholders' agreement.[5]

Shareholders agreements are commercial contracts (Article 17 of the Companies Code) and, as such, are primarily governed by the provisions of the Commercial Code. Article 3 of the Commercial Code determines the following: "if questions regarding commercial rights and obligations cannot be resolved either by the text of commercial law, its spirit, or by analogous cases provided for therein, they shall be decided according to civil law". This legal provision implies that the Civil Code is applicable only in situations where there is a gap in commercial law, and even then, only if that gap cannot be addressed by recourse to the principles or provisions inherent to commercial law itself. In other words, the Civil Code is applicable to commercial matters solely in instances where there is an absence of specific provisions within the commercial law itself, and only if such absence cannot be addressed within the framework of commercial law.[6] Furthermore, when the Civil Code is applied in such cases, its provisions must not conflict with the principles governing commercial transactions, as any such conflict would result in inconsistency.

Shareholders' agreements are also typically the result of negotiation between the parties and, as such, do not fall within the scope of the regime governing general contractual clauses established by DL no. 446/85, pursuant to Article 1. This is because the law on general contractual clauses is intended to apply to standard form contracts, not to individually negotiated agreement.

Shareholders' agreements may set out a variety of obligations concerning the transferability of shares (such as temporary lock-up periods or requirements relating to pre-emption rights) as well as provisions governing voting rights and various aspects of corporate organization. These may include the composition of corporate bodies (for example, the allocation of seats on boards of directors), non-compete undertakings, and obligations to approve capital increases, among other matters.

Shareholders' agreements are frequently supplemented with other specific arrangements to secure the performance of obligations such as the appointment of a proxy to exercise voting rights, penalty clauses, the establishment of escrow accounts, termination clauses and call or put options in favour of non-defaulting shareholders.[7]

---

[4] One may question whether, when entered into between shareholders, such agreements may also be subscribed to and/or benefit or bind other parties, namely the company itself or even company creditors (for example, lenders or future third-party acquirers).

[5] *Monteiro Pires/Hállen Cordeiro/Branco Vicente*, Arbitragem Societária, 2025, 41.

[6] *Cassiano dos Santos*, Direito Comercial Português, vol. I, 2007, 125.

[7] *Engrácia Antunes* (fn. 1), 34.

II. Remedies in case of non-performance of shareholders' agreements

A failure to comply with the obligations set forth in a shareholders' agreement constitutes a breach of contract, which may give rise to various legal consequences depending on the terms of the agreement[8]. Shareholders' agreements are frequently supplemented with other specific arrangements to secure the performance of obligations such as the appointment of a proxy to exercise voting rights, penalty clauses, the establishment of escrow accounts, termination clauses and call or put options in favour of non-defaulting shareholders.[9] Where a shareholders' agreement does not contain a sole remedy clause and does not exclude the parties' ability to pursue legal remedies available under applicable law, the parties retain the right to seek all remedies provided by law in the event of a breach. Legal remedies for breach of a shareholders' agreement may include, but are not limited to, liability for damages suffered by the non-breaching party[10] and the right to terminate the agreement. In addition to monetary compensation, the non-breaching party may also be entitled to seek injunctive relief or specific performance to prevent further breaches or to enforce the terms of the agreement.[11]

In cases of non-performance, the creditor may choose either to demand performance or to terminate the contract. Under the Portuguese Civil Code, the general provisions governing termination are set out in articles 792, 793, 801(2), 802, and 432 to 436.

---

[8] We may distinguish between agreements with an associative structure and those with a commutative structure. This distinction is based on whether the agreement pursues a common objective, with the parties' declarations aligning to create parallel legal positions (associative), or whether the parties make declarations of intent in opposition, beginning from divergent positions and seeking to reconcile conflicting interests (commutative). Against this distinction, one may question to what extent does the character of a shareholders' agreement – specifically, whether it is fundamentally organizational or associative in nature, as opposed to purely commutative – impact the determination of legal remedies for breach? Put differently, should shareholders' agreements that are primarily organizational or associative be subject to the same remedial framework as those that are purely commutative, or do their distinct purposes and structures justify differentiated legal treatment when addressing contractual breaches?

[9] *Engrácia Antunes* (fn. 1), 34.

[10] In the absence of different contractual agreements, contractual liability is dependent on the following requirements (cf. articles 798, 799 and 483 of the Civil Code): (i) an unlawful or illicit act (ii) fault (willful conduct or negligence); (iii) loss and (iv) a causal link between the unlawful act and the loss (causation) *Monteiro Pires*, Contratos, Vol. I, Perturbações na Execução, 2025, 96.

[11] In some cases, particular regarding voting rights the enforcement of obligations through specific performance (Articles 817 et seq. CC) is denied. *Cunha*, in Código das Sociedades Comerciais em Comentário, vol. I, 2025, Art. 17 n. 322., *Oliveira Ascensão*, Direito Comercial, vol. IV, Sociedades Comerciais, 2000, 296; However, a sector of the doctrine allows for specific performance among shareholders, particularly in cases involving the transfer of shares in a shareholders' agreement (*Leal* [fn. 1], 179).

1. Termination of shareholders' agreements

In the absence of express termination clauses, the circumstances under which a valid contract may be terminated for breach (in the broad sense) include: (i) partial impossibility of performance – whether or not attributable to the debtor – where such impossibility affects the creditor's interest (see Articles 793/2 and 802/2); (ii) failure to perform within a cure period granted by the creditor (Articles 808/1 and 2); (iii) delayed performance resulting in the creditor losing interest in the performance (Articles 808/1 and 2, and 792/1 and 2); (iv) non-conforming performance that leads to a loss of interest by the creditor (Articles 808/1 and 2); and (v) anticipatory breach of contract.[12]

Mere delay allows termination only if the creditor loses his interest in performance or if the debtor fails to comply within a reasonable cure period set by the creditor (See Article 808). Futile or frivolous motives are also not legitimate causes of termination, even if performance is merely partially possible (Articles 793 and 802).

Termination is not merely a remedy of last resort; it may be invoked whenever the creditor's interest so warrants and provided. According to Portuguese law, it is not necessary to set a cure period if the creditor's interest has already been compromised (see article 808(1) of the Portuguese Civil Code).

Functionally, termination serves as a remedy that produces a necessary release effect and, potentially, a recovery effect. The release effect entails the extinction of the parties' future obligations – this effect is essential, though not always absolute, as principles such as good faith (Articles 762(2) of the Portuguese Civil Code) may require the continuation of ancillary duties to protect the legitimate interests of the counterparty. The recovery effect, by contrast, is only possible in certain circumstances: not every dissolution of the contractual relationship results in recovery, either because the obligations were never performed or because restitution in kind is not feasible – in which case, recovery is typically materialised through restitution by value.

Legal literature is unanimous in recognizing that shareholders' agreements may be terminated in the event of a breach of contract, whether such termination is expressly provided for in the agreement or arises under general principles of contract law.

The broad spectrum of breaches that may justify termination of a shareholders' agreement reflects the diverse range of clauses and objectives inherent in such agreements.[13] Shareholders' agreements are typically the product of negotiation and are designed to address a variety of matters, including the differential treatment of shareholders, the protection of confidential company information, the regulation of strategic objectives, the imposition of restrictions on certain company actions, the allo-

---

[12] Additionally, the law provides for termination in cases of a fundamental change of circumstances (Article 437.º of the Civil Code).

[13] *Coutinho de Abreu*, Curso de Direito Comercial, vol. II, 8th ed., 2024, 159, *Cunha*, in Código das Sociedades Comerciais em Comentário, vol. I, 2025, Art. 17 n. 312.

cation of information rights, the establishment of dividend policies, and the granting of veto rights, among others. This diversity in content and purpose means that breaches may arise in numerous contexts, each potentially giving rise to a right of termination depending on the terms of the agreement and the significance of the breach.

A particularly interesting issue for examination is whether the legal rules governing breach and termination of contract included in the Portuguese Civil Code are sufficient to address the full range of issues that may arise in connection with shareholders' agreements.[14]

While the Portuguese Companies Code includes a provision on shareholders' agreements (Article 17), it does not contain any specific rules addressing the consequences of their breach. As a result, issues relating to the breach of shareholders' agreements are governed by the general principles of contract law. This gap is not filled by other commercial legislation, which likewise does not regulate the matter, thereby requiring recourse to the general regime of civil law in accordance with Article 3 of the Commercial Code.

Prevailing legal doctrine does not advocate for an autonomous regime governing breach of contract in commercial agreements, and this is even more evident in the context of shareholders' agreements. In this regard, it is expressly recognized that the general rules of the Civil Code – such as the exception of non-performance (Article 428) and the termination of contract (Articles 432(1), 802(2), and 808(1)) – are fully applicable to shareholders' agreements.[15]

Notwithstanding the above, reliance on general contractual remedies for breaches of shareholders' agreements may give rise to significant complexities. The application of general contract law principles to shareholders' agreements – given their commercial nature and the interplay with corporate governance – can lead to uncertainties and practical difficulties in enforcement and interpretation.

The creditor's (shareholder's) interest is central when assessing the consequences of non-performance in the context of a shareholders' agreement. Article 808(2) of the Civil Code establishes an objective standard for evaluating the performance interest,

---

[14] It is well established that most shareholder disputes arise from disagreements over the interpretation of contractual provisions. The existence of a breach necessarily presupposes the existence and scope of an obligation, which in turn depends on the proper construction of the agreement. Interpretation is therefore crucial in determining the meaning of the contract and delineating the rights and obligations of the parties. Prevailing legal doctrine does not advocate for an autonomous or distinct model of interpretation specifically for shareholders' agreements. Instead, the interpretation of shareholders' agreements generally follows the established principles of contract interpretation applicable to commercial agreements more broadly. Paulo Câmara has a different opinion and considers that "the general rules of legal business, with emphasis on the will of the parties, should only be fully applied in relation to agreements with no organizational significance, which in this respect will be governed in the same way as non-social clauses, regardless of where they are formally regulated" (*Câmara*, in Direito e Justiça, Estudos em Memória do Prof. Doutor Paulo M. Sendim, 2012, 462).

[15] *Engrácia Antunes* (fn. 1), 34.

while Articles 801(2) and 802(1) place the burden on the non-breaching party to allege and prove the requirements for termination, including the breach itself. This raises the following question: how should the "creditor's interest" be understood in the specific context of a shareholders' agreement? In my view, unless the shareholders' agreement provides otherwise, the interest of the shareholder as a party to the agreement should take precedence over the interests of the company or other stakeholders. This is consistent with the prevailing understanding that shareholders' agreements are fundamentally contractual in nature, creating rights and obligations primarily among the shareholders themselves, rather than directly implicating the company or third parties. Accordingly, the assessment of the creditor's interest – and thus the remedies for non-performance – should focus on the contractual expectations and rights of the shareholder under the agreement, rather than broader corporate or stakeholder interests, unless the agreement expressly stipulates otherwise.

Shareholders' agreements are in principle plurilateral contracts: such agreements regulate legally autonomous interests of shareholders or of blocks of shareholders. Articles 434 to 436 of the Civil Code govern the effects of termination of contracts. In case multilateral shareholders agreement, if one shareholder terminates the agreement for breach of contract of another shareholder, would the agreement expire, or would it remain in relation to the rest of the shareholders? Whether the remaining shareholders continue to be bound by the same terms of the agreement after one shareholder terminates their participation depends primarily on the terms of the shareholders' agreement itself.

Unless the shareholders' agreement contains a clause providing for collective termination or otherwise stipulates that the agreement is indivisible, in principle the agreement will generally continue to bind the remaining shareholders. The non-breaching parties retain their rights and obligations *inter se*, and only the relationship with the breaching (and terminating) party is affected. The basis of the transaction – that is, the contractual foundation and operative purpose of the shareholders' agreement – will generally not be affected by the termination of one shareholder, unless the agreement expressly provides otherwise.

However, if the departure of a shareholder does undermine the fundamental basis or purpose of the agreement for the remaining parties, legal remedies such as those provided under Article 437 of the Civil Code may become relevant,[16] provided the circumstances fall within its scope of application. In such cases, parties may seek to revise or terminate the agreement on the grounds that the contractual equilibrium or the underlying purpose of the transaction has been fundamentally altered.

[16] Article 437(1) establishes the following: "if the circumstances on which the parties based their decision to enter into contract have undergone an unusual change, the injured party shall be entitled to terminate the contract, or to have it modified in line with equity, provided that requiring the obligations undertaken by the latter would seriously affect the principles of good faith and is not covered by the risks inherent to the contract".

2. *Contractual remedies for breach of contract*

In commercial legal transactions, the parties have appreciable latitude in shaping the content of their legal transaction, which operates as self-regulation for their specific interests (Article 405 of the Civil Code).[17] Moreover, shareholders enjoy broad autonomy to define the terms and scope of their mutual arrangements, allowing them to tailor such agreements to best advance their individual interest.

In commercial agreements, including shareholders' agreements, the parties often seek to regulate remedies for breach of contract in an exclusive manner. Such agreements are frequently contested, with the principal basis for challenge typically grounded in Article 809 of the Civil Code.

Article 809 of the Civil Code of 1966 establishes that clauses by which the creditor waives in advance the rights granted to him in the preceding sections is null and void, except as provided in Article 800(2).[18] The rights conferred in the mentioned preceding sections include, among others, the right to terminate the agreement and the right to seek compensation for losses incurred.

To comprehend the rationale behind this legal provision, it is necessary to undertake an analysis of the underlying policy objectives that motivated the legislator to deviate from the prevailing principle of freedom of contract (Article 405 of the Civil Code).[19]

The anticipated waiver of a right to exercise a certain remedy for breach of contract does not transform the obligation into a natural obligation.[20] It is evident that this does not occur in instances where alternative remedies remain available, as is customary. The fundamental nature of the obligation is not affected; the debtor's legal commitment remains intact, and failure to perform may still trigger the applicable legal or contractual consequences.

---

[17] The Civil Code acknowledges the role of freedom of contract and recognizes the relevance respecting the Parties' agreement. Article 405 establishes that "1. Within the limits of the law, the parties are free to agree on the content of contracts, to enter into contracts other than those provided for in this code or include in them any clauses they intend to include". Paragraph 2 of the same legal provision sets forth that "2. The parties may also combine in the same contract rules of two or more agreements, totally or partially regulated by law".

[18] Article 800/2 establishes the following: "liability may be contractually excluded or limited by prior agreement of the interested parties, provided that the exclusion or limitation does not cover acts that constitute a breach of duties imposed by rules of public order".

[19] On the historical context of the prohibition of antecipated renunciation of rights, vide *Mota Pinto*, RLJ 4041 (2023), 82–84.

[20] Antunes Varela argued in 1990, "seriously wishing to establish the obligation and depriving it, from the outset, of the coercive means that give life to its legal status would be a kind of alliance between yes and no, which the law cannot support" – see *Antunes Varela*, Das Obrigações em Geral, Vol. II, 4th ed., 1990, 130. The same idea is reproduced in the 7th Edition, 1999, pp. 136–137. In the same vein, Ana Prata explains that "[...] the prohibitive rule of Article 809 applies regardless of the severity of the defaulting debtor's fault, and its justification lies in the very legal nature of the obligation. It is not just a matter of preserving a penalty for non-compliance, the rationale for which would have to be graded according to the degree of fault of the offender, but, more complexly, of safeguarding a mechanism of protection inherent in every legal imperative", *Prata*, Cláusulas de Limitação da Responsabilidade Contratual, 1985, 572–573.

Objections that waivers are impermissible on the grounds of indeterminacy are unpersuasive when the waiver is limited, as such limitation ensures determinability regarding the remedies being relinquished.[21]

The *raison d' être* of the Article 809 is not *also the principle of anticipated irrevocability.* Article 340/1 of the Civil Code determines that "the act that infringes upon the rights of another is lawful, provided that the injured party has consented to the infringement". Such consent can be expressed prior to the act.

The contemporary constitutional significance of free private enterprise and private autonomy cannot be overlooked, as these principles are now firmly anchored in constitutional rights and values. The Constitution recognizes the principle of free private enterprise, which allows for the freedom of market (article 61/1 of the Constitution).[22] Individuals and companies are free to engage in economic activities and business initiatives without undue interference.

In establishing the rationale behind Article 809 in relation to Articles 800/2 and 810 of the Civil Code[23] in the context of limitation of liability clauses, it becomes evident that Article 809 is designed to safeguard the integrity of contractual commitments. A similar rationale may also extend to situations where the limitation pertains to remedies other than compensation for losses incurred by the non-breaching party.

By invalidating waivers that could potentially compromise the stability of legal relationships and the trust essential for the effective functioning of any market. Article 809, when applied to the realm of contractual obligations, serves to ensure that the contract itself – and the binding commitment it creates – is not rendered meaningless. The proposition that no individual should be left without recourse is not, in itself, a complete justification, so long as the creditor retains the ability to safeguard its interests through the remedies that remain available under the agreement or applicable law.

In the context of sophisticated commercial contracts negotiated between parties with equal bargaining power and equivalent capacity to assess and allocate risks, the

---

[21] With a different position, indicating indeterminacy as one of the justifications, alongside with other motives, *Menezes Cordeiro*, Tratado de Direito Civil, Vol. IX, 3rd ed., 2019, 439.

[22] "Private economic initiative is exercised freely within the frameworks defined by the Constitution and the law and taking into account the general interest".

[23] Article 800/2 establishes the following "liability may be contractually excluded or limited by prior agreement of the interested parties, provided that the exclusion or limitation does not cover acts that constitute a breach of duties imposed by rules of public order". This sole limitation established by this legal provision concerns public order. Article 800 addresses limitations of liability, in particular, and there is no reason to impose a stricter regime in cases where no auxiliary is used in the performance of obligations. On the other hand, article 810 (1) of the Civil Code expressly permits the parties to "agree on the amount of compensation due". This agreement may take the form of stipulating a maximum limit for compensation, thereby constituting a limitation of liability. In such cases, pursuant to Article 811(2), compensation for damages exceeding the agreed maximum is excluded, making this mechanism functionally equivalent to a limitation (or exclusion) of liability clause.

rationale for applying Article 809 cannot be grounded in the need to protect the creditor from their own decisions.[24]

At the same time, the Parties often resort to call options as a remedy for breach of Shareholders Agreements. In the case of a call option (i. e. an agreement that gives the holder the right to buy or sell an asset under predetermined conditions), the holder has the option to buy the defaulting party's share in the company's capital or, alternatively, to sell its share to the defaulting party. Sometimes the price is deducted from the value of a penalty clause also agreed in the Shareholders' Agreement.

Call options are frequently used in shareholders' agreements as mechanisms to address various contingencies, including events of non-compliance with the shareholders' agreement, allowing the non-breaching party to acquire the shares of the breaching party under predetermined term.

In the context of a limited liability company by shares, call options typically refer to a contractual clause that grants its holder the right, but not the obligation, to acquire a specified number of shares under pre-established conditions set out in the same agreement (usually a fixed price, which may be set at nominal value or determined by a formula agreed upon by the parties). Call options constitute pure option rights, classified as potestative rights and therefore the transaction is completed with the beneficiary's declaration of will, without needing a new declaration from the counterparty.

Call options involve two distinct stages: (i) the creation of the potestative right (the right to exercise the option), and (ii) the actual exercise of that right, which triggers the obligation to enter into the underlying transfer agreement. Upon exercise of the call option, the intended contract, such as the sale of shares, is formed without requiring further acceptance from the party bound by the option, as the legal effect is produced solely by the beneficiary's exercise of the right. However, the exercise of the call option does not exempt the beneficiary from fulfilling all legal and procedural requirements necessary for the transfer of shares. Rather, after notification of the exercise of the call option, the parties must comply with all applicable legal formalities to effectuate the transfer and achieve completion ("closing") of the transaction. Thus, the notice of exercise alone does not result in the automatic transfer of rights; completion is contingent upon satisfaction of all required steps. For instance, in case of titled nominative shares, a transfer declaration inscribed on the certificate, followed by registration with the issuer are needed (Article 102 of the Securities Code).

[24] A significant number of legal scholars present their analyses and opinions within works devoted to the law of obligations, yet often without examining whether the underlying rationale of a given legal provision is equally relevant to commercial agreements. This approach can result in doctrinal commentary that, while thorough in its treatment of obligations in general, cannot be transposed without further thought to commercial contexts. As a result, the literature may lack nuanced discussion of whether and how the foundational reasons for a legal rule should be adapted or reconsidered when applied to commercial transactions.

Index of Contributors

Boura, Marta, Ph.D. Candidate, Guest Lecturer, Faculty of Law of the University of Lisbon; Researcher at the Research Centre for Private Law (CIDP)

Câmara, Paulo, Professor, Faculty of Law, Catholic University of Portugal (Lisbon); Head of research group Governance Lab; Partner, Sérvulo & Associados

Coelho, Catarina, Ph.D. Candidate, Guest Lecturer, Faculty of Law of the University of Lisbon; Researcher at the Research Centre for Private Law (CIDP); Ph.D.'s Scholarships holder of the CIDP.

Cunha, Carolina, Professor, Faculty of Law, University of Coimbra; Researcher at the University of Coimbra Institute for Legal Research (UCILeR)

de Luca, Nicola, Professor of Business and Company Law, Luiss University Rome

del Val Talens, Paula, Associate Professor of Business Law, University of Valencia

Enriques, Luca, Professor of Business Law, Bocconi University, Department of Legal Studies

Ferreira Gomes, José, Professor, Faculty of Law of the University of Lisbon; Researcher at Research Centre for Private Law (CIDP)

Martins, Alexandre de Soveral, Professor, Faculty of Law, University of Coimbra, Researcher at University of Coimbra Institute for Legal Research (UCILeR)

Mendes Correia, Francisco, Professor, Faculty of Law of the University of Lisbon; Researcher at Research Centre for Private Law (CIDP)

Mock, Sebastian, Professor, Vienna University of Economics and Business, Institute for Civil and Civil Procedural Law

Monteiro Pires, Catarina, Professor, Faculty of Law of the University of Lisbon; Researcher at Research Centre for Private Law (CIDP)

Nigro, Casimiro A., Assistant Professor of Business Law, Leeds University, School of Law

Olavo Cunha, Paulo, Full Professor, Faculty of Law, Portuguese Catholic University (Lisbon School); Católica Research Centre for the Future of Law (CRCFL); Partner, Vieira de Almeida & Associados–Sociedade de Advogados, S.P., R.L.

Perestrelo de Oliveira, Ana, Professor, Faculty of Law of the University of Lisbon; Researcher at Research Centre for Private Law (CIDP)

Ramos, Maria Elisabete, Ph.D., Professor, Faculty of Economics, University of Coimbra; Researcher at the Centre for Business and Economics Research (CeBER)